BUILDING WEALTH
• IN THE '90s •

Also by Gordon Pape

INVESTMENT ADVICE
Retiring Wealthy
Retiring Wealthy software version
Low-Risk Investing
Gordon Pape's Buyer's Guide to RRSPs
Gordon Pape's Buyer's Guide to Mutual Funds

FICTION
(with Tony Aspler)
Chain Reaction
The Scorpion Sanction
The Music Wars

NON-FICTION
(with Donna Gabeline, Dane Lanken)
Montreal at the Crossroads

BUILDING WEALTH
• IN THE '90s •

Gordon Pape

Prentice Hall Canada Inc., Scarborough, Ontario

Canadian Cataloguing in Publication Data

Pape, Gordon, 1936–
    Building wealth in the '90s

Rev. and updated ed.
Previously published under title: Building Wealth.
Includes index.
ISBN 0-13-088048-5

1. Finance, Personal.   I. Title.

HG179.P37 1992   332.024   C92-094773-5

Portions of Chapters 6 and 7 originally appeared in *Canadian House and Home*
Portions of Chapter 9 originally appeared in *Flare Magazine*

Prentice-Hall Inc. Englewood Cliffs, *New Jersey*
Prentice-Hall International, Inc., *London*
Prentice-Hall of Australia, Pty., *Sydney*
Prentice-Hall of India Pvt., Ltd., *New Delhi*
Prentice-Hall of Japan, Inc., *Tokyo*
Prentice-Hall of Southeast Asia (Pte.) Ltd., *Singapore*
Prentice-Hall do Brasil Ltda., *Rio de Janeiro*
Prentice-Hall Hispanoamericana, S.A., *Mexico*

Art direction: Gail Ferriera Ng a Kien
Design: Alex Li
Cover photo: Steve Payne
Manufacturing buyer: Lisa Kreuch
Composition: Jaytype Inc.
ISBN: 0-13-088048-5

Printed and bound in Canada by Webcom Limited.

5 WC 96 95 94

TABLE OF CONTENTS

To My Children: Deborah, Kendrew and Kim

*With the hope this book will help
them enrich their lives.*

ACKNOWLEDGEMENTS

A book such as this is not possible without the assistance and co-operation of many individuals and organizations. Among those who have provided information and guidance for this edition are the Canadian Bankers Association, the Bank of Canada, the Bank of Montreal, the Toronto-Dominion Bank, the Bank of Commerce, the Royal Bank, Royal Trust, Revenue Canada, the federal Department of Finance, Credit Union Central of Canada, Richardson Greenshields of Canada, Price Waterhouse, and the Canada Deposit Insurance Corporation. My thanks to all, and to anyone I may have inadvertently left out. Also, special thanks to my daughter, Deborah, who joins me on the cover. Without her diligent research efforts, none of this would be possible.

Introduction

Our world has changed dramatically since the first edition of *Building Wealth* was written in 1987.

Here in Canada, we've endured one of the most severe recessions since the Second World War, entered into an historic Free Trade Agreement with the United States, and watched with concern as our politicians struggled with our constitutional future.

During that time, thousands of Canadians lost their jobs as plants closed down, fish stocks vanished, and commodity prices fell. The stock market crashed, inflation dropped to its lowest level since the sixties, housing became affordable again to young Canadians who had despaired of ever being homeowners, and we took out our frustration with high prices and rising taxes by going shopping in the U.S.

Throw in the Oka crisis, the breakdown of our traditional political alignments, the election of an NDP government in conservative Ontario, and our first war since Korea and it was a turbulent time.

Yet viewed form abroad, Canada looked like an oasis of tranquillity. In a world of Saddam Hussein, the break-up of the Soviet Union, civil war in Yugoslavia, the end of apartheid in South Africa, and continued violence in the Middle East, our problems seemed like small potatoes.

But we don't live in any of those trouble-spots. We live in Canada in the 1990s, and we have to find our way in that context.

Individually, we can't do much about the macro events that shape our lives. Frustrating as it is, we have to leave it to the politicians to resolve our constitutional problems and to our business leaders to finds ways to revitalize our economy in a world of increased international competition.

But we are not helpless, by any means. We have the power and the ability to make decisions that will improve our personal wealth.

I admit, it isn't easy. It takes an understanding of the principles of good money management, knowledge of how national and international developments affect our financial decisions, and a willingness to devote the time and effort necessary to succeed.

But if you're determined, you can make it happen.

When I wrote the first edition of *Building Wealth*, it was mainly with my children in mind. I wanted to impart to them, and to other young Canadians, the financial knowledge I wish I'd possessed when I was starting out in life, but didn't learn until many, many years later.

The letters and comments I've received since the book came out tell me I succeeded in doing that. There is nothing more gratifying than to have someone in their mid-twenties come up to me, as happened at the Financial Forum in Toronto this year, give me a dog-eared copy of *Building Wealth* to sign, and say: "Your book changed my life."

But I also discovered something else. *Building Wealth* had an appeal far beyond its original intended audience. There are hundreds of thousands, perhaps millions, of Canadians over thirty who, like me, never learned the basic principles of good money management in their teens and twenties.

The schools offered no guidance, parents often had little understanding themselves, and among peers the main interest in money was how to spend it.

It appears *Building Wealth* filled that void for some.

I hope this new edition will continue to do so.

If you read the original book, you'll find the principles in this edition remain the same. Sound money management strategies don't change with the economic season. They remain constant.

But tactics do change. Different times may require different approaches. You'll find those reflected here.

Tax laws also change, sometimes capriciously. *Building Wealth in the '90s* incorporates all the new developments, up to and including the 1992 federal budget, and suggests some new ways to reduce your tax burden.

You'll also find explanations of the many new financial products and services that have appeared in recent years. Some offer intriguing new ways to manage your money more effectively; others are rip-offs to be avoided at all cost.

And this edition looks ahead to the rest of the decade, to try to discern what lies ahead and how you can profit from it.

As with the first edition of *Building Wealth*, the purpose of this book is to help you manage your personal financial life more effectively, through knowledge and understanding.

I can think of no greater reward than to hear from readers that I've accomplished that.

> Gordon Pape
> Toronto, Ontario
> June, 1992

Wealth Is What You Make It

Wealth is not without its advantages and the case to the contrary, although it has often been made, has never proved widely persuasive.
— John Kenneth Galbraith
The Affluent Society

Most people think they would like to be wealthy. The problem is they have no idea what that means.

Too often, they equate wealth with money. The more you accumulate, the wealthier — and, in theory, the happier—you'll be.

I don't think of wealth in that way.

True, I like money. But I wouldn't want too much of it. I don't care for the lifestyle that accompanies super-wealth.

Cocktail parties give me sore feet.

Grand old houses make me sneeze.

I can never figure out how much to tip in five-star hotels.

I think stretch limos are fun for kids' proms but pretentious for grown-ups.

I'd rather go fishing than watch a polo match.

Charity balls bore me.

More seriously, I don't want to live in an armed compound, and I don't want to worry about my family becoming a target for kidnappers or extortionists.

I simply want enough wealth to live the type of life I enjoy. Dr. Morton Shulman, who has accumulated several fortunes in his colourful career, once observed that the purpose of acquiring wealth was to enjoy life more.

It sounds simple. But it's the key to understanding what wealth is really all about, and what it should mean to you.

As you read this book, keep that idea in the front of your mind.

You are not building wealth for its own sake. There is no joy in adding up the value of your investments each month and discovering you're five percent richer. The joy is in the use you can make of that wealth — whether to have a more comfortable home, or drive a Lexus, or own a condo in Florida or Hawaii, or to send your kids to the best universities in North America, or keep a lover, or give large amounts of money to worthy causes — whatever turns you on. The joy in wealth is in the pleasures it can bring — and they can be pleasures of the soul just as much as pleasures of the body.

In short, wealth is a personal concept. You'll have to decide for yourself what it means to you.

I have my own definition. It's simple: wealth is the ability to do whatever I want in life without compromising my standard of living. In other words, comfortable independence.

Wealth to me means not worrying about how someone else's decisions are going to affect my financial position.

Wealth, to me, means being able to help my family when they need financial assistance.

Wealth means I can take a year off and live in a beach house if I wish.

Wealth means giving the gifts I want to give at Christmas, without worrying about the cost.

Wealth means sharing fine bottles of wine with friends.

In other words, wealth means living as I want to live, without financial restraint.

Your ideas may be very different — in fact, I'd be surprised if they weren't.

And you may find your objectives change as you grow older.

A recently married twenty-eight-year old, for example, may see wealth as owning his or her own home and possessing a debt-free car. A forty-year-old may take those things for granted.

Whatever your goal, the sooner you start moving toward it, the sooner you'll arrive.

Don't fool yourself into thinking it will happen overnight, however. I still haven't achieved all my personal financial objectives.

True, I've come a long way. Our family net worth is now well over a million dollars, a considerable accomplishment given that just a decade ago I was unemployed with a wife, three young children, a hefty mortgage and no investments of any sort.

But I'm still not "wealthy," in terms of my personal definition. There's a way to go yet.

The main reason it's taking so long is that I started late. Had I known thirty years ago what I know today, I'd have reached my wealth objectives long since.

But I didn't begin to learn about wealth building until my late forties (I'm in my mid-fifties as this is written). That's late in life to be getting started.

The younger you are when you begin, the more wealth you'll be able to build and, more importantly, enjoy over your lifetime.

That's what gave me the idea to write the original *Building Wealth*. My children were in their late teens and early twenties, approaching the point in life where they'd be leaving school and starting to make their own careers.

That's one of the most critical times in the whole wealth building process. You're free from parental ties, you're on your own for the first time and you're earning more money than you ever dreamed possible. The natural temptation is to live it up. Get that car you've always wanted. Go on an expensive holiday. Buy a wardrobe full of new clothes. If you go into debt in the process, so what? You have lots of earning years ahead of you.

I don't blame young people for thinking that way. It's natural. But there's an alternative. Give up a little bit now and get it back a thousand-fold later. Instead of spending everything that comes in, use some of that money to set up a lifetime wealth building program.

I've been impressed by how much more mature young people are today compared to when I was starting out. I find that people in their teens and twenties are more aware of the world and their place in it. And I'm seeing some of them display a great deal more interest in good money management than I can remember when I was young.

They're the people for whom this book is primarily intended —

they're young enough to get the most benefit from the ideas that follow, and smart enough to know that they have to put in some effort to make it all happen.

That doesn't mean that, if you're over thirty, this book has nothing for you. Quite the contrary. You're never too old to become a wealth builder. No matter what your age, even if you haven't made a serious start until now, I believe you'll find the information that follows to be helpful. The major advantage younger people have is more time — and as we go on, you'll understand why that's important.

One other point I should make here. This is a book for people who are at the start of the wealth building process. The advice and techniques that I'll be giving are best suited to their needs. If you've been a dedicated wealth builder for years, you may find a few interesting ideas. But much of the information may seem rather basic. If that's your situation, I suggest you skim the chapters that might offer some helpful ideas. Then pass the book along to a relative or friend you think would benefit from it and go out and buy a copy of *Low-Risk Investing* and/or *Retiring Wealthy*. Those books contain more advanced money management and investing strategies especially designed for more experienced investors.

I often find myself wondering why I didn't learn much of the information in this book earlier in my life. I guess it was for the same reasons most of us don't: nobody took the time and trouble to teach me. The school system showed me how to bisect angles and scan poems, but offered absolutely zilch when it came to building wealth. (Judging by my children's experience, things aren't much better for today's generation.) My parents were hopeless when it came to building wealth — in fact, my father, God rest him, seemed to be inclined in exactly the opposite direction. He was a wonderfully talented man in the laboratory — he developed a process for artificially drying prunes and apricots in the early 1930s. But he was totally lacking in wealth building skills. That dried fruit process, on which he held the patent, eventually became the cornerstone of a multi-million dollar industry. But he sold off his rights at the height of the Depression for $5,000!

I suppose I could have learned the skills myself but, like most of us, I was always too busy. There were other priorities, like getting through school, travelling in Europe, finding a job, getting married, advancing in my career, having children. Who had time to worry about such esoteric matters as wealth building?

Sound familiar?

I come in contact with many senior business and professional people in my work — men and women at the top of their field, highly respected among their peers. They are smart, articulate, fun to be with — and most of them haven't the faintest idea how to handle money intelligently or build wealth.

I'll never forget the time I was having drinks with a friend after a curling game. He was a successful sales manager, in his fifties, very well off. It was RRSP season and he'd heard me talking about the subject in a radio broadcast. He saw a chance for a little free advice and asked where he should be investing his money. The conversation went something like this:

Me: Do you have an RRSP now?

Friend: Yes.

Me: What type?

Friend: Well, gosh, I'm not sure.

Me: Well, what kind of return are you getting?

Friend: Uh, well, I really don't know.

You don't need to hear any more. Can you imagine where he'd be if he ran his business that way?

Ironically, the more successful people are professionally, the worse they tend to be as money managers. Some of the most naive people I know, from a financial point of view, are well-respected doctors, lawyers, dentists and corporate vice-presidents — most of them with six figure incomes.

Makes no sense, you say? Actually it does, if you stop and think about it a moment. What made these people so successful in the first place? To start with, a long period of education — law school, dental college, medical internship, MBA studies. Total immersion in the disciplines of their chosen fields. And then what? Establishing a practice or setting up a partnership or climbing the corporate ladder. Hard work, long hours, learning how to be the best at what they do, coming home at night exhausted with about enough energy left to eat, watch some mindless TV and fall into bed.

When did they have time to learn about handling money and building wealth? They didn't. They were too busy launching careers and getting married (and sometimes unmarried) and starting families. Wealth building was like taking a year off to sail around the world — something everyone would like to do but no one has time for.

So what happens? Many of these people reach mid-life with big incomes, but no wealth to speak of. They're still in debt, live beyond their means, and dream of the day when they'll have some time to themselves to enjoy life. Too often, that day doesn't come.

Where does the wealth building process begin? For starters, it helps to have certain advantages. One is education. There's no question that the greater your income potential, the easier wealth building becomes.

Another, as I've already indicated, is youth. The younger you are when you begin, the greater your chances of acquiring substantial wealth over your lifetime. That's why I've done what I can to make sure my children learn about money management and investing at an early age. I don't want them to go through what I did: losing major wealth building opportunities when I was young because I didn't have the faintest idea how to go about creating a coherent plan or what to do with my money.

My oldest daughter is the first to have benefited. She and her husband decided, on their own, that they should take advantage of low real estate prices and mortgage rates to buy their first home in early 1992.

She'd scrimped and saved for a small down payment and they'd both contributed to the Ontario Home Ownership Plan. When the federal government announced that people could dip into their RRSP money to buy a house, it gave them the little extra they needed to swing a deal.

As a result, they were able to pick up a well-located townhouse in the Toronto suburb of North York at a price which I expect will look like a steal in a couple of years.

That's part of the art of wealth building — recognizing opportunities and taking advantage of them while they're available.

It's not always easy. In fact, it often involves personal sacrifice. But the hard fact is that if you want to build wealth, you have to develop the self-discipline to learn how to do it properly — and then to apply what you learn when the opportunity presents itself.

It's not something you can turn on and off. It's a lifetime commitment — like having a child, or making a marriage work, or being first-rate at your job. If you aren't prepared to make that commitment, the odds are you will never become wealthy.

As part of that commitment, you have to acquire some knowledge and keep that knowledge current. That's going to take some of the most precious thing you have — time. Not just at the outset, but all the way along. If you don't know what's going on in the world and how to relate that information to the wealth building process, you're not going to do well.

Where do you start? Books like this one — the fact you purchased it and have read this far is a positive sign. Find a couple of others that are designed to provide basic information and browse through them as well; I especially recommend David Chilton's bestseller, *The Wealthy Barber.* There are a lot of different ideas about wealth building; it pays to expose yourself to a number of them.

If you find you're fascinated by the subject — many people are — you might want to consider taking a course. The best starter course I know of in Canada is Hume Publishing's Successful Investing & Money Management program.

Mind you, there's some bias showing here — I co-ordinated a major rewriting of that program several years ago, so I happen to think it's pretty sound.

You must — and I stress *must* — become a regular reader of the financial pages in your local newspaper. You may not understand a lot of the information at first. But as you read through this book, more of what seems like financial and economic gobbledegook may start to make sense. Even more important, you'll begin to understand how to use the information on the financial pages to your own advantage.

The next step is to start reading the national business press. *The Globe and Mail's Report on Business* is a must. *The Financial Post* should be on your list and the weekly *Financial Times* also offers some useful insights. Unfortunately, there is no longer any magazine in Canada devoted to personal financial management. For reasons known only to its editors, *The Financial Post Magazine* shifted away from a useful personal finance format a few years ago to become a general business publication. *Your Money*, another worthwhile personal finance magazine, went belly-up.

That leaves the magazine marketplace to such U.S. publications as Time Inc.'s *Money*, which I generally find to be almost useless for Canadian readers because of the differences in taxation, investment opportunities, mortgages and real estate between the two countries.

Much better are Canadian-based investment newsletters, like *The MoneyLetter*, to which I'm a regular contributor. The Marpep organization also produces some quality newsletters, including *Money Reporter* and *Investment Reporter*.

Whatever you read, the important thing is to stay well informed. Self-education is one of the cornerstones to successful wealth building.

There is something else you need as well. Patience. Unless you become a rock star or win a lottery, you will not get rich overnight. As I pointed out earlier in describing my own case, wealth building takes time. Years. Skill and luck will play a role in how much time it takes *you*. Perhaps you can manage it in ten years, perhaps it will take twenty-five. But it is not going to happen in one year, or two, or probably even five. You must have patience, and you must be prepared for temporary setbacks. As long as you remain committed and follow the advice in this book, you'll make it. Others have; you can too.

One other thing before we start. You should know that I'm very conservative by nature. The advice in this book will reflect that — it couldn't be any other way. The techniques I describe may seem too cautious for a more aggressive type of person.

But before you decide you'd prefer to be a high roller, think about this: every investment professional will tell you that the cardinal rule of building wealth is NOT TO LOSE YOUR CAPITAL. Surprised? I was when I first heard it. But it makes common sense. It's easy to lose money — anyone can do it. What's hard is to retain what you have and to build on it — especially in tough economic times, such as we've recently come through. That's when prudence and patience will pay off big.

That's about it for openers. Turn to the next chapter and let's get started.

The Arab Bazaar

Have you ever wondered why more people aren't wealthy? Asked yourself what it takes? Special skills? Connections? Luck? Knowledge?

Well, none of those hurt. But it takes something else as well — determination. If you *really* want wealth, you have to be prepared to work at it.

That may sound obvious. But if you want to build wealth, you have to be prepared to devote at least as much time to it as you would to learning how to cook, or to play the piano, or to master tennis. It doesn't come overnight.

Let me give you an example. Very few people, even the pros, can name all the different ways in which you can invest money today. The financial marketplace has become the modern equivalent of an Arab bazaar — complex, colourful, filled with mysterious, eye-catching products that vendors hawk as once-in-a-lifetime bargains.

The number of places you can put your money is truly astounding, and dozens more are appearing every year. You have to know which are good, and which will devour your funds and not even spit back a chicken bone in return. And you have to know whom to buy from. After all, would you purchase a genuine diamond ring in a twenty-four-carat gold setting from a street vendor in a Cairo bazaar?

Maybe *you* would. I sure wouldn't.

Let me offer another example — taxes. Earning money is obviously important. But it's even more important to keep it — not to have it all taxed away. We live in a country that is tax-oppressive. In a later chapter I'll explain in greater detail why this is so. For the moment, just take my word that, as things stand now, you cannot build wealth in Canada unless you take advantage of some of the opportunities in our quirky tax laws. Another reality is that the tax rules are constantly changing — no sooner do you figure out a way of getting around them than the government amends the law — for example, by constantly changing the rules for the capital gains exemption. It's like building a house on quicksand. Nevertheless, you have to try.

I occasionally get letters from people who suggest it's somehow immoral to plan your financial life so as to reduce taxes.

Well, if it's immoral, it's the government's fault, not mine. It's the government — or, more correctly, successive governments, federal and provincial — that have created a tax burden that dulls initiative and destroys incentive. But those same governments have built all sorts of weird and wonderful incentives into our tax laws to encourage us to invest our money in particular ways — and to ensure that, if we do as they wish, we can keep more of our wealth for ourselves. Until that situation changes, the true wealth builder will seek out every possible way to take advantage of it. That's not immoral. That's simple common sense.

Let me go back to where I started. To learn all these things obviously takes time. If you're not prepared to commit that time, don't begin. It also takes some experience — you're going to make mistakes along the way. When you do, try to limit your losses and learn from them.

That's enough preaching. Let's begin.

We'll start with some basics — principles that you establish for yourself and stick to. You may find these are as simple as brushing your teeth. You're right, they are — and you'd be amazed at the number of would-be wealth builders who fail to apply them and end up in all sorts of trouble as a result.

Principle One: Establish an objective. It's much easier to begin a wealth building program if you have a specific reason for doing so. Remember what I said in Chapter One about defining wealth for yourself in terms of things you can enjoy? That's what this exercise is all about. Set an objective and view that objective as a reward. It can be anything. Maybe it's a short-term goal, like buying a house or paying off a car loan early. Maybe it's more long term, perhaps setting up a plan for your baby's university education. The key is to establish the motivation and the self-discipline that will be needed to set up your wealth building plan and keep it going.

Ideally, your first objective should be something that's attainable within a reasonable time. If your first wealth target is something you have no hope of achieving for ten or twenty years, you may become discouraged and lapse back into your old ways.

Once you've chosen your wealth objective, put a dollar value on it and attach a time frame. That eliminates the vagueness that so often ruins the best intentions.

But remember — and I can't stress this enough — don't set your first objective too high. Make sure it's attainable. On the other hand, don't make it too easy. You should be prepared to sacrifice something to get what you want.

Principle Two: Keep things simple. Don't try to run before you can walk. If you do, you're almost sure to fall flat on your face.

Frequently when I'm a guest on a telephone hot line show I'll get a call from someone who says something like: "I don't know a lot about investing and I've just bought some shares in Moose Pasture United Mutual Fund. What can you tell me about it?"

Forgive my bluntness, but what a stupid question to ask! The caller has just bought a diamond in a Cairo bazaar and now wants to know if it's real!

One of the most common mistakes made by beginning wealth builders is to put money into something they don't understand and know nothing about. My first response when I get a question like that is to ask the caller what he or she can tell me about Moose Pasture United Mutual Fund. If the answer is "nothing" — and it usually is — then I know the caller has a serious problem.

Unfortunately, it's one I can't do much about, except to suggest they buy a copy of my annual mutual fund guide before they invest again.

There's a golden rule when it comes to wealth building: IF YOU DON'T UNDERSTAND IT, DON'T PUT YOUR MONEY INTO IT! It's so basic, yet it's violated all the time — often by people who would never dream of spending a few hundred dollars on a new appliance without investigating it thoroughly and satisfying themselves they were getting the best possible deal. I know. I've done it myself. Never once has it turned out right.

Making an investment is like buying something. It's strictly *caveat emptor* — let the buyer beware. There are a lot of high pressure sales types out there who will call you on the phone or, even worse, come to your door trying to get you to sign up for a particular investment. And they can be *very* persuasive, believe me. I've had people from brokerage firms I've never heard of call me out of the blue and describe in glowing terms all the money I can make by getting in on the ground floor of some obscure gold mine in northern Quebec. If you get such calls, just remember the Cairo bazaar.

That's why you should never try to build your wealth on something you don't understand. Sure, that means you'll have to take time to do some research into an opportunity that sounds good. I never said building wealth was going to be easy. If you don't want to take the time, then pass, tempting as the offer may sound. There's always another bus.

Principle Three: Start small. Don't get in over your head before you know what you're doing. When you're ready to begin investing, pick something that doesn't require a large cash outlay and get a feel for what you're doing. Once you're comfortable, you can commit more funds or move on to something else.

Principle Four: Don't be afraid to build your wealth on borrowed money. Just be sure you go about it in a sensible, organized way and don't leave yourself so far out on a limb that you risk falling off if things go wrong. I'll have more to say about building wealth with other people's money later in the book.

Principle Five: Look for investments you can enjoy. As I said earlier, that's what wealth is all about. Try to hold as much of your assets as seems reasonable in investments that give you personal pleasure. A family home. A cottage on a serene lake. An antique car. A fashion boutique. Wealth building isn't accumulating cash so you can buy something you want later. It's obtaining the things you want as you go along — just as long as those things are genuine assets and not liabilities.

How can you tell the difference? Real assets will appreciate in value because of certain inherent characteristics. These include quality, scarcity, high demand and revenue potential. Not every asset will possess all these traits. But it should have at least one and, preferably, two.

Liabilities, as you might expect, have exactly the opposite characteristics: indifferent or poor quality, abundance, low demand, and on-going cost.

The family car is a liability because it will normally last for only a few years, depreciates steadily, and costs a great deal to operate. No one in their right mind is going to take it off your hands for more than you paid for it.

A classic Packard, on the other hand, is an asset because of its meticulous construction, scarcity and prestige. Antique car buffs will fall all over themselves offering to buy it from you.

So what material investments are most likely to appreciate in value? Certain types of real estate — although don't expect property values to increase in the 1990s at anything like the pace they did in the eighties. Your best real estate bet for the rest of the decade is well-located cottage property. Demographers tell us the baby boomers are just arriving at the stage in life when they're most likely to buy a vacation residence. As long as the economy holds up, that suggests properties in areas like Whistler and the Gulf Islands in B.C., Canmore and Banff in Alberta, Lake Winnipeg in Manitoba, Muskoka in Ontario, and the Nova Scotia coast are going to be hot spots over the next few years. If Quebec sticks around, add the Gatineau Hills, Laurentians, and Eastern Townships to that list.

Given the low inflationary expectations for the rest of the nineties, urban properties will probably gain value very slowly, especially now that the government has declared real estate ineligible for the capital gains exemption. Collectibles, such as fine art, do best in an inflationary environment.

Your best material asset in this decade might be a family business with low overhead and strong profit potential. It's one of the best ways I know to combine wealth building, tax advantages and personal satisfaction.

In the end, it comes down to what you know best and are most comfortable with — as long as the asset meets the criteria outlined above.

Principle Six: Remember that prices don't always go up. Just ask those who assumed that house prices in Toronto would keep rising forever. What a shock they got when the bottom began to fall out of the market in 1989!

Under the right (or, more correctly, the wrong) circumstances, anything can drop in value. Hold that thought in the back of your mind as you embark on your wealth building adventure.

Final principle: Begin. That may sound simple, but many people never get started. They have great intentions, but they keep putting things off. Next month they'll get going. But next month something comes up. That's the worst enemy of the beginning wealth builder — the old "Oh, I'll get around to it sometime" syndrome.

If you're determined to start a wealth building program, then do it! Don't make up excuses for waiting. That's a game for smokers who don't really want to quit. I don't care if it's only five dollars a month — the important thing is to get into the habit of putting some money aside. Once you start you'll find it's not as difficult as you thought. And you'll find it easier to add a little more to the wealth building program whenever your household income goes up.

Where do you find the money to get going? There are several ideas in the next chapter, but here's one that was told me recently by a couple in Cobourg, Ontario after one of my seminars.

In the fall of 1987, they realized that they weren't putting anything aside for retirement. They were both in their late thirties and had no pension plan. They knew they should be making regular RRSP contributions, but couldn't find the money.

Both the husband and wife smoked. They had been telling each other for years they should quit; now they decided to do it. They made an agreement to stop on October 1, 1987. They would then monitor the cost of cigarettes every three months, calculate how much money they'd saved, and contribute that amount to an RRSP.

By January, 1992 — just a little more than four years later — they told me that, between them, they'd contributed over $22,000 to their retirement plans!

Amazing what a little imagination — and self-discipline — can achieve!

So there you have the seven basic principles for building wealth. Establish objectives. Keep things simple. Start small. Use other people's money, with discretion. Select investments that give you pleasure. Remember that prices don't always go up. And, above all, begin. Never lose sight of those rules and the odds will always be in your favour.

One other point I want to make before we finish this chapter — the importance of timing. I'm sure someone must have said this before but I couldn't find it in my dictionary of quotations so I'll pretend I made it up. It's this: Every prediction about money comes true eventually. The problem is that you can go broke waiting for it to happen.

Building wealth is like anything else in life: good timing plays a critical role in your success. That applies to everything from buying a house to investing in the stock market. If you get the timing wrong it can end up costing you a lot of money. Get it right more often than not and you'll do very well for yourself.

Just think about the gold panic in the late 1970s. People were actually lining up in bitter winter weather to buy the stuff for over $800 an ounce! It may have seemed like a good idea at the time. But in retrospect it was crazy — a classic example of bad timing. The price hasn't been near that level since, and I don't expect it will be in this century.

Then we have our periodic housing panics — at least two of them

I can recall during the 1980s. People bidding unheard-of prices for property in places like Toronto and Vancouver. No sooner did a house go on the market than potential buyers were fighting over it, actually paying more than the asking price. Great if you happened to be the seller. A disaster if you were buying, as those that were doing so at the time have since learned.

I have a number of friends who have been caught up in this type of housing hysteria. One sold his comfortable home in a good district in Toronto in early 1981 at a profit, and then turned around and bought a more expensive property at an inflated price. The idea was to re-sell the new house for an even bigger return. It never happened. The boom collapsed as quickly as it had started. My friend ended up with a terrible loss when he had to re-sell the property in a down market because rising interest rates made it too expensive to carry. Talk about bad timing! He ruefully admits today it was the worst investment decision he ever made.

He wasn't alone by any means. When Toronto house prices were getting silly again in the late eighties, another friend decided he wanted to trade up. He bought a new home at an inflated price, before his old one had sold. You can guess what happened. The real estate market suddenly went cold. He was stuck with carrying the cost of two houses and eventually had to sell his old house at a much lower price than he'd anticipated.

Obviously, no one is going to time their financial moves perfectly on every occasion. We aren't soothsayers. Even the most sophisticated money managers frequently misread the signs. (In fact, I sometimes think they do so more often than people who use plain old common sense.) There is probably nothing more difficult in the process of wealth building than getting the timing right.

I have a few thoughts that may help, though.

The first is, don't run with the herd. As often as not, the herd is wrong. Think of lemmings. When everyone wants to buy, prices often get bid up to unrealistic levels. That's when you should be selling, if you have something to sell. If not, stay on the sidelines and wait. If you get caught up with the herd, chances are you'll end up drowning.

The time to buy is when everyone's gloomy and wants to

unload. As long as you buy good quality and are patient, you'll be rewarded.

The housing market in 1991 and early 1992 is a classic example. The recession so spooked Canadians that few were prepared to take advantage of bargain prices, even when five-year mortgage rates dropped below ten percent. Uncertainty about the future and fear of losing their jobs combined to keep potential home buyers on the sidelines.

It's a typical reaction. But unless you can overcome it and take advantage of windows of opportunity when they open, you'll have difficulty building substantial wealth.

The second point related to timing is don't be greedy. If you have a nice profit, take it. Don't hang on in hopes of more. You may miss the occasional spectacular gain. But the more modest profits will add up quickly — and you'll sleep better while they do.

Next, be flexible. Change your wealth building program to meet new conditions. Back in the 1970s, many financial advisors were telling people to buy the most expensive home they could and carry the largest possible mortgage. In a time of high inflation, which we were experiencing then, real estate values would escalate quickly. Meantime, you'd be paying off your loan in rapidly depreciating dollars.

Great idea. Except conditions changed. Soaring interest rates in 1981 wiped out many people who had taken on excessive debt. Then came a disinflation period, which made the idea of paying off the mortgage in devalued dollars less viable. Today, two recessions later, the whole tactic makes no sense at all. The concern in the nineties is to get out of debt, not to accumulate more of it.

Finally, don't try to call everything on the nose. The chances are pretty slim you'll be able to renew your mortgage just as interest rates hit their low for the decade, or sell your stock at what turns out later to have been its all-time high. What you want to avoid is being caught at the wrong end of any cycle — locking in long-term mortgages when rates are high, as many people did in 1990. Believe me, that is *not* a way to build your wealth. Just ask the folks who are still paying over thirteen percent on their mortgage loan and wondering how to get out of it.

To avoid that kind of situation, it's essential to stay informed on what's going on in the world around you — and to understand what the likely consequences of current events will mean to your money. It was obvious in early 1990 that high interest rates could not be sustained for very long. The economy was in deep trouble (indeed, the recession was already starting). As business slowed, anyone with the slightest knowledge of how the Bank of Canada works knew that interest rates would inevitably come down. It took several months, but a year later, they were in free-fall.

Unfortunately, in the trauma of the moment, many people lose sight of basic realities. They end up paying a high price for their short-sightedness.

Wealth building does not take place in isolation. The degree of your success will be influenced, at least in part, by your ability to understand the significance of national and international events and relate them to your decisions and your timing.

"No man is an island," wrote the great English poet and essayist, John Donne. The successful wealth builder needs to understand that better than anybody — and to use the knowledge accordingly.

There's No Such Thing as Riskless

The only way to be absolutely safe is never to try anything for the first time.
— Dr. Magnus Pyke

If you've ever read anything about making money, you've probably been told that the place to start is with risk-free investments.

Well, I hate to disillusion you, but there's no such thing.

There are low-risk investments, investments that guarantee to preserve your capital, and investments that promise to provide a steady income.

But risk-free? No way. I only wish there were such an animal.

Five years ago, you might have argued with me. Many people saw their home as a riskless investment. Real estate prices seemed destined to perpetually rise, especially in cities like Toronto.

But, as we've recently learned yet again, nothing is forever. The latest recession disproved the notion that real estate is a never-ending win-win game. People now understand the realities of home-owning — at least they will until the next boom takes hold.

A home is still a low-risk investment. But it's not risk-free. If you have to sell at the wrong time, you can take a financial beating.

It happened to people in Calgary and Edmonton who bought homes in the 1970s and eighties when oil was king and property values in Western Canada were soaring. When the bust came in the wake of the 1981–82 recession, property values tumbled and thousands of Albertans simply walked away from their dream homes. The houses were worth less than the balance outstanding on the mortgage.

It happened to Torontonians who purchased homes in the late eighties at grossly inflated prices and then watched unbelieving as property values nosedived. Between the fall of 1989 and spring 1992 the average price of a centrally-located detached bungalow in the modest Toronto suburb of Scarborough fell from $250,000 to $192,000 — a drop of twenty-three percent. An executive two-storey home in the trendy Annex area of Toronto fared even worse, losing a quarter of its value, from $420,000 to $315,000.

No, a home is not risk-free. A combination of bad timing, personal misfortune and general economic conditions can result in the loss of many thousands of dollars on a sale.

Don't misunderstand me. In most circumstances, owning your own home is an excellent wealth building technique, one which I highly recommend. But there are no guarantees. As with any other investment, you must make a careful purchase decision and be aware of the downside potential.

Maybe that's true of real estate, you say. But what about something as rock solid as good old Canada Savings Bonds? Surely that's a risk-free investment if there ever was one.

Sorry, no. CSBs guarantee to repay your principal, which is fine as long as the Government of Canada remains financially solvent (and with deficits continuing to run unchecked, I sometimes wonder how long that will be).

But Canada Savings Bonds carry three other risks, which many people fail to recognize. These are:

Interest rate risk. CSB rates are only in place for one year. Worse, the government removed the guaranteed floor a few years ago, which offered some protection against a sharp decline in rates. What you get now is equivalent to a one-year guaranteed investment certificate (GIC), except you're allowed to cash in a CSB without penalty after three months.

Today's CSBs have a twelve-year maturity. But that just means your money is automatically rolled over twelve times, at prevailing rates.

Big deal! If rates fall, you have absolutely no protection.

In 1990, for example, series 45 came out with a 10.75% interest rate. Not bad. The public bought $6.7 billion worth.

By fall 1991, interest rates had dropped substantially. The CSB rate was set at 7.5%. Even though you had made your purchase a year earlier, you had no protection. Your return dropped to 7.5%, along with all the other outstanding CSB issues. That represented a thirty percent decline in your yield!

That's interest rate risk.

Tax risk. The government loves to see people invest in CSBs and other interest-bearing securities. That's because all such investments take a hammering from Revenue Canada.

Unlike all other types of investment income, interest receives no special consideration from the government. You pay tax on any interest you earn — whether from CSBs, GICs, money market funds or your savings account — at your top marginal tax rate.

So if you're in a forty percent or higher tax bracket — which for the 1992 tax year included most people with taxable incomes in excess of $29,590 — you'll pay at least $40 of every $100 you earn in interest back to the government.

The only way around this is to shelter the investment in an RRSP, about which more later.

Inflation risk. When you assess the return on any investment, you have to take inflation into account. If your investment only manages to keep pace with inflation, you're standing still in terms of purchasing power.

The amount by which your return exceeds inflation is known as your "real return." For example, if inflation were to average three percent in a year when CSBs are paying 7.5%, your real return would be 4.5%.

That may not seem like much. However, by historical standards, it's very good. According to the Canadian Institute of Actuaries, the real annual return on long-term bonds over the thirty year period 1960–90 averaged only 1.33%. Treasury bills produced an average annual real return of 2.58% over that time, while stocks comprising the Toronto Stock Exchange 300 and its predecessor indexes yielded average annual real returns of 4.39%.

When inflation rises, real returns tend to decline. A CSB yield of ten percent may seem attractive. But if inflation is running at seven percent that year, the real return is only three percent.

The combination of tax risk and inflation risk makes clear just how poor CSBs are as investments outside a retirement plan.

Let's assume you're in a forty percent tax bracket, inflation is running at three percent annually, and your CSB yields 7.5%. You invest $1,000. Here's what happens:

Interest earned	$75.00
Tax assessed	30.00
After-tax return	45.00
Inflation loss on principal	30.00
Real after-tax return	15.00

Instead of a $75 return on your money, as you might expect at first glance, your real net benefit is only $15.

Hardly a way to get rich!

Guaranteed investment certificates, another popular way Canadians invest, carry the same type of risk. As well, they're only guaranteed up to $60,000 principal and interest if they're issued by a member of the Canada Deposit Insurance Corporation (CDIC). There's no limit on the amount of protection for CSBs.

Okay, so why not just hold cash? Surely that's risk-free.

Nope. Remember inflation? That chronic eating away of the purchasing power of your money? If you want to really see it at work, just try this test. Put aside $1,000. Stuff it in your mattress or bury it. Include a note of what it will buy today — how many bottles of your favourite wine, or how many litres of gas, or how much fertilizer for your lawn. Then forget about it for ten years.

You can guess what will happen when you finally retrieve the money, even if inflation stays at relatively low levels over the decade.

If the Consumer Price Index rises just three percent a year, today's ten-dollar bottle of wine will cost almost $13.50 a decade from now. At four percent inflation, the price of the wine will rise to $14.80.

A fifty-cent litre of gas will cost sixty-seven cents in ten years at three percent annual inflation; seventy-four cents at four percent.

But each dollar you stuffed into the mattress is still worth exactly that — one dollar.

Cash risk-free? Not on your life. Its purchasing power will erode every year, unless there's a major depression in the meantime. You won't have built wealth by keeping your funds in "risk-free" cash; you'll have diminished it.

I hope I've made my point. Nothing — absolutely nothing — is without risk when it comes to building wealth. The key is to manage risk effectively. That means understanding the level of risk in any wealth building decision and knowing when to take a chance, and when to pass.

To build wealth, you have to be prepared to accept some level of risk. The amount that's tolerable is a personal decision.

When you're just starting out, you should aim to minimize risk. A big loss early on could spook you for life.

I have a golfing friend who's a successful professional. He's built an excellent practice and makes a fine living from it. We have a lot of things in common — but investing is not one of them. The whole idea frightens him.

Why? Because many years ago, he put money into a business venture — a high-risk deal that seemed to offer the prospect of good returns. It went sour and he was badly burned. Now he doesn't want to hear about the stock market or bonds or anything else. He's gun shy, and will remain so as long as he lives.

That's why it's wise to minimize your risk during the early years. Stick with wealth building techniques you're comfortable with and which have low downside potential. And never, never put all your eggs in one basket, even if that basket is your own home.

As you start to accumulate wealth, you can accept a higher level of risk if you wish to try to get rich sooner rather than later. Higher risk investments should, by definition, offer the potential for greater returns — otherwise why would you be in them at all? This relationship is known as the risk/return ratio. It simply means that the more risk you assume, the greater the potential reward should be. But as you add risk, be sure to always protect your base.

Remember the rule about preserving capital. Don't put essential funds into moderate or high risk situations. Otherwise, you could lose everything and end up back at square one.

Where should you start? The first step is to accumulate some cash to invest. Easy for him to say, you may be muttering. I can barely make ends meet and he's telling me to put some money aside.

Well, come on. I didn't say this was going to be a piece of cake. But if you don't make a start, you're not going to get anywhere. Think about the Cobourg couple I told you about in the last chapter. Use your imagination. Here are some ideas that may get you going:

Tax refund cheques. Almost every salaried person gets money back from the government each year. That's because Revenue Canada's tax tables are deliberately structured to withhold more money at source than is strictly necessary. It gives the government an interest-free loan (they can certainly use the money, after all) and reduces the possibility of people reneging on their tax bill.

So what will you do with that money? Many people rush out and spend it. Don't be one of them. Decide in advance to put half of it towards your personal wealth building program. How you use it is up to you. Then take the other half and have fun — without guilt.

Child benefit payments. Lower income families with children, which includes many young couples, will receive more money each month under the child benefit program announced in the 1992 federal budget. For example, a family with three children and income of $40,000 a year will receive more than $2,400 in 1993 — over $200 a month.

Part or all of that money could be directed towards a family wealth building program — perhaps by investing for the children's future education.

Pay raises. Any salary increase you or your spouse receives is extra money. You're not using it to live on now, so you should be able to put something aside for a wealth building plan.

I suggest you earmark twenty-five percent of the after-tax

amount you and your spouse receive from each salary increase for wealth building. It may not seem like much at the beginning, but over time you'll be amazed how it will add up.

Moonlighting. If you find a way to earn additional income in your spare time, put a hefty chunk of it aside for wealth building — say half, after tax. Have fun with the rest.

Windfalls. Sometimes money can appear from totally unexpected sources — a small lottery win, an insurance claim, an inheritance, a gift from a relative. If you get lucky, at least half the money should go towards your wealth building plan.

Remember, you don't have to start big. Even small amounts will grow faster than you'd expect. But you have to make the effort — even if it involves a degree of personal sacrifice.

When you get some money, then what? Start by holding it in a money market mutual fund or something similar. If you aren't contributing regularly to an RRSP, begin doing so. When you have enough money available, consider buying a family home if the market seems right. Then adopt an accelerated mortgage paydown plan. I'll provide details of how to go about all this in subsequent chapters.

When you reach the point where you've done all this, you can start looking at some higher-risk ventures. They can be a lot of fun, especially when you score. But sometimes you have to have strong nerves.

Consider oil stocks, for example. After the oil scares earlier in the decade drove prices to near-record highs, oil prices collapsed in early 1986. The value of stocks in Canadian petroleum companies followed suit. Even blue-ribbon firms like Imperial Oil saw their share values sink to their lowest levels in years.

The doomsayers were in full cry. Oil prices were going to fall to five dollars a barrel, or even lower. OPEC was dead. They were going to hang a "closed" sign on Alberta. Shares of Imperial Oil sagged to below $35 on the Toronto Stock Exchange.

In the midst of all this, a few investors paused to think about the underlying realities. Yes, there was an international oil glut. Yes,

OPEC countries were busily undercutting one another's prices in a desperate bid to maintain market share. Yes, the result was a steep fall in oil prices.

But the world was still consuming a hell of a lot of the stuff and would continue to do so for the foreseeable future. And they weren't making any more of it. So surely, these investors reasoned, the price fall had to be temporary. Prices would recover and so would share values.

So they took a calculated risk. They bought Imperial Oil. Within a year they had more than doubled their money.

It doesn't always work out that way of course. Oil prices might have fallen further. Or they could have taken much longer to recover. Or investors might have become greedy and held their shares too long — after the Gulf War ended in 1991, oil prices again dropped sharply and by early 1992 Imperial's shares were trading back at close to 1986 levels.

But the potential reward appeared to be worth the risk right at that moment. As it turned out, it was.

Intelligent risk can dramatically accelerate the wealth building process. But you must know what you are doing, what the downside is and what the potential rewards are. If you don't know, don't go. And don't even consider higher-risk wealth building techniques, tempting as they may be, until you have a solid base firmly in place.

This book will give you what you need to build that base. The risks can come later, at a time of your choosing. You'll find the techniques of taking calculated risks in my companion book *Low-Risk Investing*.

CHAPTER
4

Real Life Monopoly

A lot of people will urge you to put some money in a bank and in fact — within reason — this is very good advice. But don't go overboard. Remember, what you are doing is giving your money to someone else to hold on to, and I think it is worth keeping in mind that the businessmen who run banks are so worried about holding on to things that they put little chains on all their pens.

— Miss Piggy

From the time we were kids, Monopoly conditioned us to believe that the Bank was the source of all wealth. It was the Banker who dispensed the cash when we passed Go, handed out the property cards, held our mortgages and seized our assets when we couldn't pay our street repairs assessment. We grew up believing the words "bank" and "wealth" were synonymous.

Of course, life isn't a Monopoly game. But you could do a lot worse than to bring out the board and play a few games again. You'll find that to succeed at Monopoly requires using many of the same principles of sound investing that work well in real life.

For instance, Monopoly winners are those who use their resources in the most effective way to acquire assets — in this case, property groups — and to generate income from them. Usually, the winner is the player willing to take a calculated risk — perhaps mortgaging some holdings to buy a couple of extra houses at a critical point in the game.

We didn't realize it at the time, but Monopoly taught us some of the basics of business negotiating — is trading Park Place for Vermont and Oriental a good idea or not? We learned the importance of retaining a cash reserve, in case one of those dreaded street repair cards turned up at just the wrong moment.

And we learned something about banking. We observed that the Bank facilitated the flow of money, as it does in the real world. We used the Bank as a source of capital when we needed to mortgage a property or sell a house. And we watched the Bank seize our assets when we got into financial difficulty.

Then we grew up — and discovered the world really does work that way.

Properly used, the Bank can be a wealth building ally. Screw up, and it can take away everything you own.

Banks operate on three main levels. At its most basic, a bank is simply a financial depository, a place that holds your money for a short time between payday and the weekly trip to the grocery store.

Even at that level, however, banking can be a complex procedure. Bad decisions can cost you money.

Take the choice of an account, for example. It's not as easy a decision as it may seem. Today's banks offer several alternatives; choosing the wrong one can be expensive.

When you're selecting a deposit account, there are two points to consider: the amount of interest you'll receive (which is taxable) and the service charges you'll pay (which are usually not tax deductible).

Too many people decide they want an interest-bearing account without thinking it through. They lose sight of the fact that high service charges can more than wipe out any interest earned if you're not careful.

There was a time when bank service charges were minimal. But that was years ago, when I was young.

Today, you can be dinged for everything from withdrawals to telephone inquiries. Many banks (and trust companies as well) assess a "maintenance fee" if your balance falls below a certain amount each month, or charge for each cheque if your monthly balance is less than a magic number, even for a day.

You can even be assessed if you don't use your account. My youngest daughter, Deborah, had all the assets in her small account seized when she was ten because she wasn't actively using it. (Yes, they can get away with that; check over the list of service charges they'll give you on request and read up on inactive accounts.)

You also pay for services that weren't dreamed of a generation ago. For example, financial institutions encourage clients to make use of automatic banking machines, which reduce staffing requirements. But if your balance is below a certain level, you'll be charged every time you do so.

When my son was in college, I once took a look at one of his bank statements. He was in the habit of making twenty-dollar withdrawals from an ABM whenever he needed some cash. The bank charged him a buck every time he did. That's a five percent fee for making a simple withdrawal! He was shocked when I pointed it out to him; he wasn't even aware it was happening (which shows the importance of reviewing your statements when they come in).

A study published by Statistics Canada in April, 1992 illustrates the extent to which banks have been socking it to their customers through service charges in recent years.

In 1980, banks earned revenue of just under $1.5 billion from service charges, according to the report. By 1991, the amount was up to almost $5.5 billion — more than three and a half times the 1980 figure. By comparison, interest revenue from loan spreads had increased about fifty percent, albeit from a much larger base figure.

With service charges continuing to escalate, you have to pay close attention to your accounts. If you want to know whether you're using the right kind of account at present, take this simple test. Collect your bank statements for the past six months. Add up the total amount of interest you've received. Apply your marginal tax rate to determine how much of that you'll have to pay to the government. The balance is the after-tax interest earned by your account.

Now add up all the service charges. If the total exceeds the amount of after-tax interest you've earned, you have the wrong kind of account. You'd probably be better off switching to a non-interest paying account with a less onerous fee structure.

Alternatively, you might want a bundled package of services — one that covers a variety of fees for a set monthly cost. Next time you're in the bank, ask what options are available.

The second level on which you may use your bank is to invest money. In the past, this wasn't a big part of a bank's normal business. But times have changed and the banking industry is changing with them.

The most common type of bank investment is a term deposit (TD) or guaranteed investment certificate (GIC). You'll find these two terms used rather loosely and sometimes interchangeably. For some reason, the financial community can't seem to agree on exactly what each means.

I'll explain the difference between them in a later chapter, as well as how to use these securities most effectively. For now, let me just make the point that bank TDs and GICs are usually the least competitive you'll find from an interest rate point of view.

In mid-March, 1992, for example, the big five banks were all offering 8.25% for five year GICs. Most trust companies, by contrast, were paying 8.5% to 8.75%, with one offering a nine percent return. A half point more may not seem like much. But over five years it will add about $350 to the value of a $10,000 investment.

The banks get away with offering less because they're perceived as safe and solid. During a period when many trust companies have run into financial difficulty, the banks have been trading on their image of stability to attract your money at lower rates.

But unless you're dealing with unusually large sums, your GICs will be protected by deposit insurance, no matter which financial institution you use. So you should have a very good reason for accepting a lower return. After all, would you buy a car for $15,000 when the dealer down the street is offering exactly the same model for $1,000 less?

GICs and term deposits are the most popular form of bank investments. But there are many others.

Mutual funds are becoming big business for banks and many are spending large amounts of money promoting them.

You'll find a detailed explanation of mutual funds in Chapter Seventeen. Those offered by banks (and trust companies) are usually of the no load variety, meaning you won't be assessed any sales commission when you buy.

They also have the advantage of convenience; most branches offer them for sale — at least in theory.

Sometimes it doesn't work out that way, however. My daughter, Deborah, decided to make an RRSP contribution for the 1991 tax year on the last possible day — Saturday, February 29, 1992. Normally, our branch of the CIBC isn't open on Saturday but, because of the RRSP deadline, this day was an exception. I called to inquire about their mortgage mutual fund, which I thought might be a good, conservative choice for her. I was told we couldn't buy the fund that day because the woman who was authorized to sell mutual funds wasn't working.

"Why are you open this Saturday?" I asked the tentative lady at the other end of the line.

"For late RRSP contributions, sir."

"And aren't your mutual funds RRSP-eligible?"

"Yes, sir."

"And you only have one person who can sell mutual funds?"

"Yes, sir."

"And she's off today?"

"Yes."

"How can that be?"

"It doesn't make much sense, does it, sir?"

No, it didn't, although it was typical of the kind of service you'll sometimes find in banks (can you imagine a trust company not having a mutual fund sales representative available that day?).

But, most of the time, you should be able to buy mutual funds at your bank branch.

That doesn't mean you should automatically do so. Just because there's no sales commission and the mutual fund counter is right there doesn't necessarily mean it's a good investment. Generally, bank and trust company-sponsored mortgage funds have a solid track record as excellent performers. But some of their other funds are still new and have not yet proven themselves.

Also, contrary to the conservative image we tend to have of banks, some of the new mutual funds are in the higher-risk category. Banks now offer funds which invest in the Canadian and American stock markets, for example, as well as some international funds.

So don't assume that because it's sold by a bank, it's a low-risk investment. Spend some time learning about mutual funds and which are the best bets before deciding.

The number of investment products sold by banks expanded dramatically when many of them crossed the line into the brokerage field in recent years. Some created their own brokerage operations; others bought up existing firms.

Toronto-Dominion was first into the field, in 1984, with its Green Line Investor Services, which has grown into the largest discount brokerage operation in Canada. Green Line is available in all TD branches across the country, making it easily accessible to almost all Canadians.

Responding to the challenge, the Bank of Montreal purchased the highly respected brokerage house of Nesbitt Thomson in 1987. Within the next two years, Royal Bank acquired the biggest full-service brokerage firm in the country, Dominion Securities (now RBC Dominion); the Bank of Commerce acquired the prestigious Wood Gundy operation; while the Bank of Nova Scotia bought McLeod Young Weir, renaming the house ScotiaMcLeod.

Some trust companies have also moved into the brokerage business. Canada Trust's CT Investment Counsel is available through all branches, while Royal Trust offers a more limited service under the name Meridian.

Except for TD's Green Line, brokerage services have not yet been fully integrated with banking operations in most cases. However, the banks' move into this field, and their oft-stated desire to add insurance to their product line, raises the possibility they'll be transformed into financial supermarkets in the not-too-distant future.

Before that can happen, however, the level of competence of bank employees will have to be raised considerably. Many of them have only minimal understanding of even the basic products and services they offer today, and no comprehension at all of the more complex new products being made available. This means you should be cautious in accepting investment advice from your bank; make sure the person you're dealing with is properly qualified.

To their credit, the major banks are taking steps to remedy this weakness. The Royal Bank spent more than $80 million in 1992 on training. The Bank of Montreal is building a $40 million training centre in Scarborough, Ontario. But if you're considering making banking a career, the Commerce is the one to look at. They spent millions to buy the luxurious King Ranch spa north of Toronto after it ran into financial trouble in late 1991, with the idea of turning it into the most desirable training facility in Canada. CIBC employees should be falling all over each other to upgrade their skills.

The third level of bank service is capital, in the form of loans. It may be to buy a car, or start a business, or to purchase a home, but there are very few of us who don't go to the bank for money sooner or later.

It can be a humbling experience; some even describe it as degrading. The bank will probe into all the dark corners of your financial life. The loan officer will want to know where you work and how much you make. He or she will want to know about what you own and what it's worth. You'll be asked about your credit cards, cheque writing habits and other outstanding loans. You'll have to tell the bank where you live and what it costs. And if you haven't been there very long, they'll ask you where you were before that and before that. If you're married, your spouse may be asked all the same questions as well. And, of course, they'll run a complete credit check on both of you.

If you want to use the money to finance a business, you'll have to provide all the relevant information about that too. If it's not already up and running and showing a profit, you'd better come armed with a well-thought-out business plan if you're to have any hope of getting the money.

Bank financing has become even tougher to get as a result of the 1990–92 recession, which saw many loans go sour with resulting write-offs in the millions. If you haven't already established a good credit rating with a bank, expect to go through a real grilling before you get your money — and consider yourself fortunate if you eventually do.

As this is written, the banks are in the process of adding a brand-new level of service — trust services. Until mid-1992, these were the exclusive preserve of the trust companies. But a major package of financial reforms which became effective June 1, 1992 changed all that. Banks were allowed to compete directly in the trust services field. Toronto-Dominion, the Bank of Nova Scotia, the Commerce and the Royal Bank were the first off the mark with applications to set up their own trust companies, but by the time you read this most of the other banks will probably also be competing for this business.

At some stage in your life, you'll almost certainly use every level of a bank's services, probably many times. And you'll find the more you do, the closer you'll be tied to that particular financial institution.

Many times, for example, I've suggested to my wife that we switch our business from our current bank, because I didn't like their service fees or another financial institution was offering better rates. But we never did. Our CIBC branch is close by, they know us there and we have a well-established credit record with them.

That's why it's important to make the initial choice of a financial institution carefully. Once you've set up your accounts, given them your mortgage business and opened an RRSP, switching somewhere else becomes complicated. You'd rather pay the higher service charge or accept the lower interest rate than go through the hassle of moving.

So don't just pick the branch that's most convenient. Do a little research first. Compare accounts, rate structures and services. You may find that walking an extra block will save a lot of money over the long term.

Child Labour Isn't The Only Answer

It sometimes happens, even in the best of families, that a baby is born. This is not necessarily cause for alarm. The important thing is to keep your wits about you and borrow some money.
— Elinor Goulding Smith

If you have kids, you know what it's like. You love them dearly, but boy, are they expensive! From the moment they're born, they cost. Cribs, baby toys, diapers, clothes, shoes, school supplies, bicycles, bedroom furniture, groceries, sports equipment, allowances, driving lessons, university fees. There's always money going out and the older they get, the more expensive they are. And it seems like a one-way street — it all goes out and nothing comes back.

There was a time when children were looked upon as an investment, the Victorian equivalent of a retirement annuity.

Grow a bunch of them and then let them support you in your old age. But it doesn't work that way in our society any more. I don't know anyone who wants to be dependent on their children when they retire — nor many children who want to be saddled with that kind of financial burden. Dependence on children is out. Independence is in.

So kids have become what a hard-nosed business person would describe as a cost-centre. They dissipate family wealth, in the process making it particularly hard for younger couples to start accumulating funds for investing. We accept this willingly, of course, because children bring a different kind of wealth to our lives: the wealth of family relationships, of nurturing and bonding, of a sense of parental accomplishment in watching them evolve into useful and interesting adults.

But this is a book about money, not the joys of child-raising. Still, wouldn't it be nice if you could somehow combine the two? Have all the pleasure (and anguish) of bringing up a family and turn some profit from that as well?

Well, there are ways to gain some financial rewards from your children — and I'm *not* talking here about bringing back child labour. You won't recover all the costs involved in raising them, of course. But you can certainly make the financial burden of child rearing less painful and accelerate your whole wealth building process.

The first step is to develop an understanding of our constantly evolving tax system as it relates to children and to use it to the best advantage.

Let's start with the basics. As soon as your first child is born, you become eligible to receive monthly payments from the federal government.

Until the end of 1992, one of these cheques was a universal family allowance payment. Every family with qualifying children received the monthly payment, although those with higher incomes had to pay part or all of it back at tax time.

Some parents also received a refundable child tax credit, a payment designed to provide additional financial support for children of lower-income families. The calculations to determine eligibility were quite complex — the 1991 General Tax Guide devoted a full page to explaining the credit. As a result, some families may not have claimed their proper entitlement.

A third break for children was the non-refundable child credit, which showed up on the tax return. It was peanuts, however, worth only $71 off your federal taxes for each of the first two children age eighteen or under (it doubled after that).

In the 1992 budget, the Federal Government moved to consolidate this patchwork quilt in a new program, to be called the Child Benefit. It becomes effective in 1993.

Unlike the old Family Allowance cheque, the Child Benefit is not a universal payment. Many higher income families — about 600,000, according to the government's estimate — will get nothing. But lower income families should receive higher payments than in the past. And even some upper middle income families will benefit, depending on the number of children they have. For example, a family with three children and $75,000 annual income will receive $681 a year under the new plan. And that amount won't be taxable, unlike the old Family Allowance payments. You get to keep it all!

The budget proposal was in the form of a White Paper and some of the details may be amended before the Child Benefit program goes into effect. But this, in brief, is Ottawa's plan:

• Eliminate Family Allowances, the refundable child tax credit and the child credit.

• Consolidate all these support programs into a new non-taxable Child Benefit, for which all children under age eighteen are eligible.

• Add an annual supplement of up to $500 for low-income families.

• Give families not claiming a child care expense deduction an extra $213 a year for each child under seven. If the claim for child care expenses is small, a portion of this amount may still be paid.

• Begin payments January 1, 1993. The refundable child tax credit and the child credit will apply for the 1992 tax year.

Because the program is designed to provide increased assistance to families who most need it, the amount you receive will be determined by income. The additional supplement for less advantaged families will also be calculated according to income, using a different formula.

Unfortunately, all this is going to retain, and even compound, the complexity of the refundable child tax credit and will certainly create confusion.

As this is written, final details of the Child Benefit haven't been approved. However, here's a way to figure out how much money you should be entitled to each month under the new plan in the first half of 1993, assuming it is implemented more or less as described in the budget proposal.

Step one: Calculate the basic benefit.

Number of children 18 or under x $1,020	_____	(a)
Number of children beyond two x $75	_____	(b)
Number of children under age seven for which no child care expenses are deducted x $213 (note: if your deduction is for less than $850, multiply the amount by 25% and subtract the result from $213. Enter the result here)	_____	(c)
Total Annual Child Benefit (total lines a, b, c)	_____	(d)
Divide by 12 to determine monthly payment	_____	(e)

Step two: Earned income supplement.
(Applies only if family income is less than $25,921)

Total family earned income (wages, etc.) in 1991	_____	(e)
Subtract exempt income	−$3,750.00	(f)
Income eligible for supplement (e − f)	_____	(g)
Multiply line g by 8%	x .08	(h)
Basic supplement (line g x line h)	_____	(i)
Family net income for 1991 tax year	_____	(j)
Multiply line j by 10%	x .1	(k)
Supplement deduction (line k x line j)	_____	(l)
Earned Income supplement (line i − line l)	_____	(m)
(Maximum $500)		
Annual child benefit (line m + line d)	_____	(n)
Monthly benefit (divide line n by 12)	_____	(o)

Step three: Calculate your income offset.

Family net income as per 1991 tax returns	_____	(p)
Subtract allowable income	−$25,921.00	(q)
Net income subject to reduction (p − q)	_____	(r)
Multiply line q by 2.5% if you have one child; by 5% if you have more	x .025 or .05	(s)
Benefit reduction (s x r)	_____	(t)
Monthly reduction (divide line t by 12)	_____	(u)
Reduced monthly benefit (Subtract line u from line o)	_____	(v)

I said it was complicated, didn't I? To make matters even worse, this calculation will only determine your monthly benefits for the first six months of 1993. From July on, your benefits will be based on 1992 tax information.

If you want a rough estimate of how much you'll receive, here's a table the government published in the White Paper that was released with the budget. These figures do not include the extra payments for families with children under seven not claiming any child care deductions.

	Annual Value of Child Benefit		
Family Income	**One Child**	**Two Children**	**Three Children**
$10,000	$1,520	$2,540	$3,635
20,000	1,520	2,540	3,635
30,000	918	1,836	2,931
40,000	668	1,336	2,431
50,000	418	836	1,931
60,000	168	336	1,431
75,000	0	0	681
100,000	0	0	0

Source: Government of Canada

The government plans to adjust these payments annually to compensate for inflation. However, as with most other government programs, the adjustment will only take into account changes in the Consumer Price Index in excess of three percent. The effect will be to gradually erode the purchasing power of the Child Benefit over time.

For example, if inflation runs at three percent annually, there would be no increase in the benefit from year to year. After ten years, a $2,500 benefit in 1993 would buy only about $1,840 worth of goods. After twenty years, the purchasing power would be down to about $1,350.

Clearly, this will reduce the value of the new system as a means of assisting parents as time goes on. For the 1990s, however, the program will provide genuine additional support for families who need it most.

Many people will rush out and spend the cheque as soon as it arrives. In some cases, they'll have no alternative; the money will mean the difference between a hungry child and one who is reasonably well fed.

But if your situation is such that you can save part or all of the Child Benefit cheque, the money can become an integral part of a family wealth building program.

In the past, many parents used Family Allowance cheques to set up an education fund for their children. There was a tax advantage to this because Revenue Canada took the position that interest earned from invested baby bonus cheques belonged to the child for tax purposes. Since most youngsters don't earn enough to pay taxes, the family received this money tax-free.

This mini-tax shelter remains and is actually strengthened with the Child Benefit. The federal Department of Finance, after first declaring that any income earned on money invested on the child's behalf would be attributed to the parent for tax purposes, did an about-face in May, 1992 and said the same rules would apply as for Family Allowance payments.

That means any income from invested Child Benefit cheques will be attributed to the child for tax purposes. Since kids don't normally earn enough income to pay taxes, that money will, in essence, be received by the family tax-free.

Not all families will be able to save part or all of the Benefit, of course. But for those who do, the wealth building potential is significant.

For example, a family with two children and income of $40,000 a year will be eligible for annual benefits of $1,336, according to the Department of Finance.

If that money were invested in the children's names at eight percent a year, it would grow to over $50,000 in eighteen years. A ten percent rate of return would produce a fund of more than $60,000.

A family with two children and $30,000 annual income will get $1,836 a year when the plan takes effect. Invested at ten percent a year, that will grow to about $84,000 over eighteen years.

The Child Benefit offers one great way to use your family to build wealth. However, there are other ways to put money aside for your children in a way that minimizes taxes. Here are two ideas:

Set up a Registered Education Savings Plan (RESP). These programs are designed to provide funds for a child's post-secondary education. You're allowed to contribute up to $1,500 per child each year. There is no tax deduction for your contribution. However, once the money is in the RESP, any interest earned will be attributed to the child when it is withdrawn for education purposes in future years. One word of caution. If the child does not go on to college or university, you'll lose all the interest earned by the plan over the years (you'll get your principal back, however). So be sure to choose a program that allows you to switch the beneficiary at any time. That way, if the child for whom you originally set up the plan decides not to continue his or her studies, you can switch it to another child without penalty. For this reason, I don't recommend an RESP for each child in a family. Retain some flexibility; not all children aspire to higher education.

Invest in an equity mutual fund. Revenue Canada's attribution rules apply to interest and dividend income. They do not, however, apply to capital gains. So by investing money on your child's behalf in a security that will mainly generate capital gains, you'll avoid having to pay tax on most of the child's profits. A good equity (stock) mutual fund is the easiest way to do this. Many companies offer plans which enable you to have a specified amount deducted directly from your account each month and used to purchase mutual fund units.

Obviously, the older your children are when you read this advice, the less effective any sort of a savings program intended to help pay education costs will be. There are fewer years to make deposits and less time for the magic of compound interest to work.

But if your kids are older, there are other things you can do. And you can also bring your spouse into the act.

The point to remember always is that our tax system treats each of us as individuals. Revenue Canada does not consider the combined income of married couples or family units in making its assessments (although it does so for purposes of determining certain entitlements, like the Child Benefit). That provides some opportunities for wealth building through tax saving, as well as by splitting income within the family. For example, you're far better off putting $5,000 in additional revenue into the hands of a child with no other income than in having it end up in the taxable income of the highest earning family member.

There used to be many ways to obtain tax advantages within a family unit. Unfortunately, Ottawa has been systematically tightening up on these in recent years. Still, there are some ways to obtain tax benefits if your family situation allows.

IF YOU'RE PAYING DAY CARE COSTS
Child care expenses are tax-deductible, within certain limits. The 1992 budget raised the limit to $5,000 for children under seven at the end of the year, or those who are disabled. For older children under fifteen at year-end, the maximum deduction is $3,000.

IF YOU HAVE CHILDREN OVER EIGHTEEN
You can make interest-free loans to them. The kids can then invest the money. The return on that investment is considered income in their hands. If they have little or no other income, that money will end up being received tax-free.

IF YOU HAVE CHILDREN AT COLLEGE OR UNIVERSITY

Post-secondary tuition fees are tax deductible. Also, full-time students at college or university are allowed an education credit of $13.60 per month of study (this is calculated by multiplying the maximum monthly education amount of $80 by seventeen percent).

In the past, many students couldn't take advantage of these credits because they did not have enough taxable income. Now the credits can be transferred to a supporting person (usually a parent) if the student can't make use of them. The maximum tax credit that may be claimed in any year is $680 (it was raised from $600 in the 1992 budget). It's not much compared to the cost of a college education these days, but every little bit helps.

IF YOU HAVE A FAMILY BUSINESS

Hire your spouse and your kids. They have to perform a legitimate function and be paid a fair wage. As long as you're careful about that, you should have no problem. But what can my kids do, you may ask? Lots of things — use your imagination. One of my daughters handles all my filing. It saves me a lot of time, and the small amount I pay her is more than worth it. Another one works for me in the summer, doing much of my research and handling correspondence. My son, who's a skilled cartoonist, does drawings which help illustrate my seminars, as well as computer work. My wife looks after all the company finances. There's a lot your family can contribute, if you give it some thought.

The advantages are substantial. The children learn the discipline of working for their money from an early age. Because the company pays them, their income is tax deductible to your business. And who knows — they may find the work interesting enough to want to join the company full time when they complete their education.

IF YOU'RE A TWO-INCOME FAMILY

You have to be especially careful in planning your wealth building program. Recent tax changes in Ottawa have created both new pitfalls and new opportunities. Start by taking a close look at your combined income and decide where and how you can begin accumulating some money. Your current lifestyle and financial obligations will obviously figure prominently in this exercise, but unless you're flirting with personal bankruptcy you should be able to find some cash to put aside. If you need some ideas, review Chapter Three again.

Once you've worked out a program with which you're comfortable, your strategy should be to implement it in such a way that the lower income spouse receives any investment income. That's because he or she will be taxed on that money at a lower rate, leaving more money for future investing.

You achieve this by having the lower income spouse provide all the investment capital. For example, suppose the husband is earning $40,000 a year as an office manager while the wife earns $15,000 a year as a free-lance writer. And let's say their provincial tax rate is fifty percent of the basic federal tax payable.

On this basis, the husband's 1991 marginal tax rate would have been about forty percent. The wife's rate, however, would only be about twenty-six percent. So for every $100 in interest income received by the husband, about $40 will go to Revenue Canada. If that interest is received by the wife, only $26 of every $100 will be taxed away.

Clearly, if this couple decided that, between them, they could put aside $100 a month for wealth building, they'd be much better off if the wife made the investments from her personal earnings. That's because Revenue Canada would regard any interest earned on that money as hers alone — and assess tax at a lower rate.

How much of a difference can this make? Let's say this couple put aside $1,200 a year in a non-tax sheltered interest-bearing investment (like a GIC) for ten years, with the money compounding at ten percent annually. At the end of that time, they'd have about $19,000. That would be generating interest at a rate of $1,900 a year. If the GIC were in the husband's name, the tax bill would be $760 annually (assuming his tax bracket hadn't changed). In the wife's name, the tax bill comes to less than $500. It's clearly worth the planning involved.

Finally, before we leave the subject of family, I'm often asked how to teach children about money. It's not easy. You don't want to put so much emphasis on the subject that your children become obsessed with it — something that is very easy to do. On the other hand, you want your children to develop a sensitivity to the value of money and a basic understanding of the purposes it can serve beyond being just a medium of exchange. It's a fine line but one that's worthwhile trying to draw. Wealth building is a long-term process, one that should involve all members of the family unit. If your children learn the right techniques and attitudes at home, they'll benefit when it comes time for them to establish their own families.

But be careful. Avoid trying to do too much too soon. That's a mistake I made in the case of my own family. My lack of early financial training undoubtedly contributed to it: I didn't want my children to waste the most efficient wealth building period of their lives because of a failure on my part to give them the grounding they needed.

But like everything else in life, timing is critical in imparting this kind of information. Pre-teens simply aren't ready for it. In fact, most of them can't handle anything more complicated than allowances, a bank account and some simple explanations of the relationship between value and money.

It's around the time children hit their mid-teens that they become more sensitive to the subtleties of money management. This often coincides with a first job or a highly prized but expensive objective they want to achieve, such as paying the additional insurance costs so they can drive the family car. That's the point at which you can start going beyond the basics in laying the groundwork for a more sophisticated approach to money and wealth.

You're going to have to commit some of your time and imagination to the process, though. You can't just hand them a copy of this book and tell them to read it — it will sit unopened on the shelf. The time will come when they'll seek out more information on their own and absorb it avidly. But not at the outset.

So how then? By exposing your children to some of the building blocks of wealth in a way they'll find exciting and stimulating.

One of the most successful things I ever did in this regard was to give my children stocks as a Christmas gift. If that sounds unusual, consider this: lots of people give their children or grandchildren cash or Canada Savings Bonds as Christmas or birthday or Hanukkah gifts and don't think it strange. All I'm suggesting is that you be a little more imaginative in the type of financial asset you choose to give. If you approach it right, you may open up a whole new world for your kids.

Even though we live in a capitalist society, most children have no understanding of what the stock market is or how it functions. That's because they are never exposed to it: very few schools offer courses in investing, and most parents don't have a clear idea of what the stock market is about or how to make money in it.

Giving your children stocks as a gift is a way to spark their interest and encourage them to learn more on their own. It's not as easy as buying a plain old Canada Savings Bond, of course. But CSBs are tucked away in a safety deposit box and forgotten. They don't exist as far as the kids are concerned, except in an abstract way.

Stocks, on the other hand, are a real financial adventure. It doesn't end with the certificate they get in their Christmas stocking; in fact, that's just the beginning.

If the stocks are registered in their names, all sorts of things will start to happen. The mail will begin bringing quarterly and annual reports about the company's activities and performance. There will be invitations to shareholders' meetings, proxy solicitations and dividend cheques. If your kids are lucky, they may benefit from stock splits or rights issues or special dividend declarations. Each of those occasions is a chance for them — and perhaps you — to learn something more about the stock market, how companies operate and the way in which a capitalistic society works. And it will all happen in a painless and interesting way.

You'll find your children getting fired up by the idea that they actually own a piece of a major company. The key is to give them stocks in a firm that interests them. It would be nice if it had great growth potential as well, but it's more important that the idea of the company and the things it does turns them on.

When I first bought stocks for my kids, I thought this part through pretty carefully.

Deborah, the youngest, was just entering her teens at the time.

She was still in the cuddly stuffed animal stage, so I decided Irwin Toy would be a logical choice for her.

My son, Kendrew, was about two years older and was into pop music. He got shares in the CHUM broadcasting empire and was especially excited when he found out that meant he owned a small piece of the MuchMusic cable-TV channel.

My oldest daughter, Kimberley, was in her last year of high school and was taking a basic economics course. I bought her shares in what was then Goliath Gold Mines, on the theory that, since she was learning about the role of gold in our economy, it might excite her if she owned some.

I bought the shares through a brokerage house that was having a pre-Christmas special with reduced commission fees to encourage people to give stock to their kids. (One easy way to buy a few shares today is at a financial trade show at which a mini stock market is featured. The Toronto Financial Forum in February is one such.)

The shares were registered in the children's names, and I got hold of a copy of the latest annual report from each company to include with the certificates. I completed the package by taking a recent listing from the stock market pages and circling their companies so they would know what the stocks were worth and where to track them.

The reaction that Christmas morning was terrific. The kids were totally surprised and genuinely excited about becoming shareholders. The results were as I had hoped: all three became more interested in the stock market, especially my son who starting tracking the performance of his CHUM shares on a regular basis.

And though I didn't buy the stocks for their profit making potential, it turns out they did quite well. The CHUM stock split three for one within a year, which meant he received three shares for every one he owned. Goliath Gold was rolled into the new Hemlo Gold Mines company and my daughter sold her shares about a year later for more than twice what I'd paid for them. Irwin Toy didn't perform as spectacularly but produced a small capital gain and a quarterly dividend cheque for Deborah. All in all, a profitable education.

A couple of years later, the son of a close friend was having his Bar Mitzvah. The kid was an avid hockey player and a Toronto Maple Leaf fan. As his gift, I bought ten shares in Maple Leaf Gardens.

Unknown to me, his father had arranged for Leaf tickets the following night, dinner at the Hot Stove Club and a car to chauffeur his son to the game. The stock topped off the evening. When the boy pulled up to the Gardens in his white stretch limo, he wasn't arriving as another ordinary fan. He was a shareholder!

The success of the stock experiments inspired me to find other fun ways to teach the kids about wealth building techniques. My next venture was into mutual funds.

Here again, the idea was to introduce the children to an investing technique through the reality of actual ownership, rather than in an abstract way. The kids were starting to put some money aside for university so I suggested it might be interesting to invest some of their savings in mutual funds. I explained how such funds work and picked out a no-load fund that allowed minimal quarterly deposits. I proposed they put in $100 every quarter, which they felt they could handle. And I suggested they sign on for the distribution reinvestment plan, which meant all their earnings would be used to buy additional fund units.

The results were intriguing. The children received regular reports from the fund and reviewed them carefully. They became very conscious of the fund's performance and the current value of their investment. And they were highly critical of the fund's managers when asset values declined! It's at those times that I would sit them down and tell them about market forces and what moves fund values up and down.

As a result, they developed a basic understanding of how mutual funds work and a critical faculty for assessing good, bad and indifferent performance. The result, I hope, will be to make them more effective at wealth building in the future.

So how do you teach your kids about money? By bringing the subject to life for them. Involve them in real world financial situations. Teach them about different kinds of investments by encouraging them to undertake them themselves, within the limits of their financial ability. When an investment prospers, spend some time with them discussing why it went well. Even more important, spend time talking about why a particular investment turned out to be a loser.

If you don't know much about investing yourself, then learn with them. It's a terrific opportunity to spend quality time together.

One word of warning, though. Not all kids will be interested in money and wealth, just as all kids aren't interested in sports. If you've introduced the concept in an imaginative way and your child doesn't take to it, don't force the issue. Maybe the timing's wrong. Or maybe he or she just couldn't care less, even though the subject fascinates you. I was an ardent stamp collector when I was young; my children just yawned when I brought out my old collection and tried to interest them in the hobby.

A surprising number of youngsters today have the potential to be seriously interested in the whole concept of wealth building. They just need to be exposed to it in an exciting and challenging manner. If you want them to have the best possible future, it's up to you, as a parent, to do that job. Nobody else will — most certainly, not the schools.

Your Home Is Your Financial Castle

Real estate is the closest thing to the proverbial pot of gold.

— Ada Louise Huxtable

What you've read up to now has been the *hors d'oeuvre*. Now comes the main course — the actual steps you need to take to put together a successful wealth building plan.

Perhaps not surprisingly, it starts with the most basic of all assets, the family home. That's because I believe there is no better way to begin accumulating wealth than to own a home.

Oh sure, it is possible to lose money on a family home, as I explained in Chapter Three. But frankly, you have to work pretty hard at it or be very unlucky. For most people, their own home is the best investment they've ever made. That's why it's one of the cornerstones of wealth building. If you're still in the rental stage of your life, buying a house should be near the top of your priority list.

That doesn't mean you should rush out and buy regardless of what the market is doing. As with every other type of purchase, there are times when a home is a bargain and times when it isn't. The best strategy is to save your money and wait for a window of opportunity. When it appears, pounce. It may not be open long.

While there is some financial risk in owning a home, proper timing can reduce it considerably. That's why it's important to move quickly when the moment is right. There's no way of knowing how long an opportunity will be available; the housing market can turn within the span of a couple of months. So if there's a home in your future, start preparing now and be ready the next time the window opens.

The beauty of owning your own home is that it meets all the criteria of a first-class asset. In fact, it's hard to conceive of anything better.

To begin with, it's an appreciating asset. Like anything else, residential housing is subject to short-term market swings. But over the long haul, any well-located property which is properly maintained is going to increase in value, usually substantially. Just check out the house prices in some of the better older sections of your town or city. When well-located and properly maintained sixty-year-old homes can be sold for upwards of $400,000, as they can in places like Toronto and Vancouver, there's a message which any aspiring wealth builder would be foolish to ignore.

Second, your home is a tax shelter — probably the best one you'll ever own. The government won't tax the capital gain you realize when it's sold, no matter how large it is. And if anything happens to you, it can pass tax-free to your spouse.

Third, it's a bankable asset. Many people don't make use of the equity they build up in their homes over the years and allow the money to sit idle. That's a classic example of inertia at work. Financial instruments such as home equity lines of credit now make it possible for you to tap in to the profit you've built up in your property without actually selling the home or locking yourself into a rigid mortgage repayment schedule. That means you can use the money in your home to take advantage of other investment opportunities that may come along. Another option, which is attracting many retired people, is the reverse mortgage. This plan, which is best suited to people over seventy, effectively converts mortgage equity into tax-free income.

Finally, your home is a usable asset. It's not a piece of paper or a bar of metal that may represent wealth but has no function in your daily life. Your home fulfils a number of basic physical and emotional needs, which is perhaps why many people don't consider it an investment. It provides shelter, acts as the central focus for the family, and offers (I hope) a tranquil refuge from the problems of the world — in short, your home is your spiritual base.

Apart from being all those things, it is also a major investment. If you go about it intelligently, you can pyramid the equity you build in your home into a financial base larger than you may think possible right now. But if you screw up. . . .

Let me describe a couple of ways in which you *could* screw up, so you'll be on the lookout. These are real-life, true stories and they explain why some people end up taking a terrible financial beating on their homes.

The first involves the friend of mine I referred to briefly in Chapter Two, the one who got whipsawed by speculating in housing just when prices were at their peak. I'd like to tell you the whole story because it clearly illustrates how buying a family home for the wrong reasons can hurt you.

This friend bought a small house in a good section of north Toronto in the late 1970s. It was a nice little place, nothing spectacular but very comfortable for him and his wife. A good starter home.

Then came the great housing craze of the early 1980s. It started in Vancouver and rapidly spread east. House prices went sky-high. Bidding wars became the order of the day: you put your house on the market at a wildly inflated price and then stood back and watched as frantic buyers bid it up yet another ten or twenty percent. The speculators had a field day as people who feared prices were going out of sight scrambled to buy while they could still afford a home. It was our own version of Germany's famous 1920s inflation, when people rushed to buy everything they could before the prices went up again.

My friend got caught up in all this. He sold his small home for a very good profit and decided to get in on the housing action himself. After all, everyone else was making big money, why shouldn't he? So he went out into the market, found a much larger place that he figured was undervalued and could be turned over quickly, and bought it.

It was a disaster — total and unmitigated. To begin with, the house he bought was in deplorable condition. In his haste to close the deal, he hadn't checked it out as thoroughly as he should have. When he and his wife went in after signing the papers, they were appalled at what they found. I won't sicken you with the details; let's just describe it as filthy. They had to work day and night for weeks to put the place into habitable condition. By the time they were finished, they were both exhausted.

Even worse, that was just about the time the housing market collapsed. Mortgage interest rates had shot up to ridiculous levels. Buyers were vanishing from the scene like flies in a frost. The speculators had fled the market. And people like my friend were left holding the bag.

And what a bag! He put the house up for sale at close to what he had paid for it. No takers. He dropped the price. Still no takers. He dropped it again. Still none, and now residential housing was a glut on the market.

In the end, he took a $70,000 beating on the property, a horrendous loss by his (or anyone's) standards. He learned a lesson, as he ruefully admitted later. But it cost him a small fortune in the process, plus months of frustration and aggravation. And it was several years before he was able to accumulate enough capital to buy another house.

You can learn the same lesson free. It's very simple: don't speculate with the family home. Choose a property that is well located, that suits your needs and is priced fairly. Pay down your mortgage quickly (more on that in the next chapter). If there's a sudden run-up in prices in your area, don't be tempted to sell and get into the speculation game. Remember, your home is your key wealth building tool. Use it wisely.

How else can you lose money on a home? By a sudden, unpredictable shift in economic conditions. This is a tougher situation to cope with, because it's not of your own making.

As I mentioned in Chapter Three, this is what occurred in Alberta in the mid 1980s. As in most other Canadian cities, house prices in places like Calgary and Edmonton had shot up during the boom. When the boom ended, they fell, just as they did everywhere else. But the situation in Alberta was somewhat different.

For years, the province had enjoyed good times. The petroleum industry was strong and expanding. Agricultural products were bringing in high prices. Industry and governments were teaming up to create visions of multi-billion-dollar mega-projects which would reshape the face of the West and create thousands of new employment opportunities.

It was the time to be an Albertan. Unemployment was down, taxes were the lowest in the country, consumer spending was high, the provincial government operated with a budget surplus, and new millionaires were being created almost daily. Companies like Dome Petroleum enjoyed unlimited access to banking capital — debt counted for little alongside the tremendous growth opportunities. The future belonged to Alberta.

In the midst of all that euphoria, a lot of people went out and bought houses. In many cases, they stretched themselves to the limit financially to do so. But why not? The economy was good, jobs were plentiful and it was time to make a commitment.

And then it all went sour. Not only did the housing boom go bust; so did Alberta. The good times collapsed under the weight of the Trudeau government's ill-conceived National Energy Policy, an international recession and a slump in commodities prices. The sharp drop in oil prices, which came later, further exacerbated the whole unhappy situation and heavily leveraged companies like Dome disappeared from the Canadian scene.

And the proud new homeowners? They saw the value of their properties tumble with the Alberta economy, to the point where many homes were actually worth less on the open market than the value of the mortgages that were being used to finance them. To make matters worse, the slowdown in economic activity had thrown many of those homeowners out of work. They found themselves facing the prospect of keeping up mortgage payments on a devalued property with income that consisted mainly of unemployment insurance cheques.

The predictable happened. People in record numbers simply turned the key in the lock and walked away from their homes, leaving the financial institutions to pick up the pieces. There hadn't been anything like it since the Great Depression. In 1984–85, more than 5,000 people defaulted on their mortgage in Alberta, according to Canada Mortgage and Housing Corporation. That was five times as many as in Ontario, which has a much greater population. For those folks, owning a home was not a great wealth building experience.

Politics of another kind contributed to a loss in real estate values in many parts of Montreal. Every surge of separatism depresses house prices, especially in traditionally English-speaking areas of the city. For example, in Westmount, long a solid English-speaking enclave, the price of an executive detached two-storey home fell steadily from $600,000 in the fall of 1988 to $405,000 in the spring of 1992, as the constitutional showdown neared. That represented a drop of thirty-two percent in value. By contrast, a similar home in the French-speaking Quebec City suburb of Sillery rose in price from $245,000 to $270,000 during the same period, according to Royal LePage.

I'm not telling you all this to frighten you away from home ownership. Far from it. I believe owning your own home is a basic step in the wealth building process.

No, I'm relating these horror stories to illustrate that things can sometimes go wrong and to emphasize the importance of treating the purchase of a home as an investment decision. It's often too easy to get caught up in the emotion of home-buying and to lose sight of the investment implications as a result. And that problem isn't the exclusive preserve of first-time buyers; many supposedly seasoned home purchasers allow themselves to fall into the same trap. Don't be one of them.

Before you get turned off the whole idea of home ownership, let me describe the other side of the housing coin. A close friend of mine moved to Toronto in the late 1970s. He and his wife bought an older home on a pleasant street in the city's northern district. The area was desirable enough, but certainly wouldn't rank as one of the most expensive in the city.

They paid just over $100,000 for the property. Over the next few years they put a lot of work into the place, fixing it up. They put on a deck, remodelled the kitchen, added a top-floor bedroom, turned the basement into a comfortable lounge and put in a wine cellar. It wasn't cheap, but the additional amount they invested added greatly to the house's value — as did a rising real estate market.

In 1992 — fifteen years later — the house was sold for well over $400,000! Just by living in their home and fixing it up in ways they enjoyed, they had added hundreds of thousands of dollars to their net worth. That's what I call effective wealth building.

How do you look at a house as an investment? In the same way you consider any other investment decision.

Start by examining the profit potential. The last thing most people think about when they buy a home is what will happen when the time comes to sell it. That's something to worry about years from now; right now that little two-bedroom vine-covered cottage is too adorable to pass up.

But pass it up you should. Two-bedroom homes are notoriously hard to sell. And many people dislike having vines which clog their eavestroughs and attract insects.

The reality is you *will* sell your home some day — whether to move to a better neighbourhood or another city, or to trade up to a larger house, or because the kids have gone off on their own, or for some other reason. When that day comes, the price you get — and therefore the profit you make — will be determined to a large extent by the wisdom you showed when you made the initial purchase decision. In the meantime, if you've chosen a property with better-than-average growth potential you'll have more equity in your home to use to finance other investments.

Let me tell you my own unhappy story in this regard. When we moved to Toronto in the mid-1970s, we had already bought and sold two houses. But despite that experience, I was not as aware of the importance of assessing the investment potential of a home as I might have been. Like most people, we did our shopping on the basis of our perceived needs and our financial situation. Other considerations didn't really enter into it.

In the end, our choice narrowed down to two properties, both in the same area of the city. One was priced at $128,000. It was a pleasant, comfortable home on a good street, backing on a ravine. Nothing spectacular, but okay.

The other choice was a classic two-storey executive home in a prestigious neighbourhood about a mile away. It was on a quiet cul-de-sac, close to schools and shopping and had every amenity, from a swimming pool to a screening room in the basement. It also carried a higher price tag — $175,000.

We perhaps could have afforded it, but it would really have stretched us to the limit. So we opted for the less expensive home. If I had looked at the decision from an investment point of view, we would have made a different choice.

By 1992, the home we bought had a market value in excess of $500,000. That's a respectable appreciation, of course. But the house we passed up was worth a million or more. A difference of less than $50,000 in 1975 had soared to half a million dollars in seventeen years!

That's why I stress looking at a property's investment potential before you buy. Sometimes paying a little more at the outset for the right home can end up producing big financial dividends down the road.

What sorts of things will make a home attractive to future buyers and thereby maximize its profit potential? Start with the classic real estate cliché: location, location, location. Where you choose to live is going to have the greatest influence on what you pay today and what your house will be worth tomorrow. If you're in a major metropolitan centre, that means the farther out you go, the more house you'll get for your money. Try it yourself. Take one of the main highways out of town. Once you get beyond the city limits, check the prices of comparable homes at each successive exit. The downward pattern will become apparent quickly: the farther away you are, the lower the price.

The converse is equally true: the closer to the city centre, the higher the price, all other things being equal. If you're looking for the best appreciation potential, that tells you to buy as close to the centre as you can afford.

What else should you consider? You should pick a quality neighbourhood, preferably one that's well established. Look for good access to schools, shopping and transportation — but ensure none of them is right in your backyard. Houses bordering on school property, for instance, suffer from a higher incidence of vandalism and break-ins than other homes in the same area. Avoid corner lots — for some reason, Canadians don't like them.

In choosing an architectural design, stick with the traditional. The more off-beat you get, the smaller your potential resale market and therefore, the lower the appreciation potential. Most people want a detached, two-storey single family home. If you're into modern design with glass walls, fine — but don't expect the market to share your tastes.

You should check out the local planning act and zoning regulations before you make any offer. That pretty green space right behind you may already be earmarked for an apartment building or, even worse, a major commercial complex. I can't think of a faster way to ensure a rapid drop in the value of your new home than to have a gas station open up right behind you.

Local planning regulations can be capricious. Rules may change after you purchase the property (it happened to us recently when we learned of plans to build a thirteen-storey apartment building across the ravine, a project made possible only because the city had changed its green space rules). That can be frustrating, but, as a property owner, at least you're in a position to make a strong protest. If you buy and then learn about pending construction, you don't have much recourse; you should have done your homework in advance.

Once you've found a place you think fits the bill, spend a little money to have it properly inspected before you submit an offer. Don't be stampeded by an agent's warnings that the house may be picked off by another buyer; his or her interest is often to close the deal and get a commission and any conditions attached to the offer may impede that. A thorough building inspection shouldn't cost more than a couple of hundred dollars, although you should get a few quotes. When my daughter Kim and her husband bought their townhouse in early 1992, they received home inspection quotes ranging from $150 to $270. Some inspectors charge according to the price of the house, others use a flat rate system.

A proper inspection could save you thousands of dollars in repair bills. At the very least, it will alert you to potential problems and provide cost estimates for repairing them before the deal is completed. I didn't have an inspection when we bought our Toronto house (they weren't as common then) and it was only after we moved in that we discovered the place was poorly insulated, had a shower stall that leaked and that the heating system was improperly balanced. It cost a lot of money to put all that right, something I would have insisted the previous owner do, or negotiated a reduced price, if I'd had the foresight to use an inspector.

Obviously, you'll have to examine your own financial condition when deciding whether to buy a home. It's not much fun being "house poor," spending a disproportionate amount of your income on mortgage payments, property taxes, utilities and maintenance. In that sense, homes are like children — both can absorb a lot of money.

I've been house poor, unable even to go out to a restaurant occasionally because the budget was so tight. It's not a condition I want to experience again. But there are times when the sacrifice is worthwhile. If we had been willing to spend a few years being house poor back in the mid-1970s, for instance, our family net worth would be $500,000 more than it is today.

Deciding on the extent to which you're prepared to make a financial sacrifice to acquire a home is a tough personal decision. But if you treat it as an investment opportunity, it becomes more manageable. The greater the prospect for capital gain, the more acceptable short-term financial pain should be.

But a word of caution. You don't want that short-term pain to turn into long-term disaster. Remember those Albertans who ended up walking away from their homes. That's not a sensation you want to experience!

It's one thing to be house poor. It's quite another to stretch yourself so thin financially that one bad break — a sudden upturn in mortgage rates, for instance — might put you in a situation where you could no longer afford the house. That's why financial prudence is essential in making a home purchase decision.

Before you plunge in, take some time to carefully analyze *all* the costs involved. What does the house cost to heat each year? How much are the water taxes? How fast have the property taxes been going up? How much would the monthly mortgage payments go up if interest rates increased by one percentage point? Two points? When will the house likely need a new roof? A new furnace? If you're buying a condo, what are the monthly fees and what exactly do they cover? How much have they historically increased each year?

It may be tiresome but you have to look at those numbers before going ahead. You need to be sure you can handle all the existing costs and that you have at least a little flexibility in the event something unexpected hits you later.

The general rule of thumb is that not more than thirty percent of your gross family income should be eaten up by principal, interest, taxes and energy costs. If you want to be conservative and give yourself something of a cushion in the event mortgage interest rates move up, reduce that percentage by a couple of points.

You can exceed the thirty percent ratio slightly if you exercise discipline in your other financial commitments. But if you pass the thirty-five percent mark, you're entering high-risk territory. An unexpected development — anything from a sharp increase in mortgage interest rates to the loss of a job — could leave you with no alternative but to sell. If you're over the thirty-five percent mark now, I suggest you set up a mortgage reduction plan and get your payments down to a more manageable level as soon as possible. More on that in the next chapter

If you work out all these numbers beforehand, give your real estate agent firm instructions accordingly. Tell him or her what you're prepared to pay. Stay a little on the high side in your estimate — you don't want to miss out on a good buy that may be priced a few thousand dollars higher than the limit you've calculated. But make it clear to your agent that you don't want to look at anything beyond the price point you've established. The country is full of people who fell in love with a house that was beyond their means and lived to regret it. Don't join the group.

The timing of your home purchase will be a major factor in these calculations. There are periods when you can pick up homes at good prices and times when the chances are you'll pay too much. Clearly, you want to choose the best time to buy so as to minimize your financial risk.

When is that? When the marketplace is deserted. The other buyers have fled to the sidelines. Sellers are desperate. Prices are being slashed, but even that doesn't move more houses. Uncertainty and fear are the dominant emotions.

One such window opened in southern Ontario in 1991–92. With the economy battered by recession and manufacturing jobs in the province disappearing by the tens of thousands, the booming housing market of the 1980s went bust. The cost of a bungalow in the Willowdale area of Toronto fell from $350,000 in the fall of 1989 to $235,000 in the spring of 1992, a one-third drop.

While prices were tumbling, mortgage interest rates were also falling. In the fall of 1989, the rate on a five-year mortgage was 14.5% at most major financial institutions. By the early summer of 1992, it was down to 9.25%.

As a result, many renters were suddenly able to afford homes. The monthly cost of carrying the average Willowdale bungalow (assuming a twenty-five percent down payment and a twenty-five year amortization) fell from $3,176 in late 1989 to $1,488 in summer 1992 — a drop of more than half!

Even in Vancouver, where housing prices rose in the early nineties in contrast to the real estate depression in eastern Canada, lower mortgage rates made homes accessible to more people. In North Vancouver, a detached bungalow increased in value from $190,000 in the fall of 1989 to $240,000 in spring, 1992. But the decline in interest rates over the period actually *reduced* the monthly carrying cost from $1,698 in 1989 to $1,520 in 1992.

As if this wasn't enough, the federal government offered still more inducements to buy. The minimum down payment on mortgages insured under the National Housing Act (NHA) was cut in half, to five percent. Then, in an unprecedented move, Ottawa temporarily allowed buyers to dip into their RRSPs for up to $20,000 to acquire a home.

Still, many potential purchasers sat on their hands. Often, it was because of a combination of inexperience and fear. They lacked the experience and the knowledge to recognize the opportunity. Or, if they did, they were too worried about the future to seize it.

Psychologically, it's not easy to be a buyer in down times. It's always easier to run with the herd, to buy when the world is bullish. But be assured it will cost you a lot more if you try it that way.

A couple of other tips on the psychology of house buying.

First, keep your cool. Don't go wandering through a house raving about how wonderful it is and publicly falling in love with it. The vendor will notice. The real estate agent will notice. And it's in both their interests that you pay as high a price as possible. Keep your enthusiasm to yourself. If both the agent and the seller think the sale may be shaky, they'll be a lot more flexible in meeting your terms.

Second, don't buy too quickly. It may be tough, but waiting a few weeks, or even a few months, could save you thousands. Don't go into the market in the spring or early summer, for instance. That's when the big rush is on, because people want to have their plans settled and their moves completed before the start of the next school year. Bide your time. By late summer, those sellers who have committed themselves to a move and haven't been able to unload their old home yet will be getting desperate. That's the time when there are real bargains to be found.

One last thought: one of the best ways to judge the value of a particular type of investment is to talk to people who have already tried it. If they've done well, chances are you may also. If you don't already own a home, try it. Talk to people that do. Ask them if they think it was a good idea and if they're satisfied with their home as an investment. Then ask if they would do it again, knowing what they know now. I'll bet at least ninety percent of them say yes.

I'll also bet that if you follow the guidelines in this chapter, you'll end up making a lot of money on your home. And you'll have established the first cornerstone of a successful wealth building program.

Of course, you have to pay for the house. So that's what we'll look at next.

Living Mortgage-Free

CHAPTER 7

A man's home is his hassle.
— Al Boliska, 1968

The good thing about mortgages is that they enable you to buy that all-important family home years before you might otherwise be able to afford it. The bad thing is that mortgage lenders charge you an arm and a leg for the privilege.

You think I exaggerate? Consider this:

You live in an area where housing prices haven't gone out of sight. You're about to buy your first home, a pleasant little townhouse, well located. The price is $80,000.

You've scrimped and saved to pull together $20,000 for the down payment. The balance will be financed by a $60,000 first mortgage, amortized (a fancy term that simply means spread) over twenty-five years, at an initial rate of 10.5%.

Assuming the interest rate were to remain unchanged (it won't, of course, but this is just a simple example) and that you were to take the full twenty-five years to pay off the mortgage, how much do you think it would have cost you by the time you were finished?

Hold your breath for this one! Would you believe $167,100? No, that's not a misprint. That $60,000 mortgage would end up costing you over $107,000 in interest payments by the time you managed to pay off the original principal. No wonder financial institutions are in heavy competition for your mortgage business!

The aspiring wealth builder doesn't have to read any further to understand the message. Pay off the mortgage as fast as you possibly can! The more quickly you do so, the faster funds will be freed up for use in other aspects of your wealth building program.

It's especially crucial to start paying down the mortgage with extra payments as early as possible. That's when it will have the greatest money-saving impact.

As one mortgage expert put it to me: "The interest rate you're paying on your mortgage is, in essence, the tax free rate of return you'd have if you didn't have to pay it."

In other words, if your interest rate is 10.5%, you'd have to find an investment that paid you more than that, *after tax*, for it to be a better alternative than paying down the mortgage.

To understand why paying off a mortgage quickly is so important, you need to know something about how mortgage payments are structured. Essentially, they are a mixture of principal and interest, calculated in such a way as to reduce the outstanding balance you owe to zero at the end of the amortization period.

In practical terms, this means that the early payments on a mortgage will be almost entirely interest. You don't start to make a real dent in the principal for several years. On the other hand, the earlier you start reducing the principal, the more interest you'll save over the life of the mortgage.

Let's go back to that dream townhouse with its $60,000 mortgage. The monthly payments will amount to $557. At the end of five years, therefore, you will have turned over $33,420 of your hard-earned money to the financial institution holding the mortgage. And how much will you still owe them at that point? A total of $56,640. You've only managed to reduce the principal by $3,360 during that long, five-year period. The rest of the money you paid — just over $30,000 — went to cover interest charges. Sorry, folks.

The mortgage bind is especially acute here in Canada because there's no tax relief from the government on those payments. Even after their sweeping tax reforms, our American neighbours retain that particular tax plum. We can only look on with envy.

All of this dictates a strategy of mortgage reduction early in the game. Even a small amount can have wondrous effects.

Suppose, for example, that at the end of the first year you made an extra payment of $1,000 to reduce the outstanding principal. Nothing else changed. Any idea how much interest you would save over the life of the mortgage? Again, you may not believe this, but it works out to $9,669.21!

What happens is this: that single payment at the end of the first year reduces the total time it will take to pay off the mortgage by 19 months. Instead of taking a total of 300 months (25 years x 12 = 300) it will take 281 months. The interest you save as a result is almost ten times your $1,000 payment. Not a bad return on that modest investment!

Now suppose you kept doing that for the next four years. Remember that by making only your regular payments, you managed to reduce your principal owing to $56,640. By making five extra $1,000 payments, though, you'll reduce the total amount of interest you'll spend on paying off the mortgage to $75,991.62. That's a saving of $31,105.22 over what you would have paid in interest had you not made those annual $1,000 payments. I know those numbers seem amazing — most people can't believe that $5,000 in prepayments made in the early years of a mortgage can save that much money. But it's true — they can. That should be more than enough incentive to get you started on this particular wealth building strategy.

Those numbers emphasize the importance of ensuring your mortgage has a generous prepayment clause. That means doing some careful shopping when you select a lender, especially if you plan to sign up for a longer term. (The "term" of the mortgage is the period for which you agree to pay the lender at current interest rates. Typically it will be for a minimum of six months to a maximum of five years, although there are some seven and ten-year terms now available and even a twenty-five year term. Don't confuse term with amortization; they're two different things. You'd have to sign up for five consecutive five-year terms to pay off a mortgage with a twenty-five year amortization.)

When you're out mortgage shopping, there are a number of things to consider. The first is whether you want a "conventional" mortgage or a "high-ratio" mortgage.

A conventional mortgage is the most common. To obtain one, you must have a down payment of at least twenty-five percent of the purchase price of the home and meet certain requirements relating to your total debt.

High-ratio mortgages are available to qualified borrowers who don't have a twenty-five percent down payment. These loans are insured under the National Housing Act (NHA) to protect the lender in case of default. You'll be charged a one-time premium of up to 2.5% of the amount of the loan. So, for example, on a $100,000 high-ratio mortgage loan, your premium can be as much as $2,500. This amount can be paid up-front, but is more commonly added to the principal and amortized over the life of the mortgage.

You also need to understand the distinction between a "closed" and an "open" mortgage. A closed mortgage restricts the amount of extra payments that can be made against the principal without incurring a substantial penalty. Open mortgages allow you to pay off the full balance at any time, without penalty. But you're often charged a higher interest rate for that added flexibility.

Generally, it's not worthwhile to pay extra for an open mortgage. The exception is if you think there's a good chance interest rates will rise soon and you want maximum flexibility to lock in to a longer term at any time.

If you choose a closed mortgage, be sure the prepayment provisions are good. Typically, you'll be allowed to pay up to ten or fifteen percent of the original principal on each anniversary date. So on a $60,000 mortgage, you should be permitted to pay down the principal by $6,000 to $9,000 each year, without penalty. In addition, many lenders now allow additional prepayments. These will vary, depending on which company you borrow from. Royal Trust, for example, has a "Double-Up" plan that allows you to double your monthly mortgage payment as often as you wish, with the extra amount applied to reducing your principal. Flexible mortgages such as this can be extremely valuable if you want to pay off the loan more quickly.

The longer the term you select, the more important those prepayment provisions become. At the end of each term, you're allowed to reduce the principal as much as you like. So if you're planning on consistently choosing six-month or one-year terms, prepayment clauses aren't a big issue. But if you plan to lock in for several years in order to protect yourself from the impact of whipsawing interest rates, be sure you get a mortgage with generous prepayment provisions. There's nothing worse than having a five or ten-year mortgage with no flexibility to pay it down.

Some people tend to shrug off this advice, saying they won't have enough money to make prepayments in any event. That's being short sighted. You don't know what may be coming a year or two down the road: a big raise, a new job, an unexpected inheritance, maybe even a winning lottery ticket. If some extra money does show up, the first place the wealth builder will direct it is towards the mortgage. But if there are no prepayment provisions, you're stuck. Make sure you get a mortgage that has them.

Another technique for reducing the onerous interest costs of carrying a mortgage is to choose a shorter amortization period at the outset. It will cost you more in the short run. But it will save a heck of a lot of money in the long term.

Once again, let's go back to the townhouse with its $60,000 mortgage. Suppose that, in this case, you opted for a twenty year amortization period instead of twenty-five years. What would happen?

To begin with, your payments would go up. Instead of $557, you'd be writing a cheque for $590.09 every month. But that extra $33.09 would mean big savings down the road. If you took the full twenty years to pay off the mortgage, the total cost would be $141,622. That's over $25,000 you've saved by choosing the twenty year amortization; that's cash you can put into your pocket. And it's after-tax money, too!

If you selected a fifteen year amortization, your monthly payments would go up to $654.99. But your total cost of paying off the mortgage would drop to $117,898. That's almost $50,000 less than the twenty-five year amortization would cost.

Clearly, it's to your advantage to select the shortest amortization period you can afford. The sooner you get that mortgage paid off, the less it will cost you — and the faster you'll have funds available to do more interesting things with your wealth building program.

As long as you have a mortgage, you should have two overriding objectives in mind: to minimize the amount of interest you pay the financial institution that holds it and to reduce the principal as quickly as possible. Prepayments and shorter amortization periods are two techniques for achieving those goals.

Another strategy involves the term you select for your mortgage. This is the decision that gives homeowners the most sleepless nights. There are many factors involved: your best guess as to the future course of interest rates, your financial position, your risk tolerance level and your basic psychological make-up. No wonder the choice of a term drives many people up the wall and then leaves them second-guessing themselves for months afterwards.

Unfortunately, I can't solve the problem for you. But I can give you some things to consider that may help you make the right decision.

First, let me go back a decade. In the summer of 1984, the *Financial Times of Canada* interviewed five experts, asking them what strategy should be used by people who had mortgages coming up for renewal. At the time, one-year mortgages were going for 12.75% and five-year terms were 14.5%, with the rates for intermediate terms somewhere in between. The experts were asked what term they would advise people to select. Two suggested a five-year term, two opted for three years. Only one counselled a one-year term.

It was bad advice. Interest rates were clearly in the process of coming down from their 1981–82 highs. They had taken a temporary upward blip at the time, but few people expected that to continue. The disinflation psychology had set in and the cost of living trend line was heading still lower. Yet here were four so-called experts, telling people to lock in their mortgages at high rates for another three to five years. Mortgage lenders love that kind of advice!

Just a year later, in mid-1985, five-year mortgage rates had dropped to 11.75%. Anyone who had followed the "expert" advice and selected a five-year term the previous summer would have been paying over $1,600 more in interest *each year* on a $60,000 mortgage at that point. And rates continued to decline after that.

A similar situation occurred in 1990. Mortgage interest rates were pushed up by the Bank of Canada's determined efforts to reduce the rate of inflation. In May, five-year rates stood at fourteen percent, while one-year mortgages were half a point higher (an unusual situation, known as an inverted yield curve).

Again, I saw some suggestions that borrowers should lock in for five years, although nothing quite as blatant as the *Financial Times* article of several years before. Anyone who chose a longer-term mortgage at that point was making an expensive error, however. It was clear to anyone paying attention that the economy was running into trouble and that interest rates would have to be eased before long. Sure enough, a year later the five-year rate was down to 11.25%. By early 1992, it had slipped below the magic ten percent mark.

There are two morals to this story. The first is: put not your faith in experts. The second is: don't go long when rates are high.

In fact, I'm tempted to say don't go long, ever. In most circumstances, I feel the best mortgage strategy is a short-term one. There are exceptions, of course, but here's why I favour short over long when it comes to choosing a mortgage term.

Let's go back to my two basic goals in dealing with mortgages: pay as little interest as possible and reduce the principal as fast as you can. A short-term mortgage strategy permits you to do both, although you have to exercise some self discipline. It also helps if you have good nerves.

To begin with, you have to understand exactly what you're doing when you choose a longer term for your mortgage. You're really purchasing an insurance policy. In this case, you're covering yourself against the possibility of higher interest rates in the future.

Now, some people like lots of insurance. They pay big premiums to protect themselves against everything from flash floods to plane crashes. If you're one of those, then perhaps the longer-term mortgages are best for you — they'll give you the peace of mind you crave.

But you'll pay for those restful nights. In fact, when you discover how much it actually costs you, you may decide the price is way too high. You may even start tossing and turning with worry about how much money you're throwing away!

Let's return to 1984 and those five-year mortgages. Suppose you had bought your townhouse then and you'd signed up for a $60,000 mortgage for five years at 14.5%. What would have happened?

By the summer of 1989, the fifth anniversary of your unfortunate decision, you would have paid the mortgage company $43,557. Of that, only $1,894 would have been applied against the principal. The balance would all be interest.

Now let's suppose that you had chosen a one-year term in 1984 — the approach I recommended at the time. What would have happened?

Your interest rate would have been 12.75%. By mid-1985, when it came time to renew, you would have made payments totalling about $7,810. Of that, $376.32 was applied to principal; the balance was interest.

By mid-1985, one-year rates were down to 10.5%. At that point, you decided to renew for one year. Over the next twelve months, your payments totalled $6,703. Of that, $602.80 went towards reducing your principal; the rest was interest.

Now it's summer, 1986. You're up for renewal again. Now your one-year mortgage is going for around 9.75%. The next year costs you just over $6,352 in payments — $743.18 applied against your principal, the balance in interest.

By mid-1987, most one-year rates are sitting at 10.25% for a closed mortgage, 10.75% for an open one. Because you've adopted a short-term strategy, you continue to opt for the closed mortgage at the lower rate. Your payments for the next year come to $6,579, with $764.25 applied to the principal, the rest to interest.

In mid-1988, a one-year closed mortgage goes for 10.75%. Payments for the next year come to $6,803.28. Of that, $6,011.15 is interest, $792.13 is principal.

So what's the scorecard by mid-1989 — the year the original five-year term would come up for renewal?

The homeowner who listened to the "experts" and chose a five-year term back in 1984 has made total payments of $43,557 and reduced his principal by $1,894.

The person who adopted a one-year strategy has made total payments of about $34,250, more than $9,000 less. His principal has been reduced by almost $3,300, the balance has gone to interest. He's also had to pay renewal fees of, say, $75 each year, an additional outlay of $300.

So the five-year "insurance policy" cost about $10,400, calculating the increased interest paid and the difference in the principal still owing. That's the "premium," if you like. If that's the sort of thing that makes you sleep better at night, be my guest. I'd rather have the money.

Obviously, if interest rates had been moving up instead of down, the story would have been quite different. So if you're in a period when a long, steady rise in interest rates looks like a real possibility, locking in for a longer term might be a good idea.

Frankly, though, I think the odds are against coming out ahead by choosing longer mortgage terms. High interest rates are bad for the economy; they can only be tolerated for relatively short periods. The natural tendency for business people, bankers and politicians is to want to see interest rates stable or lower, rather than heading up. If you stick with a short-term strategy, you may end up getting burned occasionally. But those high interest rate periods shouldn't last long.

One warning, though. If you're on such financial thin ice that even a slight upward nudge in mortgage interest rates would put your home at risk, lock in for a longer term. In any financial decision, you have to look at the downside — and if that means you risk losing your home, it isn't worth it.

I made the point earlier that there's a certain amount of self discipline involved in the short-term strategy. Here's why. Even though staying short can mean hundreds or even thousands of extra dollars in your pocket, I don't want you to spend that money. I want you to use it to reduce the outstanding principal on your home at each renewal. It's a second, essential part of the short-term strategy — and one which will help cushion the shock if interest rates do move up sharply at some stage.

Basically, your goal is *to pay down principal instead of making interest payments.*

Here's how it works. Let's say that back in 1984 you chose a one-year mortgage term. But you decided the money you saved by going that route, instead of signing up for five years, would be used to reduce your outstanding loan balance. Using the same interest rate structure as before, let's look at the results.

Year one (1984-85). Your 14.5% mortgage will cost you $8,711.40 in annual payments. The 12.75% mortgage costs $7,809.72. Your saving is $901.68. Renewal charges are $75, leaving you a net $826.68 ahead. You apply that to reducing the principal at renewal time. Including the reduction in your principal through your regular monthly payments, you now owe the bank $58,797.

Year two (1985-86). The annual cost for the 14.5% mortgage hasn't changed. But your one-year mortgage is now at 10.5% and so costs you only $6,609.72. Your savings this year are $2,101.68. Again, you use that balance, less the renewal fee, to reduce the principal. Now you owe the financial institution $56,176.

Year three (1986-87). Rates are down again, so your cost for carrying the one-year term is reduced to $6,046. After deducting your renewal fee, you're left with $2,590 to put against the principal. Now you're into the bank for $52,878.

Year four (1987-88). The one-year interest rate moved up slightly over the previous year, but you still saved another $2,667 to pay against your principal. Now your mortgage loan is down to $49,518.

Year five (1988-89). The one-year rate is at 10.75%. You save $2,853.96 on your payments which, after deducting the $75 renewal fee, you again apply to the principal, reducing it to $46,739.

By way of comparison, remember that the poor fellow who took the five-year mortgage at 14.5% has paid out exactly the same amount of money to this point as you have. But he still owes the bank $58,106, while you've now reduced your loan to $46,739.

That's how this short-term strategy cushions you from the impact of interest rate hikes. Your loan is being retired at a much faster rate, which means that if interest rates do go up at some stage, you'll be paying those higher rates on a lower balance.

Now I know there are going to be some people who read all this and groan. They're locked in to long-term mortgages and only now, for the first time, do they truly understand the implications of what they've done. Now they want to get out and switch strategies. But it's too late. Or is it?

I have a friend who bought a new house when rates were high. To finance it, he took out a $100,000 mortgage with a twenty-five year amortization. The term was five years at 13.25%.

Three years into the term, he realized this wasn't such a great deal. Other people were signing new mortgages at around ten percent, while he was still saddled with one at 13.25% that had two more years to run. On $100,000, that meant he was paying more than $3,000 a year in additional interest costs.

So he pulled out his mortgage agreement, which was with a large trust company, and read it over. He discovered the arrangements were quite interesting.

The mortgage was so tightly closed for the first three years that he wasn't even allowed modest prepayment privileges. But for the last two years, the terms changed. He was allowed to pay off as much of the principal as he liked, subject to a three-month interest penalty.

So he did some calculations. He found he was paying about $1,000 a month interest on his existing mortgage. His penalty for getting out of the contract would therefore be about $3,000 plus fees of around $85. Let's call it $3,100.

He then worked out how much interest he would save if he replaced his old mortgage with a new two-year term at 10.25%. It came out to just over $5,700. In other words, by paying the penalty and getting out of his five-year mortgage, he would save himself a net $2,600 in interest costs over the two years.

He decided to go for it and called the trust company. They weren't thrilled, to say the least. In fact, they did everything they could to discourage him from going ahead. First, they told him flatly he couldn't do it. When he insisted the clause was in the mortgage agreement, the tone switched. Well, yes, the trust company acknowledged, the agreement says that. But that clause was really intended to be used only if he sold the house. And he wasn't doing *that*, was he? The implication was that they had tried to do their customers a favour and they were being taken advantage of by some unscrupulous wretch.

My friend insisted. After all, the clause was there. And it didn't say anything at all about resale of the house. He was told grudgingly he would have to take it up with the manager. All of this, remember, for a privilege that was clearly spelled out in the original contract.

In the end, he got his way — because when it came right down to it there was nothing the trust company could do to stop him. After all, *they* had drafted the contract in the first place.

Now all good stories should have a moral, at least in this book. This particular one has two.

The first is that you should never assume you're irrevocably locked in to an unattractive mortgage deal. If, after reading this chapter, you decide you want to change your strategy, get out your contract and go over it line by line. Look especially for prepayment and penalty clauses. If you find a loophole, then do the same sort of calculations my friend did to see if you can save money by refinancing.

Even if there's nothing in your mortgage agreement, you may still be able to get out from under a high-interest mortgage. All mortgages insured under the National Housing Act are automatically open for repayment after three years, with a three-month income penalty. Alternatively, if your residential mortgage is for a long term, the Canada Interest Act allows repayment after five years, again with three months' interest penalty.

The second moral is don't be intimidated by financial institutions. Remember, they don't want people paying off high-interest mortgages prematurely — it costs them money. So they may go out of their way to make the process difficult. Don't let them bluff you! If you have a legal right to discharge the loan, insist on it. They'll back off.

Before I end this chapter, I want to restate one more time the two basic principles that should guide your mortgage strategy, because they are central to using your home to build wealth.

First: Pay as little interest as possible.

Second: Reduce the outstanding principal as quickly as you can.

Follow those two simple guidelines and you will be astounded at how quickly the equity in your home will grow.

CHAPTER 8

The Interest Rate Rollercoaster

A boom is a situation in which over-optimism triumphs over a rate of interest which, in a cooler light, would be seen to be excessive.
— John Maynard Keynes

Anyone under thirty probably assumes that wildly gyrating interest rates are a normal condition of economic life. After all, that's the way it's been in Canada since the late 1960s.

The inflationary seventies saw rates bounce around like a bungee jumper at the end of an elastic cord. But that was just a warm-up for the wild eighties. In 1981, the prime soared to over twenty percent, carrying mortgage and loan costs up with it and pushing bond yields to unheard-of levels. That was followed by a rate deflation, which was followed in turn by another run-up in 1984, which was followed. . .well, you get the picture.

The nineties began the same way. The prime rate as the decade began was 13.5%, and quickly moved up from there to 14.75% in April, 1990, pushed to that level by the Bank of Canada's concern about inflation and an overheated economy. But by late that year, it became obvious Canada had entered into a severe recession. Throughout 1991 and early 1992, rates steadily moved down, with the prime falling to 7.5% before bouncing back up in March, 1992 in response to a Canadian dollar crisis. By mid year, it was back down below seven percent.

The result of all these gyrations has been a wild, often unnerving interest rate rollercoaster ride that has driven borrowers crazy while offering both great opportunities and tremendous risk to aspiring wealth builders.

But, believe it or not, none of this is normal. Historically, interest rates are usually far less volatile than what we've witnessed over the last twenty-five years. In more settled periods, interest rates tend to be relatively stable, moving only slowly up or down over an extended period. During such times — the 1950s and sixties were recent examples — planning is easy. Mortgages are available for long terms at fixed, modest rates (some readers may even remember the days when twenty-five year terms for mortgages were standard). Investments in interest-bearing vehicles pay low, guaranteed returns over several years. Borrowing costs can be budgeted with confidence, knowing that unexpected events aren't going to suddenly create a major cash flow problem.

Safe, solid and stable — all good words to describe those conditions.

You might also add "dull" to the list, although many Canadians would welcome a little such dullness about now.

That's exactly what the federal government is hoping to provide through the rest of the nineties. One of the main goals of the 1992 budget was the stabilization of interest rates at relatively low levels. The target rate for ninety day commercial loans in 1993 is 6.5%, falling to an average of six percent during 1994-97. By way of comparison, the 1991 average was 8.9%. Long-term government bonds, which yielded 9.8% in 1991, are expected to return 8.3% in 1993 and slightly less in subsequent years.

If events actually unfold this way, it would mean a return to a stable, low-interest rate environment unlike anything we've seen since the 1960s. However, that's a big if. There are so many factors affecting interest rate movements that an extended period of rate stability will be extremely difficult to achieve.

These factors do not, perhaps surprisingly, include bank profiteering. In fact, our financial institutions prefer low interest rates to high ones. Lower rates encourage more people to borrow, reduce the risk of loan defaults and carry a built-in disincentive to pay off a loan quickly.

So what does influence the rates? Here are the main forces:

General economic conditions. When times are bad and the economy is sliding into recession, or is already there, the natural tendency is for interest rates to fall. That's because lower interest rates encourage business investment and consumer spending, two forces which act to stimulate the economy and help to get things moving again. Conversely, when the economy is strong and tending to overheat, interest rates will usually move up as the Bank of Canada attempts to put a brake on growth before it reaches an unsustainable level.

Inflation. As a general rule, the higher the inflation rate, the higher are interest rates. There are a couple of reasons for this. First, investors demand a reasonable "real" return on their money — that's the difference between the rate of interest they receive and the inflation rate. For example, if the inflation rate is three percent and interest rates eight percent, the real rate of return before taxes is five percent. Second, higher interest rates will tend to slow down the economy, which in turn should slow the growth in the inflation rate. The 1981 experience is an excellent example: a government fearful of runaway inflation kept jacking up interest rates until the economy almost collapsed. The long-term result was a period during the mid eighties in which we experienced disinflation — a time of declining interest rates. A similar pattern, although not as extreme, occurred in the early nineties.

The Canadian dollar. Interest rates will sometimes spike up for no other reason than the fact that international currency traders are driving the value of our dollar lower than the government and the Bank of Canada would like it. That happened in the winter of 1986, when our dollar hit a then all-time low of less than 70¢ U.S. The government responded with a major jump in interest rates, the idea being to attract more foreign capital into the country. That, in turn, means foreigners are buying rather than selling Canadian currency, which increases its value. We saw a similar occurrence in early 1992, after the dollar had declined rapidly from above 89¢ U.S. the previous fall to slightly more than 83¢ U.S. Although the economy was fragile, the Bank of Canada pushed interest rates back up in an effort to stabilize the dollar. Such currency-driven rate movements are usually temporary in nature and thus create some excellent opportunities for wealth builders who know how to profit from them.

The U.S. dollar. Simply a variant on the Canadian dollar scenario, except in this case it's the U.S. buck that's under seige. U.S. interest rates move up to defend it and ours dutifully follow suit. This is exactly what was happening in the spring of 1987.

U.S. financial policy. Canada has relatively little independence when it comes to interest rate policies. We're especially constrained in terms of our ability to move rates lower in relation to U.S. rates. We are too closely integrated into the North American economic structure (read U.S.) and we are too small to exert much influence on its policy direction. So no matter how much we fume about it, the reality is that the general direction of our interest rate structure is going to be governed to a large extent by decisions made in Washington. Another reality: our interest rates will almost always be somewhat higher than those in the U.S. That differential is needed to attract foreign investment — the sad truth is that international capital needs substantial inducements to put money into Canada rather than into the U.S.

International developments. Our increased reliance on foreign capital to fund our runaway deficits has added to our interest rate vulnerability. Political and economic developments in places like Europe and Japan can influence the flow of money into Canada from such areas and may require Canadian bond issuers to offer better rates of return (in other words, higher interest rates) to attract offshore capital. For example, high interest rates in Germany will tempt European investors to keep their money closer to home unless they have an incentive to send their money here. Weakness in the Japanese stock market may force investors there to raise cash to cover debts, with a resulting sell-off of Canadian bonds.

Politics. There's no doubt our constitutional turmoil contributed to keeping interest rates at artificially high levels in 1992. Foreign investors became increasingly nervous as Quebec separatism and the break-up of Canada loomed as a real possibility. As a result, they demanded a "danger premium" for investing their money here — and Canadians paid the price in higher mortgage and loan rates. Money gravitates to stable political climates; anything which adds an element of political risk for overseas investors ends up costing all of us.

All of this suggests that a prolonged period of stable interest rates in Canada through the nineties seems unlikely, despite the government's good intentions. But it's not impossible. So it's important to be prepared to deal with whatever situation arises.

Your investing and borrowing strategies will be quite different, depending on the prevailing interest rate climate. Let's consider first what you should be doing if the government's projections come true and interest rates remain at relatively low levels for the rest of the decade.

Borrowing strategies. Low, stable rates are a borrower's dream. No more restless nights worrying about what to do about the mortgage. Stable rates enable you to obtain the cost advantages of short-term mortgages and avoid the "insurance premium" of locking in for a longer term at a higher rate for protection against sudden jumps. Other loans also become easier to manage; variable rates, which move up or down with prime, become less dangerous. The main objectives of borrowers in such conditions are to minimize interest costs and to avoid locking in for the long term at higher rates. The risks involved in pursuing those goals are reduced substantially when rates are stable.

A word of caution here. If rates are low but you see signs they may be about to move up (you'll find some examples below), it's a signal to lock in. Watch carefully for such indicators through the nineties, especially given my reservations about the likelihood of a prolonged period of rate stability.

Investing strategies. While borrowers love low rates, investors hate them. A low rate climate makes it much more difficult to obtain a reasonable return on conservative interest-bearing investments. For example, many retired people were shocked in 1992 to find that

GICs that had been paying up to twelve percent were being renewed at around eight percent. For those relying heavily on the interest for regular income, that decline represented a loss of one-third in buying power and a resulting decline in their standard of living.

The alternative is to look more carefully at other types of investments. Dividends, for example, become more attractive in a low interest rate environment, especially when the impact of the dividend tax credit (which gives dividends a tax advantage over interest income) is taken into account.

Whatever you do, don't make the mistake of locking in long-term interest rates on your investments while they're at relatively low levels. There's nothing more frustrating than investing in a five-year GIC at eight percent and then watching the rate move up to the eleven percent level. More on GIC strategies in the next chapter.

A volatile interest rate environment will call for somewhat different approaches. Here's what I suggest:

Borrowing strategies. Your main objective during times of interest rate turmoil is to avoid locking yourself in for a long term when rates are high. Wait for periods when rates are down to do so. As basic as this advice sounds, many people don't follow it. The result is financial disaster — long-term commitments at inflated rates. Remember the folks who locked in 14.5% mortgages for five years that I told you about in the last chapter!

If you're borrowing during periods of fluctuating rates, the message is simple: stay short. Don't lock in to long-term commitments unless you're absolutely convinced rates are heading up for an extended period. Some signals to watch for: general economic conditions should be strong and heating up still more, labour unions should be obtaining progressively higher settlements, the cost of living index should be moving up, and you should already have seen some upward movement in interest rates. If those signs are present, lock in your borrowing rates. If they're not, stay short term.

During times of interest rate volatility you may also find significant differences in the rates charged by financial institutions. A personal line of credit offering about the same privileges may cost one to two percentage points more at Bank A than at Trust Company B. That makes it essential to shop around before signing anything. And if you think a couple of percentage points isn't a big deal, consider this: the difference between a ten percent loan and a twelve percent loan can add up to several hundred dollars a year in borrowing costs. For example, a $10,000 loan at ten percent will cost $1,000 a year to service; at twelve percent the cost is $1,200. That's an additional $200, after tax, you'll be paying out unnecessarily. Surely you have some better use for that money!

Investing strategies. The opportunities to make money in a volatile interest rate climate are terrific. There are some downside risks too, of course. But you should be able to keep them within tolerable limits.

The easiest way to score big is with bond mutual funds. I'll explain how to go about it in more detail in Chapter Ten; right now I'll just whet your appetite a bit by telling you that the average investor in bond mutual funds in 1991 walked away with a gain of 17.5% and some enjoyed profits of more than twenty percent. They achieved these results by putting money into a predictable, low-risk investment during one of the worst recessions in years. Not bad!

Another good strategy during such periods is to invest in money market mutual funds (MMFs) during times when rates are high or rising. These funds hold short-term securities such as Government of Canada Treasury bills and high-quality commercial paper, such as Banker's Acceptances. Canadians discovered money market funds in a big way in 1990, when they poured over two billion dollars in new money into them. They were well rewarded that year, with an average return of 11.8%, according to the *Globe and Mail Report on Business.* But then many made a classic error. They held on to their money market funds, and even invested new money in them, as rates dropped all through 1991. Because money market funds invest in short-term securities, they reflect current interest rate movements. As rates declined, therefore, so did MMF yields. The rate of return in 1991 fell steadily and averaged only 8.7%. Those who stayed in these funds watched their returns plummet; they also missed out on the opportunity to score big gains in the bond market. By the summer of 1992, most Canadian dollar money market funds were yielding between five and six percent, and the return was still falling.

If you have enough cash, you can avoid the fees charged by the managers of money market funds and invest directly in Treasury bills.

Until recently, trading in T-bills was strictly a rich person's game. If you didn't have at least $50,000 to put up, you couldn't play. Now that's all changed — you can get in on the action for as little as $1,000 — thanks to the aggressiveness of the brokerage industry. More on that a bit later.

T-bills are short-term borrowings by the federal and provincial governments, with maturities of less than a year. The 91-day bills are the most common, but they also come in maturities of 182 and 364 days. You buy them at a discounted price and redeem them at maturity for their face value. The difference is your interest on the transaction. For example, you might pay $970 for a $1,000 T-bill that's due in 91 days. When it matures you collect the face value of $1,000; the difference is your interest on that transaction. (In this case, you're collecting interest at an annualized rate of about twelve percent.) Since the bills are government guaranteed, they're as solid an investment as you're going to find.

As a short-term place to park your money, T-bills are excellent. But there are some things you should be aware of if you want to use them.

To begin with, you may have to do a bit of searching to find someone who will actually sell you the bills. The brokerage industry has led the way in making them available to the smaller investor (the chartered banks still only want your T-bill business if you have big bucks to invest). But different brokerage firms have different policies in selling them.

Minimum purchase requirements, for example, can vary all over the lot. Some firms will take $1,000 if you're a regular customer. Others will require $5,000 or even $10,000 minimums. You have to do some checking.

And while you're at it, find out what interest rate they're paying. The retail T-bill market is highly competitive and interest rates can vary from one brokerage firm to another. You want to get the best rate you can.

As you're checking the market, be aware that for many brokers Treasury bills are almost a loss-leader — they make relatively little profit from them. Instead, they're frequently used to attract other business. I once had to listen to a long sob story from a broker about how little money he made from T-bills. He'd be happy to sell me some, of course — but only if I sent some other business his way. I took my purchase elsewhere.

This approach to selling T-bills means you often won't get the same kind of service as you would if you were buying stocks and bonds. For example, I like to use them as short-term investments in a self-directed RRSP. But the trust company administering the plan requires that the actual certificates be delivered to them for safekeeping. Many brokerage firms won't do that, claiming that even something as minor as delivery costs can make the whole deal uneconomic.

When you do find a source for your T-bills, don't be surprised to discover that they're available in maturities other than the standard 91, 182 and 364 days. That's because brokerage houses buy them wholesale and hold them in inventory. You buy from their holdings at retail rates. This is done by the broker quoting you an interest rate slightly below what the firm receives on the bills — that's where they make their profit. A typical spread is half a point — if the brokerage firm is holding nine percent T-bills, they'll sell them to you at 8.5% and pocket the difference. So the interest rate quoted daily in the financial pages of the paper is not what you'll actually receive when you purchase the bills from a broker. That's why it's so important to check out the retail rates before taking any action.

T-bill strategy is the same as for money market funds. T-bills are excellent investments when short-term interest rates are high or rising; poor investments when rates are low or falling. Your capital is equally safe in both situations, as long as the Canadian government honours its debts. But your returns will vary considerably and holding large amounts of T-bills at the wrong time can result in missed opportunities elsewhere.

As you've undoubtedly grasped by now, volatile interest rates require constant changes in investment strategies to keep up. This isn't a time to lock yourself into a long-term game plan and fall asleep.

Before we end this chapter, a word about Canada Savings Bonds (CSBs). These have always been immensely popular with investors and in the first edition of *Building Wealth* I said they had a place in everyone's portfolio.

I no longer believe that, for two reasons.

First, some of the most attractive features of CSBs have been eliminated. For example, the interest rate on Canada Savings Bonds has always been guaranteed for one year only. But in the past, the bonds carried a base rate for subsequent years which ensured that, no matter what happened, you were guaranteed a minimum return. That changed in 1987. The CSB issue that fall did not include a base rate and this policy has been maintained in all subsequent issues. As a result, CSBs should be considered strictly as one-year investments. You receive no special consideration for owning a bond for several years; when a new rate is announced each fall, all bondholders, old and new, get the same amount.

The second reason I've fallen out of love with CSBs is the appearance of more attractive competitive products. One of these is the savings certificate (also known as the cashable GIC) issued by some smaller trust companies. I'll explain how they work in the next chapter; for now, let me just say they represent an excellent alternative to CSBs.

Frankly, given the decreased attractiveness of CSBs and the new options available, I'm amazed the federal government continues to sell as many as they do every year. I guess it just proves once again that old habits die hard.

Our Love Affair With GICs

The rate of interest is the reward for parting with liquidity for a specified period.
— John Maynard Keynes, 1936

Canadians are in love with guaranteed investment certificates. Each year we pour billions of dollars into GICs and similar investments. At the end of March, 1992, we had over $112 billion of our hard-earned money tied up in this type of security, according to Bank of Canada figures.

Unfortunately, we often put our cash into GICs for the wrong reasons. Perhaps it's because they are so easy to purchase (every financial institution sells them). Maybe it's because they're easy to understand. Or perhaps it's simply a case of not knowing what else is available.

Well, here's the lowdown: GICs and their cousins, term deposits (TDs), are sometimes a good place for your money. But not always, and only after you've looked at all the other options.

The first thing you need to understand is how GICs and term deposits differ. Many people are fuzzy on this point — including some so-called experts. A recently published dictionary of financial terms suggested that the only essential difference between them was that term deposits were issued by banks and GICs by trust companies. Otherwise, the dictionary said, the two are the same.

Well, don't believe it. Nor is another widely held belief correct, that term deposits are short-term investments while GICs are longer term.

Unfortunately, even the financial community hasn't gotten its act together on this one. The terms are sometimes used interchangeably and, often, with a total ignorance of any distinction.

Technically, however, they're not the same animal, although the lines between them are sometimes blurred.

GICs are medium-term investments, usually of one to five years duration, that are firmly locked in. Once the financial institution has your money, you normally can't get it out before maturity no matter how much you beg, whine or plead, although there are a few exceptions. You're compensated for this inflexibility by a higher interest rate. But before you invest, you'd better be darn sure you won't need the money before maturity.

Term deposits, by contrast, are not locked in. If you need your money, you can get it out at any time. But you'll pay an interest penalty for early withdrawal. And you'll receive a lower rate of interest over the life of a term deposit than you would from a comparable GIC.

Many financial institutions offer both, for either short or long terms. If you're investing for less than a year, you'll usually need a minimum of $5,000 for a term deposit and substantially more for a GIC. (Short-term GICs are rarely used by individual investors.) Investments for one year or longer usually have a $1,000 minimum, although some institutions will issue a $500 certificate. The return on a GIC will typically be one to two percentage points higher than on a TD, depending on the term you choose. For example, in April, 1992 the Bank of Commerce was offering to pay 7.5% for a five-year term deposit. But if you were willing to tie up your money for five years in a GIC, you received 8.5% — an extra percentage point for loss of flexibility.

Usually (but not always) the longer the term you select, the higher the interest rate you'll receive. At the time the Commerce was paying 8.5% for five-year GICs, it was offering 6.75% for one-year deposits and eight percent for three years.

Those differences can add up over a period of time. Suppose, for example, that you invested $1,000 in a one-year Commerce GIC in April, 1992. At maturity, you'd have $1,067.50, your original deposit plus $67.50 interest. If rates stayed the same and you repeated that process each year for the next four years, reinvesting the principal and accumulated interest each time, you'd end up with $1,386.24. Not bad, considering you started with $1,000.

But now let's suppose you'd locked in for five years from the outset, at 8.5%. When the GIC matures, the bank will pay you $1,503.66. That's $117.42 in additional interest, thirty percent more than you would have received by opting for annual renewals.

Either way, you'd be much better off than by leaving the money in a savings account. The Commerce's daily interest savings accounts were paying just 2.5% at that time.

That's a key point to remember. The interest rate you earn by putting your money into instruments like this will always be higher than you'd receive in an ordinary savings account. So it's a way to make your savings work harder for you and build wealth more quickly.

In fact, your savings and chequing accounts should never have more cash in them than is necessary to pay bills and avoid service charges. These are not good places to build wealth. The interest being paid on ordinary savings accounts is, to put it bluntly, lousy. You'll never become wealthy by leaving your money there; all you're doing is allowing the financial institution to borrow that money from you for its own use at very low cost. If you think subsidizing banks and trust companies is a good idea, fine. I have better uses for my money.

There are other things you can do with that cash which are every bit as safe and which will give you a far better return. One option is a premium savings account. These pay higher rates of interest if you leave a significant amount of money on deposit. Check with your financial institution to see what they offer and the conditions attached to them. Money market funds are another possibility. Many financial institutions now offer them and some even have limited chequing privileges.

It's important to maximize the rate of return you receive on your savings because Revenue Canada takes a large chunk. Interest income is taxed at your marginal rate (the tax rate that applies on the last dollar you earn). If your taxable income is over about $30,000, that means you're going to pay the government upwards of forty cents on every one dollar of income you earn.

This is one of the major weaknesses in using GICs and TDs as investment vehicles outside a tax-sheltered savings plan, especially during periods when interest rates are low. If you're in a forty percent tax bracket, your annual after-tax return on a $10,000 GIC paying nine percent is only $540. If your marginal tax rate is fifty percent, you'll keep only $450.

That return will be further eroded by inflation. If inflation is running at three percent annually, a $10,000 investment will decline in value by $300 each year. The combination of taxes and inflation can reduce the real after-tax return on a GIC to a pitifully small amount.

Inside a tax-sheltered plan, such as an RRSP, it's a different story. The tax factor is removed from the equation, at least until such time as the money is withdrawn. So interest that would otherwise be taxed away by Revenue Canada accumulates in the plan and your wealth increases at a much faster rate. For example, if you're in a forty percent tax bracket and invest in a $10,000 GIC paying ten percent interest outside a registered plan, you'll have $13,382 at maturity, after tax, assuming the reinvestment of all interest earned. The same GIC inside a registered plan will grow to $16,105 after five years.

So there are ways to use GICs effectively as wealth building tools. Let's look at some other possibilities.

TERM DEPOSITS (SHORT)

Look at these when you want to park your money for a short period of time while receiving a better rate of interest than your bank account offers. For example, suppose it's November and you have a $25,000 GIC maturing. You plan to buy a house in the spring and use the money as part of the down payment. You could always hold the funds in your daily interest account until May, when you plan to make the purchase. But you'd be further ahead opting for a 180-day term deposit, which offers a higher interest rate. By the time the term deposit matures and you're ready to make the down payment, you'll have some extra money to spend on household items. How much extra will depend on the interest rate differential between your savings account and the term deposit. Two percentage points more on $25,000 over six months will generate an extra $250 interest. After the tax is paid, you'll still have earned enough extra money to buy some pots and pans for the kitchen.

Before you decide on the term deposit, however, look at the financial institution's money market fund. See what the current yield is compared to the rate offered on the TD. Then consider which way interest rates are moving. If the yields are comparable and interest rates seem to be moving up, the money market fund is the better choice because you'll benefit from the higher rates. If rates appear to be softening, go with the term deposit, which guarantees your return until maturity.

TERM DEPOSITS (LONG)

This is an option to consider if you want to improve your rate of interest but retain the flexibility to withdraw the money if you need it. Go back to that $25,000 you received when your GIC matured. This time, let's assume you still plan to use the money to purchase a home, but you're not sure when. It might be two or three years down the road, but it could be sooner if a big raise comes through. You don't want to lock your money into a GIC again. But you'd like a better rate of return than your savings account offers. The future course of interest rates worries you — they've been falling for some time and they might drop still more. But you don't want your money locked away.

Here's where a term deposit may be a solution. You could obtain a better rate of return than by leaving the money in an ordinary savings account. And you could get your money out early if you decide to buy the house sooner than you expect, although you'd have to pay a penalty in the form of reduced interest if you did that.

Net result: You'll sacrifice some interest income, but you preserve your flexibility. And you protect yourself against the possibility of lower interest rates over the next two or three years.

In this case, you have to weigh the effect of any potential penalty against your desire for a better return. Penalties for cashing term deposits early will vary depending on the circumstances and the financial institution you're dealing with, but they can be substantial.

Suppose you put your money into a thirty-day term deposit. Two weeks later an emergency arises and you *must* have the funds. In most cases, you'll receive no interest at all. In effect, your penalty is 100% of the interest that would have been due you.

Now let's assume you have a two-year TD paying, say, seven percent.

At the end of the first year you want the money. In this case what you'll receive depends on whom you do business with. For instance, most of the big banks would charge you a three to four percent penalty in this situation. That means your penalty for cashing in early is about half the interest you would have otherwise collected. But this policy isn't universal. Some banks and credit unions will do much better. So if you think there's a strong chance you might want to cash in the term deposit before maturity, check out the policies of various financial institutions and go with the one that will penalize you the least.

Alternatively, consider a money market fund, even if the interest paid is lower. You can withdraw cash from a MMF at any time, without penalty, so you have maximum flexibility in the use of your money.

Guaranteed Investment Certificates

When you purchase a GIC, you tie up your money for a fixed period of time. In return, you receive a competitive interest rate, usually about the best that's available to the average fixed-income investor. Before you make that kind of commitment, you should ask yourself two questions:

1. Am I reasonably certain I won't need that money before the GIC matures?

2. Do the signs indicate that interest rates are going to remain stable or in a downward trend during the period I'll be holding the certificate?

Clearly, the second question is tougher to answer than the first. But if you review the interest rate indicators I described in the last chapter, you'll at least be in a position to make an informed judgement before going ahead.

I stress this point because one of the most frustrating experiences in building wealth with interest rates is locking into a five-year GIC and then seeing the rates take off. You don't want to be one of the many people who tie up their funds at ten percent and then fume as rates rise to twelve percent. You want to be part of the other, smaller group — the people who invest at twelve percent and then sit smiling as rates fall to nine percent.

As you might expect, GICs significantly outperform such investments as Canada Savings Bonds when interest rates are declining. Let me give you a personal example.

In the fall of 1982, the new issue of CSBs came out. They offered twelve percent in the first year with a guaranteed minimum of 8.5% after that. At the same time, five-year GICs were available from large trust companies at thirteen percent. I had nearly $9,000 that I wanted to put into some form of interest-bearing vehicle. My decision came down to CSBs or a GIC. Looking at all the signs, my feeling was that interest rates were on the way down. I chose the GIC.

When it matured in the fall of 1987, that GIC was worth almost $16,300. If I'd invested the same amount in compound interest CSBs, it would have been worth about $14,200. That's a difference of nearly $2,100 over the five-year term. Considering the size of the original investment, that's a lot!

That's how to use GICs to your advantage — lock in your returns when interest rates are high so that you can keep building wealth at a better-than-average pace when they're low.

SAVINGS CERTIFICATES

In recent years, a new type of GIC has appeared which combines some of the features of conventional GICs, term deposits and Canada Savings Bonds. It's variously known as a savings certificate or a cashable GIC, depending on where you buy it.

I love these things. They're a terrific idea, great for small investors who want to retain flexibility. The problem is that only a few financial institutions offer them.

Savings certificates are usually issued for one-year terms. The rate of interest is slightly lower than you'd receive for an ordinary one-year GIC, but higher than on a term deposit. The big attraction is flexibility. Depending on where you buy them, you can cash in any time after sixty or ninety days and receive the full amount of interest earned up to that time. No penalty. This makes them an ideal place to hold short-term money. You'll receive a better return than a savings account will offer, plus you can withdraw your cash whenever you wish.

Unlike Canada Savings Bonds, these certificates are always available. So if interest rates move up after you make your initial investment, you can simply roll over the full amount into a new certificate at the higher rate. I've personally done this many times; in fact, much of the short-term money within my company is now invested in this way.

So far, only some of the smaller trust companies and a few credit unions have chosen to make this attractive product available. Since these firms usually have only a few branches, most people aren't even aware the product exists. The most convenient way to buy them I've discovered is through the telephone service offered by Sun Life Trust. They'll quote you current rates and take your order by phone any time of the day or night, including weekends.

Buying ordinary term deposits and GICs depends on what you want. Banks and many credit unions offer all these options. Trust companies tend to be more limited: they normally offer term deposits for up to 364 days only. If you want to deposit your money for a longer period with a trust company, it usually has to be in a GIC.

Normally trust companies will offer better rates than the major banks, and the smaller the trust company, the more attractive the interest rate is likely to be. The rate difference arises from the fact that smaller trust companies need to attract more business. Since the spate of failures among trust companies during the eighties and early nineties, many people have become reluctant to deposit their money in smaller, less well-known financial institutions. To get business they often must offer more, just as Canada has to offer higher interest rates than the U.S. to attract international investment.

That situation can produce some good investment opportunities and innovative products, like the savings certificate. Keep an eye on the more aggressive smaller trusts; they'll sometimes have special promotions to generate new business which may prove attractive.

If the interest spread between the banks and the small trust companies on comparable products is significant, you might want to consider the options carefully before passing up an opportunity to earn more.

One major factor in your decision should be that term deposits and GICs of not longer than five years are protected by deposit insurance for both principal and interest, up to a maximum of $60,000. So as long as you don't invest more than that with any single financial institution, you're protected by the Canada Deposit Insurance Corporation in the event of a bankruptcy. Credit unions are protected by similar provincial plans; ask for details if you're considering a credit union deposit.

You should also do some homework before investing in a term deposit or GIC. The financial papers (*Globe and Mail Report on Business, Financial Post, Financial Times*) regularly publish a list of current interest rates. So do most major daily papers. If it's too much trouble to look up the best rates there, call a stockbroker or a financial planner. Most of them monitor the fluctuation of GIC and term deposit rates on a daily basis. Since rates change frequently, you'll want the most up-to-date information.

Now, let's suppose you've done all your homework and satisfied yourself a GIC is the way to go. You've locked in for five years at what you think is a great interest rate. Then disaster strikes. Your company is taken over by a larger firm. As part of the rationalization process, you lose your job. Nothing to do with your performance, they assure you. We just don't need two people doing the same thing and old Fred over there has been around for twenty-five years.

Suddenly you really need to get at that GIC money. But you're locked in. Or are you?

If you had the foresight to purchase a GIC that's transferable, or can be made so, you may not be.

Not many people know it, but stockbrokers run a secondary market in GICs. That means they're in the business of buying and selling GICs issued by financial institutions. So if you're locked in for

several years and suddenly need the money, you have an alternative. The bank or trust company that issued the certificate usually
won't redeem it. But you can take it to a broker and sell the certificate there — *as long as it is transferable*.

You're not going to get rich doing things this way. The broker will
pay you a discounted price for your piece of paper. For example, suppose you have a $1,000 five-year compounding certificate at eleven
percent with four years left to run. You've already earned $110 inter-
est, so the GIC right now is worth $1,110. The broker will pay you
something less than that to take it off your hands — how much less
depends to a large extent on where interest rates are when you want
to sell it and how much time there is left before maturity. If interest rates have gone down since you bought the certificate and it still
has four years to run, you'll get a better price for it. That's because
it will be offering a higher return than someone could get buying a
new GIC. Conversely, if interest rates have gone up, the amount you'll
receive will be less — you may even sacrifice part of your principal
just to get it off your hands. But at least it's a way to get most of your
money out. If you're ever in this situation don't go to just one broker for an offer; you may get a better price somewhere else.

The broker who buys your certificate will then turn around and
offer it for sale to his or her clients. That means you can *buy* a "used"
GIC from a broker if you wish. Usually the return you'll receive will
be slightly higher than if you deal with a bank or trust company,
perhaps by a quarter of a percent or so. This could happen in one
of two ways: either the interest rate on the GIC is higher than current rates, or the broker will sell it to you at a discount from face
value to make the real interest yield more attractive.

If you want to compare returns on "used" and "new" GICs, contact a broker and ask for the current list of GICs they're offering.
These will be certificates issued by banks and trust companies; the
only difference is that they've gone through the buying and selling process I've just described.

Compare the rates being offered by the broker to what you could
get if you went directly to a financial institution. Remember,
you'll be taking over the GIC for the balance of time remaining until
it matures. If the term and the interest rate is right for your pur-

poses, take advantage of it.

One reminder before I end this chapter. If interest rates appear to be moving up, don't lock away your funds for a long period. The time to do that is when interest rates are high. Those opportunities don't come along too often but when they do, grab them.

Bonds:
The Easiest
Investment

Gentlemen prefer bonds.
> — Andrew Mellon, 1926

Let me begin this chapter with a sad story.

Once upon a time, many years ago (it was back in the early 1960s as I recall) my mother-in-law asked me for some investment advice.

She wasn't a wealthy woman, far from it. But she'd managed to put some money aside, about $2,000. That may not sound like much now, but in those days, when $10,000 a year was a big salary, it was quite a bit.

She didn't want to keep it in her bank savings account, which paid virtually no interest. She didn't trust the stock market. What could she do with it?

Bonds, I said.

You mean Canada Savings Bonds?

No. *Real* bonds. The kind that people trade. I'd never invested in a bond in my life at that stage. But I'd read an article.

Bonds, I repeated. A rock-safe investment that will pay you a good return.

Well, okay, she said dubiously. She should have known better. I should have known better.

She put her hard-earned $2,000 into Manitoba Telephone bonds, paying seven percent interest and maturing in 1993. They seemed safe and sure — bonds issued by a public utility and guaranteed by a provincial government.

For a couple of years, all seemed well. She received a $70 interest cheque twice a year and never gave the bonds another thought. The fact that interest rates were starting to creep up didn't bother her and I'd forgotten at that point I'd ever put her on to the bonds. All was well.

Or at least it was until one day, several years later, when she decided she'd like to sell the bonds and get her money out. She visited a broker with the certificates and was told that, yes, the bonds could be sold. She'd receive, let's see, $1,200 for them.

Naturally, she was stunned. Here was a supposedly safe investment, suggested by her son-in-law of all people, that had lost almost half its value. She couldn't figure out why — and at the time, neither could I.

Her Scottish blood refused to allow her to sell the bonds and take the loss. When she passed away a few years later, she still had them. My wife inherited them and put them into an RRSP. It was only in the mid-1980s, when interest rates dropped and the maturity date drew near, that those Manitoba Tel bonds returned to a market value that was something close to what my mother-in-law had paid way back in the early sixties. Some financial advisor I was! Fortunately, I've learned a little bit since.

One of the things I've learned is that bonds are one of the easiest ways to build wealth — if you understand what you're doing and you apply your observations of interest rate trends to your investment strategies. GICs, savings certificates and money market funds are all perfectly valid ways to make money via the interest rate route. But for maximum returns in relative safety, nothing beats bonds. And no, I'm not giving you the same line I gave my mother-in-law so many years ago. Or at least, I'm not giving it to you for the same reasons.

You can, of course, still lose a lot of money in bonds, as my mother-in-law did, along with everyone else who held them during that long period when interest rates were steadily moving up. So be careful.

There is one basic fact you have to fix firmly in your mind about bonds. When interest rates go up, bond prices fall. Conversely, when interest rates go down, bond prices increase. Once you've grasped that, all you have to do is figure out which way interest rates are moving and then sit back and cash in. Easy, huh?

Of course that's overly simplistic. If it *were* that easy everyone would be a millionaire. The trick, of course, is guessing right on which way interest rates are moving and then having the courage to take advantage of the situation.

Let me give you a simplified example — and I stress, it *is* simplified. Suppose you bought a $1,000 bond when interest rates were ten percent. You'd get $100 interest a year. Now you want to sell it, but interest rates have gone up. Similar bonds are now paying twelve percent. Do you think anyone is going to buy your bond for $1,000? Not on your bip-bip. They'll want a twelve percent return on their money, not ten percent. So to sell the bond you'll have to price it so the $100 a year it pays in interest will give the buyer a return on his investment of twelve percent. That means you'll have to sell him the bond for around $835. You've just lost money!

If, on the other hand, interest rates had gone down to eight percent in the meantime, it's a different story. Your bond is still paying $100 a year interest. But now, with rates at eight percent, your buyer will have to pay $1,250 to get that return. Your bond just went up twenty-five percent in value and you've got a nice capital gain.

Identifying the general interest rate trend isn't as hard as it sounds. That's because interest rates move in long cycles, usually several years. There'll be blips along the way, of course. One took place in the winter of 1986, when the Bank of Canada pushed up rates as part of its battle to defend the plunging Canadian dollar. But that upward spike was temporary and only lasted a few months. By summer the crisis had passed and interest rates had resumed the long decline that began in 1981–82.

The same thing happened in March, 1992 after a run on the Canadian dollar had pushed it down six cents in a relatively short time. The Bank of Canada responded by jacking up rates, even though the economy was weak. As soon as the dollar stabilized, rates started to drop again.

The key to building wealth with bonds is to catch the trend once it's begun and ride it, rather like a surfer riding a wave. Of course, sooner or later the wave crashes and the surfer wipes out. But it's a great ride while it lasts.

You don't want to wipe out, of course. And you don't have to if you're careful and pay attention to your bond investments.

At this point, perhaps a word of explanation about bonds is in order.

As you have probably gathered by now, I'm not speaking here about Canada Savings Bonds. They aren't true bonds at all; rather they're a type of savings certificate.

The bonds I'm describing are issued by governments, crown corporations, municipalities and private companies as a means of financing their capital expenditures or operating costs. Financial people refer to them as "debt instruments," because they represent money the issuer owes — rather like sophisticated IOUs, if you like. Stocks, by contrast, represent equity — an actual piece of the ownership of a company.

Bonds are bought and sold on the Bond Market, which is one of the mythical never-never lands of the financial world. It doesn't exist, at least not in any physical form. You can't walk onto the floor of the bond market and watch the traders at work, as you can at some stock exchanges (although fewer of them still use floor traders).

Bond trading is a computer game. The "bond market" is a collection of traders across the country, sitting at their desks and networking by telecommunications. Not very glamorous, perhaps. But that's the reality.

There have been entire books written about bonds, so obviously this one chapter isn't going to point out every nuance involved in trading them successfully. But here are the four key terms you need to know for starters:

Coupon: The interest rate the bond pays, based on its face value. Bonds are normally sold to individual investors in $1,000 units. So a bond with a coupon rate of nine percent would pay $90 a year interest, usually in semi-annual payments.

Maturity: This is the date at which the bond matures and you can cash it in at face value. No interest is payable after that date.

Yield to maturity: The annual rate of return you'll receive on a bond you buy today and hold until its maturity date. It includes both the interest paid on the bond and the capital gain or loss that will result if you keep the bond until it matures. The yield to maturity may be very different from the coupon rate, depending on the price of the bond, time left to maturity and the general interest rate picture.

Rating: A measure of the safety of the investment, expressed in letters. A rating of AAA means the chances of the issuer going belly up and leaving you holding a worthless certificate are almost nil. A bond with a C rating, on the other hand, is a signal to run quickly in the opposite direction unless you're prepared to take big risks in hopes of a spectacular return.

As you learn more about bonds, you'll find you can make use of all these variables to improve your returns. But the thing I like about bonds is that you really don't have to bother with all this stuff if you don't want to.

What you *do* have to be aware of is that the longer the time to the bond's maturity, the more volatile it will be and, therefore, the more risk is involved in the investment. Bonds with twenty years to maturity will move more sharply in price than those with, say, five years left. That's why my mother-in-law's Manitoba Tel bonds did so badly; they were long-term and so reacted with greater volatility in a rising interest rate environment.

The other thing you need to know is that you don't have to go through the agony of selecting exactly the right bond. This is what makes bond trading so different from the stock market. With stocks, you not only have to identify which way the market is moving, you then have to pick specific stocks that you believe will perform exceptionally well. Bonds are different. Most bonds with similar maturity dates and ratings will tend to move in the same direction in the market. You don't normally expect to find one twenty year Government of Canada bond moving up while another is going down.

So once you decide you want to invest in bonds, you don't have to do a lot of soul-searching about which one to choose. If you're just starting out, stick with Government of Canada bonds. Don't even touch anything else until you have a clear understanding of what you're doing. Decide whether you prefer short-term bonds (which I define as those with maturity dates no longer than five years from now), medium-term (five to ten years), or long-term (over ten years).

Generally, the longer the term you choose, the greater the risk you're assuming and the larger your potential gain or loss.

Short-term bonds are less risky simply because their maturity date is relatively close. At that time they can be cashed at face value. So if interest rates rise — causing bond prices to fall — short-term bonds won't usually suffer as great a loss as long-term bonds will.

Conversely, long-term bonds are a place you can make big money if interest rates decline. Prices of those bonds will increase more, because the holders can collect the coupon interest rate, which is now substantially more than new bonds are paying, for a longer period of time.

So if you believe interest rates are in a downward trend, buy some Government of Canada bonds. The maturities will depend on your risk tolerance — you might choose a blend of short, medium and long term bonds.

That's what I did in the summer of 1984, during one of those periods when interest rates had taken a temporary upward spike. I was convinced they'd start moving down again within a few months, so I bought a mixture of Government of Canada bonds.

Interest rates did in fact drop during the autumn and, of course, the value of the bonds went up. When rates started to turn around again in February, 1985 I sold some (not all) of the bonds and took some profits.

On one, my profit worked out to about twenty-three percent on an annualized basis — this was a combination of interest and capital gain. On the other, my annualized profit was just under twenty-five percent. Given the very low risk involved in this particular investment, I consider that a respectable rate of return, certainly much more than I would have received by investing in CSBs or GICs. I only wish I'd known all this when my mother-in-law asked me for advice back in the sixties.

An easier way to achieve the same results is with bond mutual funds. This relieves you of the decision of which bonds to purchase; the fund manager assumes that responsibility. Bond mutual funds also enable you to invest with much less money. In some cases, you can open an account for as little as $500.

The most recent opportunity to make big money in bonds came in 1990. Interest rates were high, but the economy was clearly weakening. Those two signals convinced me the time had come to shift large amounts of money from cash into bonds and bond funds, and I urged people who attended my seminars that year to do exactly that.

It didn't take a genius to figure out what was going to happen. It's simply a case of economic history repeating itself. As the economy plunged into recession, the Bank of Canada and the Federal Reserve Board in the U.S. responded by reducing interest costs. As rates declined, bond prices went up. The average return for all bond funds sold in Canada was 17.5% in 1991. Some bond funds produced gains in excess of twenty percent that year. Easy money for those who had seen the signs and acted accordingly.

I'm not suggesting that you should become a bond speculator. Normally I hold my bonds for much longer than a few months. But when the opportunity presents itself, you'd be foolish not to take advantage of it. Once interest rates appear to have bottomed out, take some profits and switch a portion of your money elsewhere.

If you're just starting out, a bond fund is certainly the best route to take. However, if you'd prefer to build your own portfolio, consider buying only Government of Canada bonds with a maturity of less than ten years to minimize risk. Another good rule is to buy only when the interest rate is at a level you'd be content to live with if you held the bond to maturity. And, of course, you should only be buying if you feel interest rates stand a good chance of moving lower.

Follow those basic rules and you won't wipe out — even if the wave does crash.

Finally, a few words about stripped bonds, which have become popular in recent years. Strips, or zero-coupon bonds as they're also known, can either be treated as a conservative, long-term investment or as a short-term speculation. In other words, they have a Jekyll and Hyde personality. Here's how they work.

Let's take a Government of Canada bond with a face value of $1,000, maturing in fifteen years and paying ten percent interest. If you purchased one of these, you'd receive two separate components. One would be the bond itself, guaranteeing repayment of the principal on the maturity date. The other would be thirty coupons, one of which you'd cash every six months to collect your interest.

When you buy stripped bonds (or stripped coupons) you are buying these components separately. You can buy the bond alone, without the coupons, at a discounted price and hold it until it matures. The increase in value during that period would be, in effect, the interest on your investment.

There are two advantages to the investor. The first is that your yield to maturity is guaranteed. With an ordinary bond, you have to reinvest interest payments as they are received; if rates fall, you won't receive as high a return as you anticipated. The second advantage is that you can buy more assets because of the discounted price. For example, a fifteen year stripped bond priced to yield ten percent until maturity would cost about $240 to purchase — its "present value" in financial terms. That means you could hold four such bonds for every one regular bond. That, in turn, increases your profits if interest rates fall and bond prices rise — or your losses if the opposite happens.

Buying stripped coupons simply means you're purchasing the other component of the bond, the semi-annual interest coupons. Again the same principle applies: you buy the coupons at their present value and cash them in at maturity. The advantage here is that, because the coupons become due every six months, you can vary the maturity dates to suit your own needs.

Stripped bonds and coupons carry the magic of compound interest to its ultimate degree. Unlike GICs or CSBs, you can lock in a guaranteed interest rate for fifteen, twenty, even thirty years into the future. That offers some intriguing possibilities.

For example, when interest rates were sky-high in the early 1980s, think how great it would have been to guarantee yourself a seventeen or eighteen percent return on your money for as far ahead as you can see.

Or in mid-1984, when brokerage houses were strongly promoting strips, you could have locked in returns of thirteen to fourteen percent. I bought strips with a face value of $77,000 at that point, with various maturity dates into the 1990s. They cost me just under $26,000 and yielded 13.6% to maturity. They turned out to be one of the best bond investments I ever made. My only regret was that I didn't buy more.

Another good opportunity for buying strips came in early 1990, when yields topped eleven percent for a time.

Strips are sometimes over-hyped by brokers. But claims which appear to be exaggerated may, in fact, be true. You can, for example, turn $2,000 into $25,000 — if you can get a 13.5% return and you're prepared to wait twenty years. If you wait five years longer, that original $2,000 will balloon to over $47,000.

Sounds terrific. But there are some pitfalls to be aware of.

First, if you hold the strips until maturity you have to make your purchases with care. It doesn't make a lot of sense for a seventy-year-old person to buy a strip with a twenty-year maturity. A younger person doesn't have to be as concerned. But if you're approaching retirement age, choose maturity dates that will ensure you have cash regularly becoming available.

Second, strips don't pay any income. You only collect when the bond or coupon matures. If you need a steady income flow today, this isn't the way to go.

Third, the interest rate that looks good right now may not seem so hot five or ten years in the future. Remember my mother-in-law's Manitoba Tel bonds. You'll have to decide whether the rate being offered on strips is likely to seem reasonable over the long haul.

Fourth, some brokers charge excessive commissions on strips. Depending on the broker and the term, it can range anywhere from one to ten percent. Unfortunately, it's not easy to determine exactly how much commission you're paying because it's buried in the price of the bond, instead of being broken out separately as in a stock transaction. Ideally, the provincial securities commissions would step in to require brokers to show the commissions as a separate item on each transaction slip, but that doesn't seem likely to happen soon. So make a point of inquiring how much commission you're paying before you place an order.

Fifth, stripped bonds are very volatile. Their value will rise and fall much more sharply than ordinary bonds, as interest rates move. At one point the Ontario Securities Commission felt it necessary to issue a warning about the volatile nature of this type of investment. If you intend to hold the strips to maturity or you want to speculate in them, fine. But be aware that the prices can swing wildly.

Sixth, there are important tax considerations in owning strips. Revenue Canada requires you to declare the accrued interest and pay tax on it annually — even though you haven't actually received one cent of real income! For that reason, strips should only be purchased as a long-term hold within a tax-sheltered environment, such as a Registered Retirement Savings Plan, Registered Retirement Income Fund, pension plan or Registered Education Savings Plan. In that case, no tax would be payable — you just let the money accumulate until you're ready to cash in.

Like any other bond, strips offer the best opportunity for profit when interest rates are high. So keep your eyes open for buying opportunities — periods when interest rates, particularly long-term rates, are up. That's when the odds are in your favour. Take advantage of them.

The Credit Card Squeeze

CHAPTER
11

You can't put your Visa bill on your American Express card.
— P.J. O'Rourke

In the first edition of *Building Wealth*, I made an offer to readers. I asked them to open their wallet or purse and count the number of credit cards they were carrying. Every person who had two or less would receive five dollars from me. Every person who had more would send me a dollar for every card over two.

I received a couple of requests for the five dollars. No one sent me any money for their extra cards, however.

Since only the winners seem inclined to accept the bet, I have to withdraw it or face potential bankruptcy. But the challenge is still on the table.

Try it yourself. Unless you have a bad credit rating or simply don't believe in using plastic money, I'm sure you'll find you're carrying too many cards around with you. Perhaps you'll even discover some you weren't aware you owned. There were fifty-one million credit cards in circulation in Canada in 1991. The average adult Canadian carries between two and three cards; most people with higher incomes have more. And we're being bombarded with sales promotions for new cards all the time.

What have credit cards to do with wealth building? A lot. An essential part of any wealth building program is the effective management of your financial resources. You must be able to handle credit well and to make intelligent choices in the credit instruments you use. Credit cards are the first experience many people have with borrowing. Unfortunately, that first experience often turns into a financial disaster which can take years to put right.

Part of the fault for this lies with our credit granting institutions themselves. Some of the gimmicks that are being used in the hot pursuit of credit card market share smack of hucksterism at its worst. As a result of all this intense promotion, we tend to lose sight of the real purpose of a credit card — as a convenient substitute for cash.

Card issuers entice us to sign up with every form of inducement, from frequent flyer points to free life insurance. Some cards offer merchandise bonuses; for example Royal Bank's Premier Visa Card gives points for the dollars you spend, one point for every $100 charged to the card. The rewards can be anything from a golf umbrella (forty-five points) to a grandfather clock. The clock requires 6,500 points — $650,000 worth of purchases. That would take even a heavy credit card user like me a few years to achieve.

The big U.S.-based Citibank promotes its prestige Visa card by borrowing a merchandising device from Canadian Tire. Card users receive one Citibank dollar for every $10 charged. The Citibank bucks can then be redeemed for partial payment on a variety of merchandise, but you have to sign up for a card to find out what you can receive. When we were researching this edition, we were firmly told that lists of prize merchandise are not provided to non-cardholders.

Royal Trust introduced a much simpler device with its Gold MasterCard — a one percent rebate on everything purchased on the card. Some other prestige cards now offer a similar feature, including the TD Gold Elite Visa Card, which was launched in 1992. The rebate is another merchandising ploy to grab a respectable share of the market. But, as I'll explain later in this chapter, it's one the smart credit card user can turn to his or her advantage.

It's not just the premium cards that are aggressively pursuing your business. My daughter Deborah worked briefly one summer for an outfit which kept dozens of people busy every day doing telephone solicitations for Bay cards. The pay was poor but the bonus incentives for signing customers were good. At one point, my daughter confessed later, she pleaded with a potential customer to sign up so she could meet her quota, telling the surprised man on the line to cut up the card and flush it down the toilet if he didn't want to use it after it arrived in the mail. Real salesmanship!

In the past few years, another type of credit card has made its appearance — the affinity card. If you're a university graduate, you've probably been asked to sign up for a Visa or MasterCard (the latter has been the most aggressive in developing this business) issued to the alumni of your *alma mater*. The typical affinity card is a handsome piece of plastic, perhaps bearing a picture of one of the landmark buildings of the school. You're offered a special inducement to sign up (perhaps a reduced annual fee). The school receives a small percentage of the total purchases made by its card holders. Since every college and university in Canada needs financial help these days, there's been a rush to get on the affinity card bandwagon.

Affinity cards are also available to members of some recreational organizations, environmental associations, clubs and similar groups. In the U.S., you can even get an affinity card that bears the logo of your favourite National Football League team.

The fact that banks, trust companies, credit unions, department stores, oil companies, universities, clubs and a variety of other organizations are going to such lengths to persuade you to sign up should tell you something. In many cases (although not all), credit cards are a very profitable business for them. They are not, conversely, very profitable for you — unless you use them correctly.

If you're a normal credit card user, you can probably save yourself hundreds of dollars each year by applying some basic financial management discipline. That's money that could be channelled into productive wealth building activities. And by handling your cards more effectively, you'll reduce the risk and inconvenience of having them lost or stolen.

How? Here's a guide to intelligent credit card use that may help.

To begin with, a suggestion: Don't carry more than two personal cards. Unless you have some unusual credit requirements, you don't need any more. This isn't just an exercise in keeping a neat purse or wallet. Most major credit cards now charge annual user fees, so you're paying a lot of money for the privilege of carrying around all that plastic, especially if you're not making regular use of it.

Which two cards should you keep? That depends on how you use them. Take out all your credit cards and spread them on a table in front of you. Pick up those you used less than four times over the past year. They have to go — any card used that infrequently isn't worth keeping.

I'll admit, it's not always easy. But it's a necessary exercise. Let me tell you what happened when I did it a few years ago.

The first casualty was my En Route card, the one that used to be issued by Air Canada (it was recently taken over by Diner's Club, after years of losing money). I carried one for a while but never found myself in a situation where I wanted to use it. When En Route announced they were going to start charging an annual fee, I cancelled it in a hurry.

Next to go was Diner's Club, for basically the same reason. I was paying for a card I rarely used. The only reason it stayed in my wallet so long was that I'd forgotten I even owned it.

After that it was the turn of Visa to get the chop. I used to carry two Visa cards. Don't ask me why; I'd picked up a second one at some point and since it kept arriving automatically in the mail, I never bothered to cancel it. Then they introduced user fees. That was all the motivation I needed. I cancelled one immediately. Then, after shopping around a bit, I found a Visa issuer that still gave the card free. I cancelled the other card I'd been carrying and switched.

Finally came American Express. I'd owned an American Express card for years, ever since the time I travelled through Europe as a student and the local American Express office became a second home, a place you could pick up mail, get cheques cashed and meet fellow North American nomads. So it was a real wrench to cut up my card — almost as if I was being disloyal to the company that had been so helpful when I was young. But when I discovered I hadn't used my card for fourteen months, I decided the money I was paying for the annual fee might be better spent somewhere else.

There are situations when a card like American Express is useful, because it has no fixed spending limit. If you tend to run up large travel and entertainment bills, you don't face as great a risk of having a disdainful waiter hand your card back because you've exceeded your credit limit. (This *can* happen if you switch your spending patterns, however; I've seen several complaints from people who were denied credit because they were spending more than they normally did. AmEx says it's a safety mechanism to reduce fraudulent card use.)

I was never in the position of worrying about exceeding a credit limit, however. I always pay off my bills as they come due and the credit limits on my cards are more than adequate for my needs. So AmEx got the chop.

There has only been one occasion since then that I've been financially embarrassed because I didn't have an AmEx card. Ironically, it occurred just a few days before this chapter was written. We had dined with friends at a fine restaurant in Naples, Florida. When the bill arrived, I presented my MasterCard in payment.

"I'm sorry, sir," the waiter said. "We do not accept MasterCard or Visa. American Express only."

Given the fact that many restaurant owners were complaining at the time about the high rates charged by AmEx, I was astonished. Fortunately, my wife had the foresight to bring some travellers' cheques (American Express, of course) in her purse, so we escaped without having to wash dishes.

So there can be occasions when the two credit card policy can backfire. Fortunately, it doesn't happen often.

Incidentally, in the months following the cancellation of my American Express account, I received several form letters telling me, in polite terms of course, what a fool I was and offering me the chance to reconsider. They pointed out all the benefits I was foregoing and implied that without an American Express card my social status would fall to zero. I read all these sales pitches carefully and looked again at the benefits they described. They only reinforced my decision — I had never had occasion to use a single one of the advantages offered by the card, besides simply charging things, of course. And, when I thought about it, I realized I wouldn't use them in the future either. After a while, the letters stopped. I guess I'd finally been relegated to AmEx Siberia.

Back to the card selection exercise. By now, you may have three or four cards left on the table. Of those that remain, select the two with the widest acceptance. These will most likely be Visa and MasterCard. Now look again at the others that are still there — maybe a gasoline card and a department store card. Ask yourself whether you couldn't just as easily use one of the bank cards when you're making the purchases you normally use those cards for. If you can, add them to the discard pile.

There are a few exceptions. Sears is one; it's the only major department store in Canada that still accepts only its own card. If you do a great deal of shopping there, you'll probably have to keep their card as well.

Once you've made your final decision, don't just cut up the cards you don't need and forget them. Cancel them with the issuer, otherwise you'll continue to receive replacement cards at the expiry date, with accompanying invoices. I'm still receiving monthly invoices from Diner's Club (always with a zero balance, of course), even though I haven't carried a Diner's Club card in my wallet for years.

And, of course, pay off any outstanding balances that may remain. This isn't an exercise in ruining your credit rating.

When you've completed this whole process, you should be down to two basic cards. Now let's consider how to use them most intelligently.

Rule one: Reduce your user fees to an absolute minimum. Ideally, aim for zero net cost. It's still possible, but you have to work at it.

I'm reluctant to pay credit card issuers for using their product. It may be because I remember when most credit cards were free. It's only in recent years that they've added all kinds of user charges and transaction fees. Plus there's the fact that I know the merchants are paying the card companies a percentage of everything I charge, which of course is built into the price I pay. I figure the issuers are getting enough from me.

There are still free credit cards around, although they're becoming rarer. And since card issuers are constantly changing their policies, a good deal one year might be a lousy one the next. Here are a couple of places to look, though.

Central Guaranty Trust (if they're still around when you read this). For years Central Guaranty offered the best deal on a Visa card: no user fees and no transaction charges. This is still the policy as this edition is being written, but many of the assets of Central Guaranty have switched hands or are in the process of doing so, so I can't guarantee the free Visa card is still available.

Bank of Montreal/National Bank of Canada/National Trust. Many MasterCard issuers have moved to user fees, but as this edition was prepared these institutions maintained a no-fees policy for a basic MasterCard. If that's still the case when you read this, a MasterCard from any of them is a good value.

Rule two: Use status cards wisely. You can get gold cards, platinum cards, emerald cards, prestige cards, premier cards and heaven knows what else. They'll all cost you — sometimes a lot. And the merchandising can be tempting, as we've already seen. The range of extras these cards offer runs all the way from membership in an exclusive wine club to free medical insurance coverage when you travel outside Canada. If you really feel you'll make good use of these, fine. But be sure.

A few years ago, my view was that the main difference between these cards was the colour. Gold cards — which most of them were and still are — were little more than an expensive status symbol. Sure, they offered some perks, like a twenty-four-hour travel hotline. But how often do you want to call a travel agent in the middle of the night?

Times have changed, however. Today's premium cards offer a wide range of services and bonuses. Whether you should pay the hefty fee most charge depends on how much use you'll make of the card's features.

Each premium card has its own smorgasbord of goodies. You'll have to do some research to find which combination of features best suits your needs.

Here are some of the most common:

Travel health insurance. If you travel outside Canada, you should have some form of supplementary health coverage in the event of accident or illness. Otherwise, your medical costs could be staggering.

114

Many provinces have cut back the amount they'll pay for medical care outside Canada. Ontario, which drastically reduced the fees payable for out-of-country health services in the fall of 1991, took out large newspaper ads strongly advising travellers to buy supplementary insurance to protect themselves.

Some premium credit cards offer this protection as part of their package. But watch out! All the plans aren't the same and some issuers are getting out of this field altogether because of the increasing costs involved.

Royal Trust Gold MasterCard holders, for example, received notices in the spring of 1992 advising them that health insurance coverage outside Canada would no longer be automatically available after August 31. They were given the alternative of buying special insurance for a fee instead. Several other premium card issuers were reviewing their out-of-country coverage as this edition was finalized. If you're counting on your card to provide such protection, make sure it's still in force before you leave home.

If your card does offer health coverage, check out all the details. See whether it's a matter of having to pay first and collect later. The CIBC Gold Convenience Card, for example, offers a Blue Cross Deluxe plan which eliminates the need to work through government agencies to collect small claims. This can save a great deal of aggravation.

You should also look carefully at the fine print of the plan. See if it imposes limits on the maximum amount paid or the length of time you can be abroad. Check out the status of dependants. In short, if medical coverage is an important factor in choosing a premium credit card, look at the terms as carefully as if you were buying a policy directly.

Collision damage waiver. Renting a car is expensive enough. If you accept the agency's collision damage waiver coverage, you can add another ten dollars a day or more to your bill.

Many premium cards provide this protection free, when you use the card for the rental. If you rent frequently, that saving alone could be enough to justify the extra cost of the card.

But be sure you really need the coverage before using this as a rationale for going gold. You may already be protected through your personal automobile insurance policy. Check with your insurance agent.

Travel insurance. This is always nice to have, but only if it covers you for the most likely contingencies. Most premium cards offer some form of accidental death or dismemberment (what an awful word!) protection. But it's not likely you'll ever use it.

Far more valuable, in my view, is trip cancellation and trip interruption coverage. This protects you in the event illness or a family emergency forces you to cancel or cut short your trip.

Only a few cards offer both, including the Visa Gold cards issued by the Bank of Nova Scotia, the Royal Bank and the Toronto Dominion Bank. All place dollar limits on their coverage; only the Gold Visa card issued by the Quebec-based Caisses Desjardins offers unlimited protection.

Extended warranties. American Express has done most of the promotion for this feature, but almost all the premium cards now offer it. Protection typically covers loss or breakage of any item purchased with the card for ninety days, plus extension of the manufacturer's warranty for up to one year.

Discounts, bonuses. Increasingly, the big selling point of many premium cards is some form of discount or reward program.

As I mentioned earlier, the Royal Trust Gold MasterCard and TD Bank Gold Elite Visa Card offer a one percent discount on all purchases, as long as you pay on time. Canada Trust's Gold MasterCard will also pay a one percent rebate, if you use it to buy more than $5,000 worth of goods and services in a year.

Purchases made with the En Route card earn Air Canada mileage points, as do those made with the CIBC Aerogold card. Royal Trust and Canadian Airlines have hooked up with a similar deal on the Canadian Plus card.

Other cards offer bonus points good for merchandise or travel discounts with each purchase.

So is a premium card worth it? You'll have to do your own

cost/benefit analysis. Including a card for your spouse, the annual fee could be anywhere from $60 (Bank of Montreal Gold MasterCard) to $700 (American Express Platinum Card, if both of you have one. You can get a Platinum Card for yourself and supplementary Gold Card for your spouse for $400.)

You'll have to weigh the cost of the card against the money you'll save by using it. If you travel a lot, or plan to spend $10,000 or more annually on the card, it's probably worth it. Otherwise, stick with the low-cost basic model.

Rule three: Don't use your credit cards to finance purchases. If you don't pay off your balance in full every month, you're actually using them as a means to borrow money. That is an absolute no-no. If you need to borrow money, there are far less expensive ways to do it, which I'll discuss in the next chapter.

Even the banks, if pressed, will admit privately that carrying a credit card balance and paying interest on it makes no sense. They try not to say it too loudly, though — after all, interest on credit card balances is one of their main revenue streams from these pieces of plastic.

Almost every financial advisor I know agrees that carrying a credit card balance is foolish. I read articles in newspapers and magazines all the time that repeatedly stress this point. And yet about half the credit card holders in Canada do it — that's several million people. It's the single most common money management mistake people make.

Why do they do it? In part because of convenience — it's much easier to use a credit card to finance your purchases than it is to negotiate a bank loan. They may also feel the amount of interest they're paying isn't enough to get excited about. That's because they haven't done their math.

The spread between an ordinary loan and the interest rate on your credit card may be up to ten percent. This assumes you're using Visa or MasterCard, not one of the department store cards which charge interest at a rate of 28.8% in most cases.

If you carry a balance of $2,500 on your card, that means you may be paying up to $250 a year more in interest than you should be.

That's too much money to be throwing away. Take out a personal loan, pay off the credit card balance and make a solemn vow never to make the same mistake again. If you can't stick to it, cut up the rest of your cards. If you can't manage them properly, you shouldn't have them at all.

By the way, don't be surprised if you keep getting charged interest even after you've paid off your balance in full. Credit card issuers have some cute tricks to keep you on the hook as long as possible. Here's a letter I received a few years ago from a listener to one of my CBC radio broadcasts that shows what can happen. This particular case involved a Bank of Montreal MasterCard.

"On November 29, I discovered I had missed making my payment, which was due on November 27," he wrote. "Realizing that I would incur interest charges, I decided to leave the payment until the next statement arrived, as previous experience had taught me that the interest was the same for two days or for thirty days.

"The following statement came with an interest charge of $16.09. Fair enough, I missed the payment, I pay the interest. I paid the outstanding balance and figured that was the end of the situation.

"Much to my surprise, on my January statement there was a further interest charge of $6.97.

"I feel that this second interest charge is excessive and unwarranted and until this amount is credited to my account I will not be using my Bank of Montreal MasterCard."

You can see this gentleman's point. He had paid off his account in full, he thought, yet he was still being charged interest. Unfortunately, those are the rules of the credit card game — not just for the Bank of Montreal's MasterCard but for most other cards as well.

When I called the Bank of Montreal about this complaint, they explained it this way: the interest charge on your statement is the amount you've incurred up to the date it was prepared. But the clock doesn't stop ticking while they wait for you to pay. They keep adding interest charges based on the average daily balance outstanding in your account until they receive full payment. That means that the faster you pay, the better off you'll be.

Let's look at another example. Suppose your last statement date was February 28 and you had interest charges on that bill. If you went to the bank on March 4 to pay off the full amount, you'd be charged interest for four extra days beyond the date showing on the statement. But if you waited until March 28, you'd find another full month's interest tacked on to your next bill — even though you thought you'd paid off the account in full.

The moral of this story is, if you're incurring credit card interest charges, pay off the bill as quickly as possible and stop the meter. Better still, don't put yourself in that spot. Pay off the entire balance every month and make sure you don't miss a payment. That way you'll pay no interest at all, which is the key to good credit card management.

By not carrying a balance from month to month you are, in effect, obtaining an interest-free loan from the credit card issuer each time you make a purchase. Obviously, it's a short-term loan — it lasts only from the day you make the purchase to the date it shows up on your statement and payment is required. But that can be as long as six weeks in certain circumstances. That means you have the use of the money during that time, without cost.

That interest-free period offers an opportunity to gain another small edge in your wealth building program. If you use your credit cards frequently, as I do, it means you are constantly deferring payments on your purchases for four to six weeks. If your balances average $1,500 a month, it means you can hold that amount in a daily interest account, earning interest for you, while your credit card transactions are being processed. Assuming you spend about the same amount each month on credit card purchases, that amounts to a perpetual deferral of payment — you'll always have about $1,500 more in your bank account than you would have by paying for everything by cash or cheque. If your financial institution is paying four percent interest, that would produce an extra $60 a year in investment income for you. That's one reason why I use credit cards to make purchases whenever possible. My monthly credit card invoices are in the $3,000 range, which means I'm earning over $100 in additional interest this way, even when rates are low. (The other reason I like cards is the ease with which I can keep track of family spending through the invoices.)

I add to my credit card related earnings by using a Royal Trust Gold MasterCard. The one percent discount on all purchases is enough to pay for all the costs associated with buying the card and provide me a modest profit as well (it used to be a lot more but Royal Trust has raised the price of the card, something which often happens a year or two after a new premium card appears).

As a result of these techniques, my credit cards are actually contributing to my monetary wealth, not subtracting from it. That's the objective you should be aiming for.

Clearly, people like me — and, hopefully, you — are not terribly popular with credit card issuers. They're in business to make money from their cards, not to subsidize aspiring wealth builders. So they're looking at other options which will make it difficult, or even impossible, to use their cards for our own profit.

One such instrument is the *debit card*. It looks like a credit card, it feels like a credit card, it even seems to act like a credit card when you buy something. But once the cashier punches in the transaction it does terrible things — like electronically whisking money out of your bank account at that very instant. So long, interest-free loan.

Financial institutions have conducted numerous debit card experiments in recent years, including a major one in Ottawa which proved highly successful. It's only a matter of time before these cards are made available to the public on a broad scale.

Many people like them, because the debit card forces them to manage their money more carefully and keeps them out of debt (as long as they don't have overdraft arrangements for their account). Also, some retailers who normally don't take credit cards — grocery and liquor stores, for example — have participated in debit card tests and are said to be happy with the result. Getting people like this on board will increase the attractiveness of the debit card to the general public by reducing the amount of cash needed for a shopping trip.

Debit cards probably won't replace the familiar credit card, at least for many years. But some retailers may shift over to them exclusively as they become generally available because of the attraction of an instant transfer of a customer's money to their own account.

If that becomes a widespread trend, credit cards may gradually fade as a medium of exchange over time.

Some store owners really don't like seeing their customer use credit cards because of the cost to them. Whenever you use a credit card, merchants have to pay a percentage to the card issuer, which cuts into their profits.

In some stores, you'll now see signs saying credit cards will not be accepted on small orders. I've been told I couldn't use a credit card to purchase a major appliance at a sale price. A retailer may offer you a small discount to pay by cash or cheque. Their contracts with the card issuers say they're not supposed to do any of these things but some do anyway.

I've also seen retailers use various ploys to talk you out of using your card.

My wife, Shirley, ran into that situation a few years ago. After twenty years of faithful service, our clothes dryer passed away. We'd seen it coming for some time, as the service calls increased and the repair bills mounted. So Shirley had already been shopping and had a new one picked out. It was just a case of going in and placing the order.

So she went to the store and ordered the machine. It was a top-of-the-line model; with installation, the colour charge and tax the whole thing came to $660.

When the bill had been made up, my wife offered her credit card as payment. Now this store prominently displayed signs saying it accepted all major cards. But the owner balked. He moaned and whined about the card. He complained that if my wife insisted on using it, it would cost him about $20 in fees and processing. His profit margins were so tight, that meant he'd be just about giving the dryer away. Groan. Snivel. Couldn't she write a cheque instead? It wouldn't cost us any more and he'd consider it a favour. Grovel.

So she agreed — as I'm sure a lot of you would. After all, we all hate to see a grown man cry.

When she got home that night and recounted this little episode to me, I blew my top over the store owner's behaviour. He had to know that every time he persuaded someone to go along with him on this, he was adding to his own profit at his customer's expense.

Here's how. To pay by cheque meant we had to withdraw $660 from our daily interest account six weeks earlier than we would have had it been a credit card transaction. Given interest rates at that time, that would have worked out to about four dollars in lost interest. On top of that, we lost the one percent discount from using the Royal Trust Gold MasterCard. That amounted to an additional $6.60.

Taking the two together, writing the merchant a cheque was adding over ten dollars to the cost of an already expensive dryer. The additional twenty dollars he was making was more than half paid for out of my pocket!

Maybe that doesn't sound like such a big deal to you. But as I said at the outset, part of the wealth building process is understanding how to manage money effectively. That means you don't throw away ten-dollar bills for no reason.

I called the next morning and cancelled the deal. We went to another store which had the same dryer, ironically at a slightly cheaper price. And they didn't say a word when we offered the credit card as payment.

CHAPTER 12

Making Debt Work for You

To borrow money, big money, you have to wear your hair in a certain way, walk in a certain way, and have about you an air of solemnity and majesty — something like the atmosphere of a Gothic cathedral.
— Stephen Leacock

Debt is the number one enemy of the wealth builder. It compromises your ability to save. It erodes your asset base. In extreme circumstances, it can even destroy you financially.

Debt is the number one ally of the wealth builder. It allows you to become wealthy using other people's money. It accelerates the wealth building process. In extreme circumstances, it can even make you a millionaire years before you ever dreamed possible.

How's that for two totally conflicting views of debt? Now I'll confuse you even more. Both of them can be true, depending on your circumstances.

I don't think there's any concept in the wealth building process that's more misunderstood than the use of debt. Perhaps that's because most beginning wealth builders don't really understand what debt is all about. They tend to relate it to consumerism — the debts incurred by purchasing a car or new furniture, or by taking a vacation. They don't generally understand debt's relationship to building wealth.

That's what this chapter is all about — helping you distinguish between constructive and destructive debt and to understand how to use debt effectively in your wealth building plan.

Let's start with the most destructive kind of debt. I call it Beginner Debt, because it's the kind of debt most frequently undertaken by younger people just starting out in life. It has four main characteristics:

1. It is incurred for consumption purposes. By that I mean the money has been borrowed to purchase goods or services, not for business or investing purposes.

2. It carries a high interest rate. This is because younger people usually start in lower paying jobs and have few assets, thus making them higher risks. A large proportion of this debt may be credit card related.

3. Servicing the debt requires a disproportionate share of the household income. In other words, it costs you more each month to meet the financing payments than you're comfortable with.

4. Interest on the debt is not tax deductible.

It's extremely easy to fall deeply into Beginner Debt and our society actively encourages people to do so. Financial institutions and retail outlets make credit available to almost anyone, literally for the asking. Our newspapers and television screens are cluttered with ads offering easy terms for big-ticket items like appliances, electronic equipment, furniture and cars. Some retailers have scored huge successes with campaigns promising you won't have to pay a cent for six months or more.It's all part of the Why-Wait-When-You-Can-Have-It-Now? syndrome. It's easy, it's seductive. No wonder millions of people fall for it.

And what happens? The easy money debts pile up. Repaying them becomes an increasing financial drain on the household. There's no money left once the debts have been serviced and the necessities looked after. There's not even enough to go out to a movie occasionally; how in blazes are we supposed to start a savings program?

Debt like that is to be avoided at all costs. It undermines the wealth building process and takes control of your financial destiny out of your hands. Stay away from it!

I know that's far easier said than done, especially when you're just starting to build a family household. I'm aware that I'm suggesting you make personal sacrifices — that you live with your old car or buy second-hand furniture or pass up a trip south next winter. And I know foregoing those comforts isn't pleasant.

But if you seriously want to build personal wealth — if you want to create an independent lifestyle for yourself while you're still young enough to enjoy it — then this is a sacrifice you have to make. There are no compromises on this one. If you load yourself down with Beginner Debt, you'll face years and years of struggle just to get out from under. And, as I've said before, those are the most precious years of all in the wealth building process.

The rule is very simple: *Don't take on consumer debt under any circumstances.*

If you've already accumulated a consumer debt load by the time you read this, your number one priority should be to pay it off as quickly as possible. Above all, don't add to it.

Now, I recognize it's not always possible to avoid Beginner Debt. Many people went through some rough times in the early nineties. Wages were frozen, jobs were lost, businesses went under. In such circumstances, often no other choice exists. Fair enough. But most Beginner Debt doesn't originate that way. It comes from societal pressures which encourage you to want too much too soon. Call it what you will: greed, ambition, aggressiveness. It all comes down to spending money you don't have in order to acquire possessions before you can afford them. That's destructive debt, no matter how you look at it. The committed wealth builder will avoid it at all costs.

One of the keys to avoiding destructive debt is proper budgeting. This enables you to manage your money properly and ensures you won't accidentally overspend.

Every family needs a budget, no matter how well off you are. We still have one, even though our annual income is substantial. It's the only way I can control the outflow of cash and know how much we have available for renovations, holidays, investments and helping the kids.

The easiest way to set up and run a family budget is on a computer. If you own one, or have access to one, I strongly recommend going that route; it makes the whole process much easier to manage.

You can set up a budget by using any spreadsheet program. The more detail you put into the budget, the better. It may take a little longer to set up, but the result will be a much clearer picture of where the money is going and how much is available for savings or special purchases you want to make.

Any system that works for you is fine. But if you want a model, here's what I use.

The first column is a summary of the family's monthly after-tax income from all sources: salaries, part-time work, investments and any other revenue you receive from miscellaneous sources (gifts, a tax refund, etc.). If there is any money left over from the previous month, it can be carried forward here. The total at the bottom is your budget for the current month. It can be adjusted as the month progresses if unexpected income is received.

Each subsequent column covers a separate expense item. In each case, the total budgeted for the month is shown at the top. As expenses occur during the month, they're entered below.

Depending on your personal situation, your column headings may include:

Mortgage payment (or rent). The amount of the monthly payment you're required to remit.

Property taxes. One-twelfth of the expected annual property tax bill. In months when payments aren't required, the outstanding balance should be carried forward to the next month.

Maintenance and repairs. A monthly allocation for the upkeep of your home.

Insurance. A monthly allocation for all your insurance costs, including property, car and life insurance. Add up the total annual premiums and divide by twelve to arrive at the monthly figure.

Food and supplies. Your monthly budget for food and household necessities, like lightbulbs and cleaning supplies.

Transportation. The monthly cost of operating a car and/or taking public transit.

Clothing. Your monthly clothing allocation for the family.

Money not spent should be carried forward, as clothing expenses may vary significantly from month to month.

Utilities. Heating, telephone, cable, electricity, water and similar costs. These can be broken out into separate columns, if preferred.

Education. Any current expenses involved in sending the children to school can be included here along with savings for future education costs.

Health care. It's a good idea to build a fund to cover future costs for glasses, dental work, non-insured prescriptions and other health-related costs.

Recreation. You need to have fun, whether it's going to a movie or joining a club. Include an appropriate monthly allocation here. Money for alcohol and tobacco should also be budgeted here.

Special. There will be special occasions during the year when you'll require extra money — birthdays, anniversaries, bar mitzvahs, Christmas. This is the appropriate column for that.

Vacation. Saving for a holiday is easier if you put a little aside each month.

RRSP. If you budget something each month, you won't be scrambling for cash at RRSP deadline.

Savings and investments. Every wealth builder should enter something in this column each month, even if the amount is small.

Miscellaneous. There are always some unexpected costs, or those which don't fit into a particular category. Allow for them here.

I set up my program in such a way that each entry automatically adjusts the outstanding balance at the bottom of each column. That way, I know exactly how much I still have to spend in each category at any given time.

So a typical monthly budget might look like the one on page 128.

Income

Source	Amount
Carry-forward	$1,000
Husband income	2,000
Wife income	2,000
Interest	200
Miscellaneous	100
Total	5,300

Expenses

Item	Amount
Mortgage	$1,200
Property taxes	150
Maintenance/Repairs	150
Insurance	100
Food/Supplies	900
Transportation	250
Clothing	250
Utilities	250
Education	150
Health Care	150
Recreation	250
Special	200
Vacations	300
RRSP	400
Savings	300
Miscellaneous	300
Total	$5,300

Now, what about constructive debt — the kind described in the second paragraph of this chapter? That's debt that is used to build wealth, debt incurred to acquire assets that are going to help you move ahead financially. I call this Investment Debt. Its main characteristics are:

1. The debt is incurred for investment or business reasons. You are borrowing money for the purpose of increasing your assets, with the objective of using the funds for personal profit. (I would consider a Student Loan to be a form of Investment Debt. In this case, you're investing in yourself.)

2. The interest rate is competitive. This is because the assets you purchase with the funds from the loan can be held as collateral, thereby entitling you to a preferred interest rate.

3. The repayment program for the loan is manageable and may be covered in part by profits from the investment.

4. Interest on the loan will often (but not always) be tax deductible.

The most common type of constructive debt is a mortgage. Very few of us can afford to pay cash for a new home. And if we tried to save until we could, house prices might keep moving ahead at a pace which would make it difficult to catch up.

That's why a mortgage is a wise form of borrowing. It allows you to purchase an asset today that you couldn't otherwise afford — a family home. And that asset may increase in value as the loan you incurred to purchase it is paid off.

We've already dealt with mortgage management at some length, so I won't go into it again. Suffice to say that as long as you handle your mortgage intelligently and pay it off as quickly as possible, it is an excellent way of using borrowed money to build wealth.

Another type of constructive debt is the loan you undertake to enable you to maximize your RRSP contribution. I'll deal with the importance of RRSPs in later chapters. The point I want to make here is that you should do everything possible to make your maximum allowable RRSP contribution each year.

Now that the rules allow you to carry forward any unused RRSP deduction entitlements, I expect many people will postpone contributions to some vague future date. In most cases, I don't advise doing that. Even if you eventually make the contribution (which most people won't), you'll lose years of tax-sheltered compounding within the plan. Unless you're truly financial strapped, try to make your full contribution each year. If that requires taking out a loan, do so. Just be sure to repay it within twelve months. Use the income tax refund your RRSP contribution will generate to help you do so.

Neither a mortgage loan nor an RRSP loan is normally tax deductible (although a mortgage loan can be made so in certain rare circumstances). The government used to give you a tax break on interest costs relating to RRSPs but that benefit was dropped several years ago.

Most other types of Investment Debt are tax deductible, though. As a general rule, the interest on money borrowed to acquire an income-producing asset, or one with a reasonable expectation of generating income within a certain time, would be considered tax deductible by Revenue Canada.

That means money borrowed to purchase such things as a rental property, Canada Savings Bonds, a stock portfolio, mutual funds and the like would usually be considered eligible for interest deductibility.

Funds borrowed for a summer cottage, home improvements, a new deck and certain types of investments such as commodities or raw land would not qualify.

Your objective is to ensure that most or all of your debt, beyond your mortgage and any short-term RRSP loans, is tax deductible. If governments want to help subsidize the cost of your wealth building activities, why not let them?

At this point people often ask why they should borrow at all. Why go into debt if you don't have to?

Good question, and a natural one. Canadians, quite rightly, tend to be leery of debt. My mother-in-law's Scottish heritage — which many Canadians share — made her rebel at the very idea of owing money to anyone.

There's nothing wrong with that attitude and certainly living debt-free may cause you to sleep better at night. But the reality is that well-managed debt can help immensely in the wealth building process.

Let me illustrate. Let's say you're one of those people who refuse to get into debt for any reason, even if the risk seems low and the opportunity great. The country has just come through a period of economic turmoil, which pushed the prime rate into the mid-teens (this actually happened in 1990). Now conditions are stabilizing and it looks like interest rates have peaked and have started to turn down. It seems like a great opportunity to invest in Government of Canada bonds.

You've managed to put aside $10,000. You read in the paper the Government is about to go to the bond market with a new issue. The coupon rate is eight percent, the bonds have a twenty-year maturity and they're priced at par. You think it's a great investment and invest your $10,000.

Sure enough, interest rates do fall. At the end of one year, the market value of your bonds has increased twenty-five percent. You sell. What's the result?

Sale price of bonds	$12,500
Interest for one year	800
Gross proceeds	13,300
Profit (before tax)	3,300
Before-tax return on $10,000 investment	33%

Not bad at all. You can feel pretty proud of yourself.

Oh, by the way, I bought some of those bonds too. Like you, I only had $10,000 saved. But I borrowed another $40,000 at ten percent interest, using the bonds as collateral. So my total investment was $50,000. I also sold out after one year. How did I do?

Sale price of bonds	$62,500
Interest for one year	4,000
Gross proceeds	66,500

Less after-tax interest cost on borrowed money (assumes 45% tax bracket)	(2,200)
Less repayment of loan principal	(40,000)
Net profit (before tax)	24,300
Before-tax return on $10,000 investment	143%

Gosh, I guess I did a little bit better, even though we both started with the same amount of savings. That's because I used other people's money to purchase more assets than I otherwise could have afforded. The technical term for that is *leveraging*, and it's the way you can make borrowed money work to build wealth for you.

Oh sure, you say. But suppose it hadn't worked out that way? Suppose the bonds had gone *down* twenty-five percent instead of up?

You're right. That's the danger in leveraging. You can use it to magnify your profits. But it will also increase your losses if you guess wrong. Let's see how great a risk I took.

First, let's look at what would have happened to you if your bonds had gone down twenty-five percent and you'd sold after one year.

Sale price of bonds	$7,500
Interest for one year	800
Gross proceeds	8,300
Loss	1,700
Loss on $10,000 investment	17%

You lost money on the deal, but it wasn't a total disaster. The coupon rate on the bonds limited your risk.

Now, what happened to me?

Sale price of bonds	$37,500
Interest for one year	4,000
Gross proceeds	41,500
Less after-tax interest cost on borrowed money	(2,200)
Less repayment of loan principal	(40,000)
Net proceeds	(700)
Loss	(10,700)
Loss on $10,000 investment	107%

I ended up losing all of my original investment and more, while your loss was modest. That's the way leveraging works — it's a two-edged sword.

In effect, I put all my savings at risk to make a potential profit of over $25,000. You risked much less — but your profit was less than $4,000.

You might decide you'd be much more comfortable doing it your way — smaller profits for less risk. And there's nothing wrong with that approach, especially when the investment climate is uncertain.

But there are times when leveraging is an acceptable move — the odds appear to be strongly in your favour, the upside potential is good and the downside risk is manageable.

You're the one who has to decide when circumstances are right to take a chance and if you have the stomach, and the financial resources, to do so. You should never, never use leveraging if a wrong guess will place you in serious financial difficulty. But if conditions are right and you're comfortable with the idea, keep leveraging available to you as a possible investment option.

Let me stress one more thing at this point. Beginning wealth builders should be very cautious about using leveraging. It's far wiser to pay down your mortgage as a first priority. Only when you have achieved that goal should you consider borrowing for other investment purposes. There are risks involved in using other people's money to invest that should not be undertaken until you've established a firm financial footing.

If the time comes that you do want to try leveraging, start small. The amount of risk you undertake by incurring Investment Debt is directly proportionate to the size of your loan. Begin with $1,000 or so, just to get the feel of leveraging and a practical understanding of how it works. There'll be plenty of time to do some high-rolling later, if that's what you want. Your first priority is to gain some experience in Investment Debt without putting yourself seriously at risk. If the first attempt works out well and you're comfortable with it, you can borrow a little more for the next project. Just remember to pay off the loans as you go along; don't allow them to accumulate to the point where you wake up some morning and discover you've created a debt mountain you can't handle.

That brings us to the question of where and how to borrow.

There are plenty of people who want to loan you money and there are many types of loans. The place to start is with your bank. They know you and the interest rates they charge will be competitive. Have a talk with the manager, explain your needs and ask him or her to explain the options available. As I explained in Chapter Four, that can be a disconcerting process. But if you have a steady job, a decent salary and a good credit rating, and you present yourself well, you should get the loan. Just be aware that banks are being especially careful these days. A lot of loans went sour during the recession of the early nineties and lenders have tended to become more conservative as a result. So expected to be grilled and try not to be offended by it.

When the banker is finished, it's your turn. Ask hard questions about the loan options available to you. Find out whether the interest rate is fixed or variable. Ask whether the bank has programs that offer better rates (sometimes they do but don't mention them unless you inquire). The banker's objective is to make sure you're a good risk; yours is to pay the bank the least amount possible in return for the use of their money.

Do not, under any circumstances, finalize any deal at the first meeting. Get all the details, then visit a few other financial institutions to see what they're offering. Don't overlook credit unions in your market survey; they sometimes have the most attractive deals around.

You may be surprised at the variety of loan plans offered by different financial institutions. You can frequently save a lot of money in interest costs by taking the time to investigate.

Although there are numerous variations on the theme, you'll probably find yourself considering three borrowing alternatives once you've looked around.

1. *Some type of instalment loan.* This will involve a fixed term and an agreed repayment schedule of blended principal and interest. The interest rate may be fixed for the duration of the loan or it could be subject to review periodically. RRSP loans are usually instalment loans, with repayment over a twelve-month period.

2. *A demand loan.* It's exactly what it sounds like. There is no fixed repayment schedule but the financial institution can demand payment in full at any time. That rarely happens, but it's always a possibility you must be alert to. Demand loans are somewhat harder to obtain — you have to have collateral or be perceived as an excellent credit risk. The interest rate will usually start out at about the same level as an instalment loan, but will be variable and may change as frequently as every month.

3. *A personal line of credit (PLC).* These have become the hot way to borrow because of the convenience and flexibility they offer. You should look closely at this option before making a final decision.

PLCs have been around for a long time, but they used to be the preserve of the wealthy. Financial institutions only began to aggressively promote them in the mid-1980s. However, not everyone can get a PLC. One banking official told me that only about one-third of the people who qualify for a credit card would be eligible for a line of credit. You have to undergo a fairly intensive screening, but, if you're credit worthy and have a steady job, chances are you'll qualify.

Why should you want one? Because they are just about the cheapest way, other than a mortgage, for the ordinary person to borrow money. And, as I've said repeatedly, when you borrow money your objective is to pay as little interest as possible.

A PLC is simply an authorization by a bank, trust company or credit union that allows you to borrow money from them in any amount, up to a predetermined limit. You don't have to make use of that borrowing power until you need it and you're only charged interest on the amount you actually use.

For example, your bank may give you the authority to borrow up to $10,000 on a PLC. You pay nothing until you actually draw funds against the account. If you decide to borrow $2,000, you'll be charged interest on that amount and the credit balance available for your use will drop to $8,000.

Once you're approved for a PLC and your limit is established, personalized cheques bearing your account number will be issued to you. There will be nothing on the cheques to indicate they're being drawn against a line of credit; they look exactly like cheques drawn on a regular account. If you want to borrow, you simply use one of these cheques and it's done. No further authorizations are needed. Some financial institutions also allow you to access your PLC through a credit card.

Once you've drawn on the PLC, you'll receive a monthly statement. This will show your outstanding balance, the amount of credit you have left and the current interest rate being charged. That interest rate can vary from month to month; be sure you stay aware of what you're paying and satisfy yourself it's competitive.

The statement will also show you the minimum payment due that month — typically, it's three percent of the outstanding balance but that can vary from one financial institution to another. In some cases, the minimum payment is simply the amount of interest incurred during the previous month. You can pay the minimum amount or more if you like. There's no penalty for paying off all or part of the outstanding balance at any time, which means you have a high degree of flexibility with this type of borrowing.

The interest rates on PLCs can vary widely among financial institutions and the type of plan you sign up for, so you need to spend a little time checking out the options before you commit to anything. Usually, however, you'll find the interest rates are low compared to other types of consumer loans. In fact, in some cases they won't be far off prime, which is the rate banks charge their best corporate borrowers. If you can get almost as good an interest rate as the folks with million-dollar loans, you aren't doing too badly.

Some financial institutions offer a choice between secured and unsecured PLCs. The secured loan offers the best rate, but you have to put up top quality collateral — CSBs, a good stock portfolio, GICs or something similar. The unsecured PLC won't offer as good a break on interest rates, but it should be cheaper than other types of consumer loans.

One variation on the PLC which has attracted a lot of interest is the home equity line of credit. This type of PLC allows people with substantial equity in their home — those who followed my earlier advice about paying down the mortgage — to tap into those funds for investment purposes.

The home equity line of credit is really a cross between a regular PLC and a mortgage. It permits you to turn the equity in your home into usable cash as you need it, without tying yourself to a rigid repayment schedule.

If you're not quite sure just what equity you have in your home, call in a real estate agent and ask what price you might expect to receive if you decided to sell. From that estimate, subtract the outstanding balance due on your mortgage. The difference gives you a good idea of your equity.

If you've owned your home for some time, you may be surprised to find just how much idle cash it represents. That doesn't mean you should rush right out and spend the money. I repeat, debt of any kind is not something you should undertake lightly. Furthermore, home equity lines of credit have some hefty costs attached to them. But if you're at a stage when incurring some Investment Debt seems like a smart move, this is certainly an option to consider.

The main drawback to these loans is the upfront cost. You are actually putting another mortgage on your property, which means you'll end up several hundred dollars out of pocket once all the appraisal and legal fees are paid. The only consolation is that's a one-time charge. Once the home equity line of credit is established, it's in place for as long as you want it.

Some financial institutions also charge an annual maintenance fee for a line of credit. The amount is usually relatively small — Royal Trust, for example, charges $12. But it's an expense you should be aware of before making a final decision.

The borrowing power available to you through a home equity line of credit is immense, probably far more than you'll ever want or need. Typically, a lender will grant you a home equity line of credit of two-thirds the appraised value of your property, less any outstanding mortgage, as long as you have adequate income to carry any payments. So let's assume you have a home that's worth $125,000, with a first mortgage that still has $45,000 owing. The equity in the home is therefore $80,000. The lender will give you a line of credit for two-thirds of that amount — which means you have over $53,000 in borrowing power.

The danger is that you'll get carried away and use that money unwisely. Here's where self discipline is important. Use that money for wealth building purposes and it can help make you rich. Use it to travel around the world and you'll end up with a big chunk of consumer debt that will take a long time to pay off.

While home equity lines of credit are about as inexpensive a way to borrow as you're going to find, remember the interest rate can vary from month to month. If there's a sudden run-up in rates, you could find yourself paying much higher interest charges than you had anticipated. Don't get over your head and put your home at risk.

As far as repayments go, these are the ultimate in flexibility. Most of them allow you to pay only interest if you wish — no reduction in the principal is required. That means you can carry an outstanding balance for as long as you want and pay it off at any time. That's especially valuable if you're using the money to invest in something that doesn't pay regular income such as a stock. You don't have to pay off the principal on your loan until such time as you sell the asset and (hopefully) take your profit. At that stage you can pay off the loan and pocket the rest. Of course, your home equity line of credit remains open, ready for the next time you want to use it.

Earlier in the chapter, I said there are rare occasions when mortgage interest is tax deductible. This is one example. If you use money from your home equity PLC for eligible investing or business purposes, Revenue Canada will allow a deduction.

Let me finish by stressing two points again, because they're so important for wealth building. Borrowing to buy consumer items is something you should *never* do. Borrowing to invest is something you may undertake at the right time, *with caution*. Use debt to build your wealth, not to destroy it, and you'll have mastered one of the key techniques of financial success.

The Money Machine

Count your nest eggs before they hatch.
— Betty Jane Wylie

While I was supervising the revision of Hume Publishing's *Successful Investing & Money Management* course several years ago, the question came up of a new title for the lesson on Registered Retirement Savings Plans. Many people tend to think of RRSPs as boring; we wanted a title that would grab attention and motivate students to study the lesson carefully. In short, we wanted a single phrase that would encapsulate the incredible wealth building power of this investment form.

The title we finally chose was "The Million Dollar Money Machine." I liked it then and I still do. It may sound like hyperbole, but let me assure you it isn't. In fact, several financial institutions have now picked up on the idea and use it as part of their annual RRSP sales promotions.

A Registered Retirement Savings Plan can indeed make you a millionaire, if you start contributing early enough and make regular payments.

But let me hasten to clarify one point. By the time your RRSP has a million dollars in it, a million won't buy as much as it will today. Inflation will take its toll on purchasing power and it will add up over the years. But your RRSP million will still be worth plenty and you'll accumulate it much more quickly than you're likely to do any other way.

I'm so sold on the wealth building potential of RRSPs that I regard them as one of the two cornerstones of personal financial success, the other being the family home. In fact, I believe you should pay off your mortgage and maximize your RRSP contributions before you consider any other form of investment.

Unfortunately, many Canadians don't take advantage of this incredible wealth building tool. A study released by Royal Trust in 1992 showed that half of Canadians over eighteen had never contributed to an RRSP. Other surveys have reached similar conclusions.

Too many people don't seem to understand how valuable these plans can be. The head of a major tax preparation firm once told me that they see hundreds of people each year who don't even know what a Registered Retirement Savings Plan is. I'm sure few readers of this book would fall into that group but just in case, a Registered Retirement Savings Plan is a government-approved program which permits you to deduct your contributions from taxable income (up to certain limits) and allows investment income within the plan to accumulate tax-sheltered for many years. Funds withdrawn from an RRSP are treated as ordinary income in the year you take them out.

Even many people who have RRSPs don't realize the potential of these plans. They tend to regard them purely as retirement insurance — something that will generate a little extra income for the sunset years to supplement a company pension, Old Age Security and Canada Pension Plan payments. This attitude leads to sloppy use of RRSPs, especially when you're younger and retirement seems many years off. Contributions are made on a haphazard basis, depending on whether or not spare funds are available. Management of the money already in an RRSP is frequently non-existent. Those funds are treated almost as if they were Monopoly money. It's a sort of "The money's locked away so it isn't real" approach.

If you're one of those people, then it's time to wake up. Not only is that RRSP money real; it can be used in dozens of imaginative ways to build your wealth quickly. And the money is *not* locked in until you retire. You can draw it out any time you want — just be certain you take the tax consequences into account when you do so.

Some smart young couples have used RRSPs successfully to help them start a family. While both worked, the wife put aside enough money to make her full RRSP contribution each year. When she left the work force for a period to have children, she drew money from her RRSP to help supplement the family income and partly compensate for the loss of her salary. If there's no other income during a year, it's possible to withdraw about $7,000 from an RRSP without incurring any tax at all.

The federal government has also shown a willingness to allow people to dip into their RRSPs for specific purposes without being assessed tax. The one-year program to borrow up to $20,000 in RRSP money to buy a house, which was announced in the February, 1992 budget, was the first such example. Now that the precedent has been established, others may follow.

You can use money in your RRSP to hold a mortgage on your home. It can be a source of emergency funds, if you have other assets to swap for RRSP cash. Some people have used RRSP money to help finance a year's sabbatical from work. In short, there are many ways to use RRSP money to your advantage — long before the time actually comes to retire.

Let me give you an example of just how much wealth potential exists in your RRSP. One night after a curling game, I was having drinks with some friends and the subject of RRSPs came up. I'd been doing some research on the subject, so I tossed out a Trivial Pursuit type question for discussion.

I asked my friends to assume they had a relative who was twenty-four years old. This person was not a member of a company pension plan and his earned income allowed for a maximum RRSP contribution of $4,800. I told them to assume this relative contributed the same amount every year until age seventy-one — the last year you can contribute to an RRSP in most circumstances. That would mean forty-seven years of contributions, which would add up to $225,600 over his lifetime. I also told them to assume he was a good money manager and was able to average a fifteen percent annual return on his investments over that time. How much, I asked, would the RRSP contain when he was seventy-one?

I could hear the mental wheels clicking all around the table.

Finally, one woman suggested the RRSP might contain as much as one million dollars. Someone else guessed $1.5 million. Then another lady went way, way out on a limb and offered a guess of five million. She was quickly pooh-poohed by the rest of the group.

As it turned out, she was closest to the mark — although her guess was way off. At age seventy-one, the amount in the RRSP I described would be — wait a second. I suggest if you're reading this book standing up, you'd better sit down.

The total would work out to $26,184,018.94. I know it's unbelievable — over $26 million in an RRSP. That's more than one hundred times the value of his contributions to the plan. I couldn't accept it when I first saw the number and even after I worked through the whole calculation I still thought it was a mistake. I had to get an accountant to confirm it for me.

As you can imagine, that caused quite a sensation around the table. People don't realize how dollars can multiply in an RRSP until they're confronted with numbers like that.

To be fair, you have to be an excellent money manager — and very lucky — to average a fifteen percent return on investments over forty-seven years. Few people could do it. But even at a more realistic twelve percent, you'd still build up nine million dollars in assets during that time. And keep in mind the maximum contribution allowed is substantially more than $4,800 a year.

Of course, as I've already pointed out, $26 million won't have anything like the buying power half a century from now that it does today. The higher the average inflation rate during that time, the more the value of your money will be eroded. But even if inflation were to average ten percent a year — an unacceptably high rate by anyone's standards — that RRSP money would purchase an annuity worth about $4,000 a month in today's dollars.

So why aren't we all going to be millionaires somewhere down the road? To start with, some of us just don't have enough years left until retirement, although even if you're in your fifties when you start, you can still build a comfortable nest-egg. As for younger people, many don't have the extra cash to sock away in an RRSP; just maintaining a household is all they can manage. And, finally, too many people with RRSPs don't pay proper attention to them.

Why do RRSPs build wealth so effectively? Two reasons.

First, the tax deduction created by RRSP contributions allows you to put more money to work sooner than you might otherwise be able to. It's a form of leveraging if you like, except in this case you're not borrowing the money — the government is *giving* it to you.

Suppose you're in the middle tax bracket, with a marginal federal tax rate of twenty-six percent. If your provincial tax rate is half of the federal tax, you pay a combined rate of about forty percent on your last dollar earned.

Let's say you're allowed a maximum RRSP contribution of $4,000 this year. That generates a tax refund of $1,600, which means that your out-of-pocket cost for contributing to the RRSP is only $2,400. But you have the full $4,000 working for you inside the plan. The government has put up the difference.

That's why it pays to borrow to make up any shortfall in your RRSP contribution. Suppose you don't have enough money put aside in a given year to make the full contribution to which you're entitled. Borrow the balance for a few months and pay off the loan with the tax refund. That way you've got more money working on your behalf — and a larger government subsidy than you would have received had you only contributed the amount you'd saved.

The second reason RRSPs work so effectively is that all the investment income earned inside the plan is tax sheltered. The government doesn't get a nickel of it until you draw it out.

It's those tax-free earnings that allow the RRSP to grow so rapidly. All the interest and dividends you earn outside a plan are heavily taxed, as are any capital gains over the $100,000 lifetime exemption. But inside a plan, the money that would otherwise go to the government in taxes instead works on your behalf.

Let me give you an example of how important that is. Again, we'll assume you're in the forty percent tax bracket. Let's see how the same investment — a five-year $25,000 GIC at ten percent compound interest — would fare inside and outside an RRSP. I've assumed that the tax owed on the GIC interest earned outside the RRSP would be paid from the income received, with the after-tax balance re-invested at the same rate. I haven't allowed for the tax that will be assessed when the money is eventually withdrawn from the RRSP, since that will be deferred for many years.

	Tax rate	Total tax Paid	Value after 5 Years (Net of tax)	After-tax Return
Inside RRSP	0	0	$40,262.50	$15,262.50
Outside RRSP	40%	$6,807.50	$33,455.00	$8,455.00

As you can see, the after-tax return is over eighty percent higher inside the RRSP. It doesn't take much imagination to see how those numbers will magnify over many years, especially when increasingly larger amounts of money are involved.

RRSPs are really the last great tax shelter in Canada — and the only one that can be easily used by everyone. With the advent of tax credits, RRSPs are also one of the few ways higher income people can obtain a full tax benefit. Your contributions continue to be deducted from taxable income, not converted into credits at a lower percentage than your marginal tax rate. (Canada Pension Plan contributions, for instance, are converted to tax credits at a seventeen percent rate. This means taxpayers in the higher brackets don't receive full tax relief for their contributions.)

By now, I hope you're convinced of the value of using RRSPs to build wealth. The next step is to take a careful look at how much you're allowed to contribute so that you can start a savings program that will enable you to put in the full amount allowable each year.

There's been a great deal of confusion about RRSP contribution limits in recent years. The federal government, while remaining fully committed to the concept of RRSPs, has changed direction several times on the contribution limits that will be allowed to taxpayers. After years of uncertainty, what was supposedly the final version came into effect on January 1, 1991. Under that plan, higher-income Canadians who did not have a pension plan were allowed to contribute more to an RRSP each year, until the dollar limit reached $15,500 in 1995. (Lower-income Canadians actually ended up with lower limits because the base calculation for the maximum allowable RRSP contribution was reduced from twenty percent of earned income to eighteen percent).

But then Ottawa switched direction again. The 1992 budget suspended any increase in RRSP limits for a year, freezing the 1993 maximum contribution at 1992 levels. There's nothing to prevent future budgets from doing the same thing. But, as of mid-1992, here are the maximum dollar limits allowed for RRSP contributions in the coming years:

1992	$12,500
1993	12,500
1994	13,500
1995	14,500
1996	15,500

After 1996, the limit is to be indexed to inflation.

Note, these are maximum dollar limits. Your RRSP contribution is calculated by multiplying your earned income for the previous year by eighteen percent, to the maximum dollar amount allowed. (Earned income includes salary, income from your own business and certain special payments such as retiring allowances and alimony and maintenance. It does *not* include pension or investment income.) So for the 1993 tax year, you would multiply your 1992 earned income by eighteen percent, to a maximum of $12,500.

For example, if your 1992 earned income was $30,000, your 1993 RRSP deduction limit would be $5,400 ($30,000 x .18). If you were fortunate enough to earn $100,000, your limit would be $12,500. The formula appears to allow you more ($100,000 x .18 = $18,000). But in this case the ceiling comes into play.

Your contribution limit is calculated differently if you belong to a pension plan. In this case, your employer must calculate a "pension adjustment," or PA, which you'll find on your T4 slip. This figure is then used to determine how much RRSP room remains. Members of defined benefit plans (those which guarantee a retirement pension according to a predetermined formula) are allowed a minimum RRSP contribution of $1,000 a year in most cases.

Fortunately, you don't have to do the calculation yourself. Revenue Canada sends you a notice every fall advising you how much you may deduct for RRSP contributions on your tax return.

Now that you know all the advantages and the basic rules governing RRSPs, the next step is to decide what kind of plan to choose. Your watchword here is caution. The RRSP market has become highly competitive; everyone out there wants your business. Don't be distracted by all the shrill claims that you'll see in the ads. They may well be true — some RRSP programs have produced amazing returns. But, generally speaking, the larger the potential return, the higher the degree of risk. If you're just starting out, you're better to adopt a more conservative approach. Choose a plan that offers a guaranteed return on your money and let the magic of compound interest go to work for you. You can diversify into other types of investments later, but begin with a solid cornerstone.

There are many RRSPs available, but they can all be broken down into four types.

Savings plans. These function just like ordinary savings accounts, except they're tax-sheltered. They're safe, but the interest rates are extremely low. You should never put your money into this type of RRSP; it would take too long for the million-dollar money machine to work.

Mutual fund plans. These invest your money in stocks, bonds, real estate, precious metals, etc., depending on the type of plan. I'll discuss them in greater depth in a later chapter. At this point, suffice to say that the novice RRSP investor should consider funds with minimum risk, such as mortgage funds, if this is the way you decide to go.

Self-directed plans. These allow you to do your own managing and choose your own investments. I think everyone should have one at some point; I'll explain why in the next chapter.

Guaranteed plans. These invest your funds in Guaranteed Investment Certificates of varying maturities. They're a good alternative for the beginning RRSP wealth builder, combining safety with a reasonable return. The higher interest rates are when you contribute, the more attractive a guaranteed plan is. Just be careful not to lock in for too long if it appears interest rates are on the rise.

Most financial institutions — banks, trust companies, credit unions — offer all four types of plan. Brokerage houses usually offer only mutual fund and self-directed plans. Most life insurance companies have guaranteed and mutual fund (called "segregated funds" in their case) programs.

Finally, I want to end this chapter by discussing one of the questions I'm asked most frequently by beginning wealth builders — is it better to put money into an RRSP or to pay down the mortgage, if you can only do one?

It's not an easy question to answer. Both are excellent ways to use your money. Both are essential to the wealth building process. Which is the better route at any given time will depend to a large degree on your personal situation: your age, the interest rate on your mortgage, number of years the mortgage has to run, etc.

However, here are some things to consider in making the decision:

1. The longer your mortgage has to run, the more the scales tip towards reducing the principal. As we've already seen, any reduction in principal in the early years has a tremendous impact on the total amount of interest you pay over the life of a mortgage.

   If you have a $50,000 mortgage at eleven percent that you've just incurred and you make a $5,000 pre-payment against it while keeping the monthly payments the same, you'll clip eight years off the original twenty-five year amortization period. That will save you over $41,000 in interest costs over the life of the mortgage — tax-free money in your pocket.

2. The higher your tax bracket, the more the balance shifts towards the RRSP. That's because the government is subsidizing your contribution to a greater degree. If you're in a fifty percent bracket, the government picks up half the tab of your RRSP contribution. So if you put $10,000 into your RRSP, the government gives you a tax refund for $5,000.

147

The older you are, the more frequently the RRSP is the logical choice. That's because older people are usually better established in their jobs and occupy more senior, better paying positions which put them into higher tax brackets. They've also tended to own their home for a longer period, which means the mortgage has fewer years to run, so the impact on interest saved isn't as great.

If you're like me and would prefer not to put all your eggs in one basket, consider this option: contribute the maximum allowable amount to your RRSP and then use the tax refund that's generated to pay down the mortgage. Try that for several years and you'll find yourself with a mortgage-free home *and* a nice retirement fund. It's the best of both worlds.

CHAPTER 14

Personalizing Your RRSP

The man who makes no mistakes does not usually make anything.
— Edward John Phelps, 1899

When I first began putting money into RRSPs, I fell into a trap, one which, it turns out, is fairly common. Since the government allows you to have as many RRSP accounts as you want, I deposited money in a variety of institutions and investment vehicles. I was looking for diversification. What I got was confusion.

After a few years I had so many RRSPs I couldn't keep track of them, much less monitor their performance intelligently. Furthermore, I didn't seem to be gaining any financial ground; the combined value of the plans wasn't increasing at the rate I thought it should. Looking back, I realize I had no clear investment objectives at that stage. I was simply choosing whatever plans seemed most convenient or had the strongest advertising appeal.

At that point, it occurred to me that maybe having multiple RRSP accounts wasn't such a hot idea. It took a heck of a lot of paperwork, and some incredible frustration, but I finally managed to reduce my RRSPs to two plans (I'll explain later why I have two instead of just one). Both those plans are self-directed. As far as I'm concerned, that's the *only* type of RRSP a truly dedicated wealth builder should have, once you've contributed at least $15,000 to RRSPs.

You'll occasionally read articles suggesting that self-directed plans (or self-administered, as they're sometimes called) are for sophisticated investors only. If you don't have a thorough knowledge of investing techniques, you shouldn't be in them.

Hogwash! A self-directed RRSP is as complex or as simple as you choose to make it. It can hold investments as easy to understand as Canada Savings Bonds or as complicated as covered call options. You can spend as much as a couple of hours a week looking after it or as little as an hour a month.

In short, self-directed plans give you the ultimate flexibility in the management of your RRSP money. They enable you to move quickly to take advantage of opportunities. And they allow you to diversify your RRSP holdings to a degree that is simply not possible with off-the-shelf plans. One other important consideration: running your own self-directed plan will give you hands-on experience in managing your own investments. You won't be giving your funds to other people and asking them to make decisions on your behalf; you'll be making those decisions yourself. They may not always be the right ones, but if you're careful and follow the guidelines in this book, you shouldn't run into any serious trouble. If you do lose some money along the way because of bad calls, learn from the experience. Spend some time analyzing what went wrong and deciding whether the loss could have been prevented. And remember — the pros don't get it right every time either.

That kind of investment management is an essential apprenticeship to the art of wealth building and the earlier in life you can experience it, the better. The problem is that most people starting out don't have the money to set up an investment portfolio. Anything extra goes towards payments on a house or into an RRSP.

That's why it's important to use the RRSP funds to gain money management experience. It may be the only opportunity you have to hone your investing skills for many years.

This does not mean you should gamble with your RRSP money — far from it! A self-directed plan requires self discipline and avoidance of high-risk investments, no matter how tempting they may seem. But managing your own money and making your own decisions is essential. Investing is like anything else in life — there is nothing, absolutely nothing, that can teach you more quickly than doing it yourself.

There are some ground rules to follow, however. First, don't put your RRSP money into any investment you don't completely understand. Go back and review what I said in Chapter Two about the importance of knowing exactly what you're buying and why you're doing it. Second, keep your RRSP investments diversified. Never put yourself in a position where one particular investment is exposing a large percentage of your RRSP assets to potential loss. Third, finish reading this book before you start — and be sure you thoroughly understand the investing guidelines you find in it.

If you follow those instructions, you should be able to manage a self-directed RRSP with no difficulty. And, if you're truly interested in wealth building, you'll have a lot of fun in the process.

How do you go about setting up a self-directed plan? With great care. Most financial institutions now offer plans of this type. Some are excellent, some are mediocre, some are downright poor. Here are some of the things to look for when you're shopping for a self-directed plan:

Cost

The fees involved in having your own self-directed RRSP can vary considerably and are tending to rise. Most financial institutions charge a flat annual rate, which, as of mid-1992, ranged from $100 to $200 in most cases. Unless there's some significant advantage for paying a higher fee (such as more frequent reports), find a lower-cost plan.

Also beware of self-directed plans that charge you a host of special fees. These may include transaction fees (a charge every time you buy or sell something), opening fees, closing fees, transfer fees and similar add-on costs. You want a plan that charges one low basic fee which covers everything. There are some around, although unfortunately fewer than in the past, so you'll have to do some shopping.

It was the brokerage industry that took the lead in making self-directed plans available at low cost. Many brokers set up their own programs by making special arrangements with trust companies, which actually hold the securities and administer the plan. This bulk-buying enabled stockbrokers to introduce their own brand-name self-directed RRSPs and market them to clients for an attractive fee. Most brokerage plans now cost about $125 a year. However, you will find some brokerage plans that are less; in fact, Richardson Greenshields offers a free self-directed plan if you limit your investments to certain interest-bearing securities.

The broker's profit doesn't come from the fee you pay. It comes from the commissions generated every time you do a transaction in the account.

LIMITATIONS

My experience has been that brokers' plans offer far and away the best reports of any self-directed RRSP. The main problem with them is that you become a captive client. Every transaction you make in the plan has to be done through that particular brokerage house and they set all the rules. That's a bind. It means you may not get the best deal on Treasury bills, or that you might miss out on a new bond or stock issue because your brokerage firm isn't involved in the distribution. It means the broker will be reluctant to acquire no load mutual funds from top managers like Altamira or Phillips, Hager & North because there's no commission in it for them. Or, if they do buy the funds, they may charge you an "administration fee" for handling the transaction. Some brokers won't deal with certain mutual fund companies because — of all things! — their computer systems aren't compatible. All this adds up to frustration, lost profit opportunities and higher costs.

In some ways, you're better off setting up a completely independent plan at a financial institution. You can still designate a broker to trade for you in such a plan. But you're not limited to that particular firm; you can have as many brokers as you wish, as long as you can supply each with enough business to keep him or her interested in your account.

However, this solution isn't perfect either. Many financial institution plans have lousy reporting systems (see below). And they impose their own rules; some won't allow you to hold certain types of qualified RRSP investments, like call options, because the paper work is too complex. It has also been my experience that financial institutions tend to be less attentive to possible violations of RRSP rules that may get you into trouble (e.g. too much foreign content or an ineligible investment) than brokerage houses.

It's important to get questions like this cleared up in advance. If there are limitations on your self-directed plan, you should know about them from the outset. I hate surprises!

Taxes

Administration charges for your RRSP are tax deductible — but only if they're paid outside the plan. You may receive an annual invoice from your plan's trustee, stating that the fee must be paid by a certain date or the money will be deducted from the cash balance in your RRSP, in which case you can't claim a tax deduction. However, some companies don't send out reminders; if the payment isn't made by a certain time, it's automatically taken out of the plan. Inquire about the practice used by the firm holding your self-directed RRSP when you open the plan. If no invoice is sent, mark the due date on your calendar pad and send in your remittance well in advance of it. By the way, you don't need a receipt from the plan administrator to claim this deduction; just include it under "carrying charges" when you file your tax return. Of course, if Revenue Canada asks for evidence of payment outside the RRSP, you'll have to provide it.

One bit of bad news regarding RRSPs and taxes. The GST applies to a range of RRSP-related services, including administration fees. That increases the cost of a self-directed RRSP, which is one reason why I recommend not opening a plan until you have at least $15,000 to deposit in it.

Reports

One of the elements most frequently overlooked by people setting up their first self-directed RRSP is the frequency and quality of the reports you'll receive. If you're going to manage your RRSP funds effectively, then accurate, up-to-date information is absolutely essential. If you don't have it, you can run into real trouble.

Once you've identified some financial institutions or brokerage houses that offer low-cost self-directed plans, ask about their reporting policies. If you won't receive updates at least quarterly, look elsewhere. Monthly reports are best, although few financial institutions offer them for the basic fee, and then it often depends on the amount of activity in the plan. Semi-annual and annual reporting is not acceptable; you need to stay more tuned in to your RRSP than that.

Proper reporting is vital, especially as your RRSP grows. You want an itemized statement every month, showing a complete inventory of your holdings and a summary of all transactions, including any dividend or interest payments received. The report should also provide an updated cash balance, so you can see how much you have available for new purchases. In short, the reports should provide all the information you need to make decisions.

In your search, you may find some companies that issue reports only twice a year but will do so more frequently for an additional fee. It may be worthwhile choosing a plan with a low basic fee and this additional report privilege; that way you can select a reporting schedule that meets both your monitoring needs and your pocket book.

Before you sign the papers, ask to see a sample report. Make sure it covers all the points I mentioned above. Satisfy yourself that it's easy to read and that you understand all the entries.

While we're on the subject of reports, there's a point I must make — and it's so important I'm spelling it out in capital letters. ALWAYS REVIEW YOUR STATEMENTS AND MAKE SURE THEY'RE CORRECT. You wouldn't believe how often RRSP reports are fouled up or how serious that can be.

A few years ago, I was reviewing one of my statements and discovered two hundred shares of Gulf Oil stock had vanished since the previous month. The stock hadn't been sold, transferred or otherwise disposed of. It was just gone.

I called the trust company and drew their attention to it. The following month, the stock was still missing. At this point I became angry and spoke to one of the firm's vice-presidents. He looked into it and called me back the next day. Yes, I was correct. It was a clerical error — a junior clerk had inadvertently deleted the shares from my account. They would be back next month.

Of course, the error would have been discovered sooner or later, wouldn't it? I asked. In the annual audit perhaps. Well, maybe not, he admitted. It turned out they did only spot audits of self-directed RRSP accounts. If my account wasn't on the list, this particular error might not have turned up if I hadn't called it to their attention.

That really frightened me. The Gulf Oil stock represented an investment of about $5,000 at that time. Can you imagine losing that amount of money because of a computing error? Some trainee presses the wrong key and your shares vanish! And yet, that's what might have happened if I hadn't carefully checked my account.

In fact, most RRSP trustees do not monitor the holdings in individual accounts. You're expected to do that yourself and you'll probably receive a notice from the company's auditors each year asking you to confirm that your latest RRSP statement is correct. Don't send it back until you've verified that the trustee's report tallies with your own records.

The securities in your self-directed RRSP are held in what's known as street form. That allows you to trade them quickly and easily, without the bother of having to sign them over when you want to sell. But holding them in street form means they are not registered in your name. There is no record, other than your confirmation slips and your monthly report, that you own them. So if they disappear from the computer screen, they could disappear totally. Scary, isn't it?

I'm devoting a lot of space to this because the Gulf Oil incident was not an isolated one. I've had other people's dividends incorrectly credited to my RRSP. I've also not been properly credited with dividends I should have received. There has been at least one other occasion when some assets from one of my RRSPs have vanished into computer limbo. And my wife once had five (!) different securities with a total value of over $18,000 disappear from her plan, all at once.

The message should, by now, be very clear. Make absolutely certain the reports you receive are accurate. And raise hell immediately if they're not.

DISCOUNT SERVICES

If you're a beginning investor, I recommend you not use a discount broker for your RRSP account at the outset. Although discount brokerage houses are much cheaper, they're simply order-takers. Discount houses won't provide advice or guidance. You have to make all the decisions; they simply execute them. You're better off paying a higher commission and obtaining advice and recommendations from a full-service broker — assuming you have a good one, of course; there's no point in paying more for *bad* advice. I'll deal with the whole question of brokers in more detail in a later chapter.

There may be situations, however, when you know exactly what you want to do and why. You don't need the help of a full-service broker and you'd like to save some money on commissions.

There are a couple of ways to achieve this, assuming you've set up your plan with a financial institution and not a full-service brokerage house. One is to simply designate a discount broker as one of the dealers authorized to trade in your account. The other is to use the discount service that some financial institutions (but not all, by any means) offer self-directed clients. When you're shopping for a self-directed plan, ask whether this type of service is offered. You may not make much use of it at the beginning, but it could be an important option as your plan grows and you trade securities more frequently.

Once you've found the right self-directed plan, the next question is what to put in it. You may be surprised at the number of choices you have. The financial institution that you're dealing with should be able to provide you with a complete list of RRSP eligible investments. But the most important ones are shares in Canadian companies, bonds, mutual funds, GICs, term deposits, cash and mortgages (including your own).

While most of the investments must be Canadian, you are permitted to hold foreign securities in your self-directed plan. The book value of such holdings (book value is the price you originally paid) must not exceed sixteen percent of the total book value of your RRSP in 1992. This limit increases to eighteen percent in 1993 and to twenty percent in 1994, where it will remain unless changed in a future budget.

You should also be aware of non-eligible RRSP investments. If you make a mistake and put one in your plan, the penalties can be costly. You are not permitted to hold gold and precious metals directly, although shares in gold mines and units in a precious metals mutual fund are okay. Similarly, your RRSP may not own real estate directly, but can hold real estate mutual funds and mortgages. Commodity futures, raw land, certain foreign securities and collectibles such as art and antiques are all on the forbidden list. For more details, consult my annual *Buyer's Guide to RRSPs*.

What you put in your self-directed plan depends on how aggressive you are and the extent of your investment knowledge. You may decide to hold nothing more than Canada Savings Bonds and GICs at the outset. Or you may want to take on greater risk by purchasing strip bonds or mutual funds.

There is some debate over whether stocks are appropriate for RRSPs. One school of thought is firmly against including them, for two reasons. First, they're too risky for a retirement plan. This is the money you're putting aside for your old age, the argument runs; it shouldn't be in anything as volatile as stocks. Second, you lose the tax breaks available from stocks by putting them into a retirement plan. The dividend tax credit can't be claimed when the dividends are paid into an RRSP. And capital gains in an RRSP aren't eligible for the $100,000 lifetime exemption or for the favourable tax treatment that applies when you exceed that limit.

But wait a minute, you may say. If they're inside an RRSP, dividends and capital gains aren't taxed at all. What's the issue here?

The argument is that those profits will be taxed at your prevailing marginal rate when the funds are drawn out. That means you'll end up paying more tax than you would have had the stocks been held outside the RRSP.

All that is true, but it's not enough to convince me that stocks should never go into an RRSP. I come at RRSPs from a different perspective. I don't regard them simply as a means to save for old age. I see them as a wonderful tax sheltered opportunity to create personal wealth. On that basis, I believe in maximizing the investment potential of my RRSPs — and that means buying stocks when the conditions are right. People who held all their assets in interest-bearing vehicles during the great bull market of the mid-1980s realized a modest return on their money. But that was nothing compared to the gains enjoyed by those of us who invested at least part of the RRSP portfolio in the stock market.

Understand me well. I am not suggesting you should be reckless with your money, quite the contrary. As I said at the outset of this book, I'm a conservative by nature. I don't believe in taking undue risk or in throwing my money away on bad securities. I *do*, however, believe in using the wealth building power of the RRSP to its fullest.

As for the tax argument, I suggest there's another side to it. Yes, you might have to pay tax at a higher rate down the road on your dividends and capital gains. But in the meantime you have the use of that deferred tax money to reinvest and add to your wealth.

Let's suppose you purchased one hundred shares of a stock for $30 each. Ignoring the commissions, your investment was $3,000. You held the stock for a year, during which you received $120 in dividends. At the end of that time, you sold the stock for $4,500. Your total profit would be $1,620, of which $1,500 is capital gain.

Outside an RRSP, both the dividends and the capital gain are subject to tax. Let's assume you're in the top tax bracket and that you've used up your capital gains exemption. The tax payable on the dividends will be about $40 depending on which province you live in. The tax payable on the capital gain will be assessed on seventy-five percent of your profit; the balance is tax free. In this case, assuming you're in a fifty-two percent bracket, you'll pay tax on the gain of about $585. All told, that means you'll have to hand over about $625 to Revenue Canada. That money is no longer available for you to reinvest.

If the same thing happened inside your RRSP, no tax would be assessed immediately. Let's assume you didn't plan to dip into your RRSP assets for another thirty years. That $625 would continue to work for you during that time. If the profits were reinvested so as to earn ten percent a year, what do you think the $625 would be worth at the end of that time? Would you believe $10,900? That's money you wouldn't have had that $625 gone to the tax department years before. If you're still paying tax at a fifty-two percent rate when you withdraw the $10,900 from the plan, you'll be hit for about $5,670. But you'll be left with the balance — money you would not otherwise have possessed. That's why I don't buy the tax argument.

One other point. The experts who tell you not to put stocks into an RRSP aren't saying stay out of the market entirely. They just want you to build an equity portfolio outside your plan, not in it. That's all well and good — if you can afford a second investment portfolio. Most beginning wealth builders can't. It's a case of stocks in the RRSP or no stocks at all. You know which course I suggest.

What are the dangers in a self-directed plan? You're the main one. Don't get carried away and be tempted to venture beyond your depth. If you stick with what you know, you'll be all right.

Failure of the financial institution operating the plan is another concern, especially if you've opted for one of the smaller trust companies. But the Canada Deposit Insurance Corporation protects you for up to $60,000 for investments that would be covered if they were outside an RRSP. That includes such things as cash deposits and GICs. Other assets, such as stocks, bonds and mutual funds, are held for you in trust. They shouldn't be in any danger in the event of a financial collapse, unless criminal misappropriation has taken place. When the Principal Group went down in Alberta, for example, RRSP holders were protected — their assets were secure.

So now you've got your self-directed plan and, hopefully, some ideas of what you're going to put in it. In the next chapter, I'll discuss techniques you can use to make that money grow in a hurry.

Oh yes, I almost forgot. I said at the beginning of this chapter I'd explain why I kept two self-directed plans instead of one. Originally, it was to test investing strategies. One plan was quite conservative in its investment approach, the other more aggressive. I compared results to see which technique worked better and this helped to refine my investing strategy. Now, I run both plans in the same way. But I value the input from both the brokers I've been working with and don't want to give that up. I consider the additional administration fee worthwhile for that reason. Good advice is worth a lot more than a few dollars a year!

Building Wealth in Your RRSP

CHAPTER 15

You pays your money and you takes your choice.
— Punch, 1846

One day a friend came to me with a real dilemma. His wife had some money in an RRSP, which had originally been put into a guaranteed investment certificate. The certificate was about to mature and the trust company was asking for instructions on how to reinvest the funds.

Along with this notification, my friend received a list of RRSP investment options offered by that particular trust firm. There were thirteen of them! This couple knew a little about money but my friend frankly admitted they were at a loss. They didn't have any idea which of those thirteen options was the right one for them — or, indeed, if any of them was.

A lot of people are in exactly that situation — maybe you're one of them. There are so many RRSP options available today that try-ing to choose among them can induce mental paralysis. They all claim they have the best vehicle. How do you know which one to believe?

The answer is, you don't. If you're going to invest your RRSP money wisely and maximize its wealth building potential, you have to take the time to look beyond the advertising claims. You have to determine what investment choices really have the best track record. And you have to look to the future because, as mutual fund salespeople are obliged to constantly point out, past performance is no guarantee of future results. You have to take stock of what's happening in the world around you and what it's likely to mean for certain types of investments. And you have to give careful consideration to your own needs and objectives.

If that sounds like work, I'm afraid it is. But it's work with a big potential pay-off. Because of its tax-sheltered status, there is no way the ordinary person can build a substantial investment portfolio faster than within an RRSP. And, as I pointed out in the two previous chapters, "substantial" means just that — you could end up with several hundred thousand dollars, or even more, by the time you're through, if you play your cards right. But to make that happen, you must make the right investment decisions. You must pick the opportunities that combine solid growth potential with limited risk and reject those that carry high loss potential. You won't always be right — no one is. But if you can make the correct choice more often than not, you'll come out ahead.

The problem is that many people give very little thought to what happens in their RRSPs. Their main concern is the immediate tax benefit. So they sock their money in the most convenient place, get the receipt, claim the tax refund and forget it. I'll bet you know people who do exactly that. Maybe you're one of them.

In all fairness, the maze of choices may be partly responsible for this RRSP inertia. Many people freeze when called upon to make decisions in areas they don't fully understand; they'd prefer to do nothing rather than risk being wrong. Perhaps if we had only three or four options to choose from we'd manage our money better. But the reality is that all those options are available. If you want to use your RRSP to build wealth, you have to understand the various investments available and be prepared to choose among them.

I cannot stress the importance of this strongly enough. Next to the family home, a solid RRSP investment program is the most important component in the early stages of wealth building. If you ignore it, you might as well forget about ever acquiring real wealth. That may seem like a strong statement, but I firmly believe it to be true. Managing your RRSP provides you with the discipline, knowledge and experience you'll need to move on to other types of wealth building activities later. If you're not prepared to devote the time and effort to doing it right, you have very little chance of succeeding in other types of wealth building pursuits.

I'm not just talking here about making the right decisions at the time you make your initial RRSP contributions, although that is, of course, very important. You have to actively manage that money at all times. You must know where it is, how much it's earning and what other investment opportunities are available for it. You must be prepared to get out of one investment and into something else when the occasion arises — and you must have a clear understanding of why you're doing it.

That may sound a little scary, especially if you're not used to making investment decisions. But it really isn't all that hard. It requires some knowledge, some common sense, some time and some decisiveness on your part. Once you're into it, I expect you'll find, as I did, that it's not frightening at all. On the contrary, it's challenging, stimulating and, yes, fun.

In this chapter, I'll show you how to start. We'll look at the most common RRSP investments and I'll explain how and when they should be used to maximize your return. I'll show you how to start a plan and how to manage it successfully yourself.

Let's begin by assuming you're about to make your first RRSP contribution, for $3,000. You don't have enough money yet to consider a self-directed plan and you're a little nervous about the whole process. Perhaps you're thinking: "I'm opening an RRSP because this guy said to. But what the hell do I do now?"

Okay, let's discuss that question. When you're just starting out, the number one priority is to protect your capital base. You're probably not making a large salary and finding the money to put into an RRSP isn't easy. The last thing you want is to lose that small nest-egg. You need that money to build on — in two ways. You want to add to your capital through investment income. And you need to build confidence in your investing ability. If you get wiped out the first time around, it will probably be a long, long time before you stick your toe in the investment pond again.

With that in mind, your first RRSP investments should be conservative in nature. You should diversify them, even if the amount available is small, to give yourself experience with different types of investment choices and to reduce whatever limited risk you may have. You should not be taking any major chances at this stage. Save that stuff for later. Right now, you're just getting your feet wet.

So where do you start? Look first at some basic interest-bearing investments — those that are easiest to understand. Investments like this should be the foundation of your RRSP at any time, even when you move into much more sophisticated areas. So start using them right from the outset.

Plain old GICs are as good a place as any to begin. Shop for one offering a high rate of return. You don't have to trudge from bank to trust company to credit union to do that or even make a lot of phone calls. Just check out the financial pages of your local newspaper or the *Globe and Mail Report on Business*. At least once a week many major newspapers carry a comprehensive listing of current interest rates being offered by financial institutions for term deposits and GICs (you'll find it in the *ROB* on Mondays). Check them over carefully. You'll usually find the major chartered banks will pay you the least for your money. The larger trust companies will fall into the middle range. The small trusts and credit unions will give you the biggest bang for your dollar.

The difference between the best and worst rates can be significant. For instance, if you'd picked up the paper on March 31, 1992 and scanned the interest rate section, you'd have discovered that a one-year GIC would have paid interest of as low as 6.5% or as high as eight percent, depending on where you put your money. Let's say you decide to put $2,000 of your RRSP money into a GIC. The lowest rate GIC at that time would have returned you $130 interest over the next year. The GIC with the highest rate would have added $160 to your RRSP. If you think that $30 difference isn't significant in the great scheme of things, look at it this way: you would earn twenty-three percent more interest with the highest rate GIC than with the one with the lowest rate.

As the amount of money in your RRSP grows and you have more to invest, the dollar numbers become magnified. If you'd had $20,000 to invest in a GIC instead of just $2,000, the interest difference between the lowest and the highest rate would have been $300. Does that seem more impressive?

Training yourself to spot those distinctions early on will be invaluable later as you develop a larger financial base with which to work. The good wealth builder will be constantly on the lookout for every edge he or she can get. Extra dollars can add up surprisingly quickly if reinvested over a period of time. Even that modest $30 in extra interest you received by choosing the highest yielding GIC can yield fascinating results. Reinvested over the next thirty-five years at an average return of ten percent a year, that original $30 interest bonus will grow to almost $850! Multiply that by all the other small amounts you'll gain along the way by constantly seeking out the interest rate edge, and the total impact on your RRSP investment portfolio can add up to many thousands of dollars.

One other point here. There is nothing wrong with placing your money in a small financial institution — as long as it is a member of the Canada Deposit Insurance Corporation (the CDIC). That's an absolute must. There have been too many bank, trust company and investment firm failures in recent years to take any chances on this score. As long as the firm you deal with is a CDIC member and you're buying a GIC or term deposit directly from them, your money will be protected up to a maximum of $60,000 if anything should go wrong. Just make sure the company isn't selling investment receipts issued by someone else. There have been situations where investors thought they were dealing with a CDIC insured company only to discover that the GICs they received were actually issued by an associated firm that wasn't covered. If you have any doubts at all, take your money somewhere else.

How long a term should you choose for your GIC investment? You'll have to decide that yourself; it depends on the interest rate climate at the time you make the investment. If rates are high, you should consider locking in for three to five years to take advantage of them. If rates are relatively low, stick with a one-year GIC. You can review the situation at the end of that time and decide where to go next.

You've now invested two-thirds of your $3,000 RRSP stake in a high-yielding GIC. It may not seem terribly exciting, but it's safe and solid and provides a fair return on your investment. Now, what do you do with the last $1,000?

Since you've placed most of your money in a very secure investment, you might consider something that carries just slightly — and I mean slightly — more risk but offers a potentially higher return. Also, since you're seeking to develop investing experience, you should learn about something new. I suggest you take a look at a no load mortgage mutual fund.

These are among the most conservative of mutual funds (if you're not sure what a mutual fund is, I'll explain in more detail in a later chapter). Typically, they invest in residential first mortgages and the emphasis is on safety with a modest return to investors. Many banks and trust companies offer them and the initial investment required is usually very low. Your $1,000 will get you into most of the available mortgage funds without any problem.

Don't expect to make a lot of money from this type of mutual fund. The risk is low, but so is the potential return. However, chances are your return on the mortgage fund will be higher than from your GIC investment. There's a risk it won't be, though; in fact, you could even lose a bit of money, although it's never happened in any mortgage fund in Canada to my knowledge. If you should suffer a loss, it's likely to be small and temporary, probably in a time of sharply rising interest rates.

What are some good mortgage funds to consider? My annual *Buyer's Guide to Mutual Funds* can provide the most recent information. But some no load funds that have been solid, long-term performers include the CIBC Mortgage Investment Fund, the First Canadian Mortgage Fund (sold by the Bank of Montreal), the Green Line Canadian Mortgage Fund (available at branches of the TD Bank), the Montreal Trust Mortgage Fund and the Royal Trust Mortgage Fund.

Top performer for the five-year period between 1987 and 1991 was the First Canadian Mortgage Fund, with an average annual return of 11.6%. All of the funds mentioned above averaged better than ten percent annual return during that period.

During 1991, mortgage funds performed especially well, with returns over seventeen percent in some cases. But this was due mainly to falling interest rates during that time; normally returns on mortgage funds are more modest. During the period from

1976–91, for example, the First Canadian Fund produced returns ranging from a low of 6.4% in 1979 to a high of 22.8% in 1982. In more than half those years, however, the return was between ten and fourteen percent, according to the *Mutual Fund Sourcebook* published by Southam Business Communications. That's about what you should look for over the long term if you add a mortgage fund to your RRSP portfolio.

In selecting your mortgage fund, use the same process as you did when choosing a GIC. Shop around. In this case, you're looking for two things. First, you want a no load fund — one which doesn't charge any commission fees when you sign up or when you redeem units. Second, you want a fund with a strong and consistent track record. That's where the business press can help. All the papers publish monthly reports on the performance of mutual funds; buy a copy or spend some time at your local library checking out the information. Pick a mortgage fund that has a consistent record of solid returns over the years and go with it.

So here's where your small RRSP portfolio stands after all this:

Guaranteed Investment Certificate	$2,000	66.7%
Mortgage Fund	$1,000	33.3%
Total investment	$3,000	100.0%

It may not be exciting, but it's an excellent start. Your investments are safe, you've achieved a modest degree of diversification and you'll get a decent return. Now what?

Let's assume you don't make any changes in your RRSP portfolio for the first year and that the combined yield from your investments is nine percent. You've earned $270 in tax-free money over the year and you contribute another $3,000 to the plan. You now have $6,270 in assets, of which $3,270 is cash. What should you do now?

First, review your original investments. See if they're still solid or if you should make some changes. Perhaps you chose a one-year GIC and, based on your experience, you feel you'd rather take $1,000 of that money and move it into your mortgage fund. Do it! Never make the mistake of allowing your money to remain in relatively unproductive investments. At the same time, don't go to the other extreme and put all your eggs in one basket. Maybe the mortgage fund had a terrific year and you're tempted to put all the GIC money into it, as well as your new contribution. Don't! If the next year should be a weak one for mortgage funds, your RRSP would have no other revenue source and you'd end up with a lower return than you anticipated.

Let's assume that, after reviewing your holdings, you decide you like the mortgage fund enough to invest another $1,500 in it. With the reinvested interest your fund earned in the first year, this brings your total mortgage fund holding to $2,590 (this assumes no change in unit value).

You roll over your $2,000 GIC for another year, along with $180 you earned in interest, for a total of $2,180. Now you've got $1,500 in new money left to invest.

You still don't want to take any major risks. Your RRSP is growing, but you aren't at the point where you could afford any serious reverses. But you'd like to add to your investment experience.

This could be the time to look at another type of mutual fund — a bond fund. There's slightly more risk here than with a mortgage fund, but the potential returns are also somewhat greater.

You've already learned the basic facts about bonds from reading Chapter Ten. You know that bonds perform best when interest rates are falling and do worst when they're on the rise. So before you make any commitment to a bond fund, you should do some research to inform yourself on what interest rates are doing at the present time.

Let's assume you conclude that interest rates are stable or in a downward trend. A bond fund appears to be a good choice at this point, so you now go to the financial newspapers and check past performance. Again, you're looking for a no load fund, which will be designated by the initials NL.

You'll find several that have produced excellent results over many years. One which especially catches your eye is the Altamira Income Fund. It's been a favourite of mine for some time and I've frequently recommended it in my *MoneyLetter* columns. It meets the no load criterion (although you will be charged a small one-time set-up fee when you open an account) and is easy to order through a toll-free number. Performance has been consistently good; over the five years from 1987 to 1991, the fund produced an average annual return of 12.6%. It also has an excellent safety record; this fund has never had a losing year since it was created in 1970. Of course, this isn't the only good bond fund around. There are many others, some of which are no load, some of which have a sales commission attached. Review your options carefully before deciding.

Once you've made up your mind, you invest the remaining $1,500 in the bond fund you've chosen. Your RRSP portfolio now looks like this:

Guaranteed Investment Certificate	$2,180	34.8%
Mortgage Fund	$2,590	41.3%
Bond Fund	$1,500	23.9%
Total Investment	$6,270	100.0%

As a result of these moves, you've achieved greater diversification in your RRSP, with no more than 41.3% of your assets in any one holding. Your investments are still quite safe, but you have added to your risk (and your potential return) by increasing your mortgage fund holdings and buying the bond fund.

I'm sure you're getting the idea of how to proceed but let's look at one more year.

Let's assume that by increasing your risk and growth potential by adding the bond fund and switching money into the mortgage fund, you improve your average return in the second year to ten percent. That's $627 your RRSP earns for you. And let's say you make another $3,000 contribution. Going into the third year, your total RRSP assets are now $9,897 (see how quickly they grow?), including $3,627 in new cash to invest.

Now it may be time to consider some real diversification. So far, you've put all your money into interest-bearing assets. You should now consider adding some equity to your RRSP.

You don't know much about stocks and you certainly don't want to get involved at this stage in individual stock selections. But there are a number of mutual funds around that invest in the stock market. This may be time to look at one of them.

Again, start by doing your homework. The first thing you need to determine is which funds are RRSP-eligible; not all of them are. The tables in the monthly mutual fund reports in the business press will provide that information, as does my annual *Buyer's Guide to RRSPs*.

Next, check for the no load funds. The fact I'm emphasizing this doesn't mean you should never buy a load fund, far from it. It's just that when you have only a modest amount of money to invest, I don't believe it's wise to pay a commission up front or to put yourself in the position of having to pay a redemption fee if you decide you've made a bad decision and want to cash in.

Finally, look at the performance records. What funds have consistently done well over the years and are still going strong? Again, you'll find several possibilities. If you've already bought units in the Altamira Income Fund, you might decide to stay with that company and purchase their Equity Fund as well. It was the top-ranked Canadian equity fund for the three-year period 1989–91, with an average annual rate of return of over twenty-five percent.

Whatever your choice, you decide to add an equity fund to your portfolio. You recognize that you're getting into higher-risk territory, though, so you only commit half your new contribution to it. The balance of your cash is distributed as follows: $500 plus $196 interest into your GIC, $500 plus $260 interest into your mortgage fund, and $500 plus $171 interest into your bond fund. Now your RRSP holdings look like this:

Guaranteed Investment Certificate	$2,876	29.1%
Mortgage Fund	3,350	33.8%
Bond Fund	2,171	21.9%
Equity Fund	1,500	15.2%
Total Investment	$9,897	100.0%

In just two full years of RRSP investing, you've established a solid position. You've given your plan an excellent base of interest earning investments. You've started to add some higher growth potential, while still keeping your risk relatively low. You've diversified your holdings among four different types of investments. And you've learned a lot about new investment vehicles in the process. A pretty good start!

As your RRSP grows, continue to follow the same pattern that I've outlined above. Here are some guidelines:

1. Review your investments regularly. If any are not performing well, search out alternatives and replace them.

2. Add new types of investments gradually and only when you fully understand them.

3. Make sure that only a small proportion of your RRSP money is in medium to higher risk investments. These should never exceed a third of your total RRSP value.

4. Maintain good diversification in your RRSP. The larger your fund becomes, the lower should be the maximum percentage that's devoted to any one investment. In the example we just looked at, two assets made up the total plan at the start. But by the beginning of the third year you had invested in four different types of securities. Your largest single holding was the mortgage fund, which represented only one-third of the total.

If you stick to those basic guidelines, you'll find yourself with a solid and growing RRSP in a relatively short time. And, equally important, you will have accumulated a lot of knowledge and experience that will help you as you move into other aspects of wealth building.

Protecting Your Assets

CHAPTER 16

There's none deceived but he that trusts.
— Benjamin Franklin

In October 1986, a young Dalhousie University law student named Adrienne Scott walked into the Halifax office of Principal Savings and Trust. She'd been attracted by a newspaper ad offering investment certificates at ten percent interest, an unusually high rate at that time.

Her story, as she told it later on CBC radio in Ottawa, is relevant to every wealth builder.

She was directed to the back of the office by a woman who said the ten percent certificates weren't actually being issued by the trust company itself. There she met with a man who explained that the certificates were issued by a company called First Investors, a member of the Principal Group. Because First Investors was a separate company, the certificates weren't covered by deposit insurance. But they were fully backed by deposits in major chartered banks and were as solid an investment as she could wish for. The only money that might conceivably be at risk was that portion of the interest payment over five percent and that risk was very small.

Still, Ms. Scott was cautious. She had $64,000 she wanted to invest, $20,000 of her own money and the rest borrowed from her mother. She didn't want to take any chances with it; it was money that would be needed to help finance her university education. So after asking more questions, she obtained a copy of the investment contract and took it away with her. She read it over and showed it to some members of her family and a friend. Everyone thought it looked okay. She also talked to people who had put money into certificates issued by First Investors. They reported no problems. So she went ahead, investing her funds in several certificates with varying maturities.

Several months later she read in the paper that two companies associated with the Principal Group had effectively gone into receivership when their licenses were revoked by the Alberta government. That happened after an audit revealed their assets weren't adequate to cover the commitments they'd made on investment contracts they'd issued. It appeared that the firms, one of which was First Investors, had invested heavily in Alberta real estate in the early 1980s and had been hit hard by the subsequent drop in property values in the province.

At about the same time, Adrienne Scott received a letter informing her that she would be receiving a thirty percent refund on her deposit with First Investors within a few weeks. No mention was made of the balance of the money.

Needless to say, she was shocked. She thought she had made a safe investment and suddenly she found herself faced with the loss of a large portion of her funds. She'd been careful, but still ended up in trouble.

Ms. Scott was the victim of a bait and switch technique that is all too common in this country. She'd gone to a trust company, a member of the Canada Deposit Insurance Corporation (CDIC), believing that any funds she placed on deposit with them would be protected. That would have been the case but instead, she was sold an investment contract issued by an associated firm that was not covered by the CDIC. The guarantees she was given were worthless, but they had diverted her attention away from the fact her money would not be protected by deposit insurance by providing what seemed like a plausible alternative.

One result of all this was that CDIC tightened the enforcement of a law which forbids the staff and agents of financial institutions from telling customers that a specific deposit is insured. You're encouraged, instead, to call a toll-free CDIC number (800-461-

2342) if you have any doubts.

Ms. Scott's case is by no means unique. Some 67,000 investors were affected by the debacle within the Principal Group. Years later, they were still fighting in the courts to try to recover their money. As of mid 1992, holders of notes issued by First Investors had recovered 82.5 cents on every dollar. It was estimated at that point they would end up with 87 cents on each dollar — not as bad as it appeared at first, but a significant loss nonetheless.

Tens of thousands of other Canadians have lost large amounts of money in the collapse of other financial institutions and investment companies in recent years.

The carrot in these situations is usually above-average interest rates. People are always looking for a better deal; and an additional point or two on a GIC is very attractive, as I've pointed out in previous chapters.

Just because one financial institution is offering a higher interest rate doesn't mean it's in some kind of trouble. Many smaller trust companies have to pay a premium to get business, especially during a time when there's concern about the stability of small financial firms. As long as the investment you make is fully covered by deposit insurance, you're protected to a large extent. Just make sure the GIC you purchase is, in fact, covered. Don't accept any lesser guarantee.

The importance of CDIC protection became even more apparent a few weeks later when Principal Trust itself (which had been in business since 1954) was forced to close its doors. Many more depositors were affected when that happened. But most of their funds were protected by deposit insurance.

As it turned out, Metropolitan Life Holdings Ltd. took over the firm and created a new firm, Metropolitan Trust. But that was only made possible with the help of the CDIC, which ensured Principal Trust depositors (but not those of non-member associated companies) were protected. Adrienne Scott would have been delighted to change places with any of them.

No aspiring wealth builder can afford to sustain the kind of loss endured by those who put money in First Investors and Associated Investors, the second company involved. And yet it can happen so easily, and so unexpectedly, it's scary. Let me tell you my own story.

On November 1, 1982 I put $30,000 of my RRSP money into a one-year guaranteed investment certificate with a small trust company. The funds came in part from a pension refund and in part from a retiring allowance received when the company for which I was working folded at the height of the 1981–82 recession.

I didn't pick the trust company the money was deposited with. In fact, I'd never heard of it before. I acted on the advice of a well-known Toronto firm of personal financial consultants who had been hired to help senior executives of my organization put their financial affairs in order.

The rate on this particular GIC was fourteen percent. That was about a point higher than the rate being offered by other trust companies and chartered banks at that time.

The name of the company where I put my money? Greymac Trust.

On December 31, 1982, on the advice of the same consultants, I deposited additional pension funds worth about $13,000 in a three-year certificate with another small trust company. It was paying 13.25% — again, a higher rate than was available elsewhere at that time.

This company's name was Seaway Trust.

On January 7, 1983, only a week after that second deposit, the Government of Ontario approved a controversial takeover plan involving Greymac, Seaway and Crown Trusts. This was as a result of a complicated flip involving thousands of apartment units, a deal which eventually resulted in criminal charges against some of the people involved. The takeover of the three trust companies, which eventually put all of them out of business, took place after it became clear they had all been involved in the transactions in one way or another.

When I heard the news, I was sick. I was faced with the prospect of having years of savings wiped out by a series of unpredictable events totally beyond my control. And, of course, it wasn't just me. Thousands of other people with deposits in those companies faced exactly the same situation.

Two things saved me. One was the Canada Deposit Insurance Corporation. Unlike Adrienne Scott's situation, my investment certificates were indeed held by trust companies which had deposit insurance.

But maximum protection at that time was only $20,000. I stood to lose $10,000 of my deposit with Greymac.

That's where the other fortuitous event occurred. Parliament rushed through legislation which retroactively increased the deposit insurance limit to $60,000, thus protecting all the Crown, Greymac and Seaway depositors up to that amount.

I got my money out, although not with all the interest I should have received, which I'll explain later. But at that point I wasn't complaining. I was just relieved to have escaped relatively unscathed what could have been a serious financial setback.

There are two morals to this story. First, don't take advice from financial planners on blind faith, even if they have an excellent reputation. Do some thinking of your own as well. In this particular case, it was almost impossible to see what was coming. But often, such as in the collapse of Standard Trust in April, 1991, there are signs of trouble well in advance which should alert any prudent investor to take action.

Second, make absolutely sure your money is fully protected by deposit insurance.

Never think you're immune from the failure of a bank, trust company or other financial institution. Consider these names: Astra Trust, Pioneer Trust, Commonwealth Trust, Security Trust, London Loan, District Trust, Fidelity Trust, Western Capital Trust, Northguard Mortgage Corporation, Northland Bank, Canadian Commercial Bank, Standard Trust, Shoppers Trust, First City Trust, Bank of Credit and Commerce International, Saskatchewan Trust. What do they have in common? In every case, the CDIC had to bail out depositors after the companies fell into financial difficulties.

The reality is that North America's financial structure has been less than rock-solid in recent years. Even our major banks have had more than their share of woe. The difficulties at Olympia and York, for example, hit most of our big chartered banks hard. The Bank of Commerce, for example, was forced to make a record $1 billion provision for bad loans in the quarter ending April 30, 1992, in large part due to concerns over O&Y debt. This doesn't mean that our big chartered banks are at risk as far as depositors are concerned, however. It would take a financial earthquake of far greater magnitude than O&Y to topple any one of them. But shareholders paid the price in falling stock values.

The problems haven't been confined to Canada by any means; in fact, our system has been a model of stability compared to what's been happening in the U.S. The 1980s saw the biggest rash of bank failures in the United States since the Great Depression, and the early nineties weren't any better. Problems with the fragmented American banking system were compounded by the debacle in that country's Savings and Loan industry, which required a government bail-out costing hundreds of billions of dollars that's still draining the U.S. Treasury to this day. Why so much trouble? The reasons range from debt defaults by Third World countries, to bad lending decisions during the leveraged buy-out mania of the eighties, to plunging real estate values in many areas of the U.S.

So far, the underlying structure has swayed but not toppled. But we're not out of the woods yet and it's essential you protect yourself. Which brings me back to deposit insurance and the importance of understanding just what it does — and does not — cover.

If you think you've got a pretty clear idea of what it's all about, try the little test that follows.

Question one: You're planning a trip to Florida next winter. You want to convert some money to U.S. dollars now because the exchange rate is favourable. You deal with a major chartered bank, a CDIC member, and one day while you're in the branch you notice a sign promoting U.S. dollar accounts. You decide to open one so your Florida money can earn a little interest before you depart. Is your money protected by deposit insurance?

Question two: You've had great success in building the value of your RRSP by using the techniques I've described. Now you decide you want to invest $50,000 in a five-year Guaranteed Investment Certificate with a small trust company which attracted you with an offer of 9.5% interest, compounded semi-annually. (Forget for the moment that this isn't such a hot idea because you'd be tying up too much of your money in a single asset. I'm just trying to illustrate a point.) You leave your money on deposit for almost five years. A couple of weeks before the certificate is to mature, the trust company declares bankruptcy. But you know it's a member of the CDIC so you're not worried. Is your relaxed attitude justified?

Question three: You had $50,000 in a guaranteed investment certificate with Victoria and Grey Trust when it was announced the company would merge with National Trust. You also had a $25,000 GIC with National. How much of your money is protected following the merger?

Here are the answers:

Question one: You have no protection at all. The odds are greatly against your chartered bank failing, of course. But if the unlikely happened and it did go belly-up, you'd have to kiss your Florida vacation good-bye. The Canada Deposit Insurance Corporation doesn't insure any deposits held in U.S. dollars, or any other foreign currency for that matter. So if you really do need a U.S. dollar account, make sure the financial institution you use is rock solid.

Question two: This may come as a surprise, but you stand to lose several thousand dollars. Your $50,000 GIC at 9.5% interest, compounded annually, will be worth about $78,700 at maturity. Since the maximum CDIC protection for any single account is $60,000, you face a potential loss of $18,700. Don't be so relaxed!

Question three: You're protected for the full $75,000, even though the amount exceeds the CDIC cap for deposits in any one financial institution. The reason is that when banks or trust companies amalgamate, deposits held in each institution at the time of the merger are considered separately for CDIC purposes. This applies until the funds are withdrawn or until the maturity date, if the deposit has a fixed term. But be careful. Additional deposits made after the merger are not protected because you're already over the normal limit.

If you managed a perfect score on those questions, you don't need to read any more of this chapter. It's clear you know the CDIC rules inside out. But if you missed any of the answers, you may find the information that follows to be of help.

First, what is covered? The CDIC will protect your savings and chequing accounts in any member institution up to a maximum of $60,000 per person. However, the word "person" is interpreted very broadly. A "person" can be two people, in the case of a joint account. A "person" can be a Registered Retirement Savings Plan or Registered Retirement Income Fund. Companies and even governments are "persons" for purposes of CDIC coverage. So if you run a small business, your firm's account is safe up to $60,000. Note, however, that a sole proprietorship is not a separate "person" for CDIC purposes.

Apart from Canadian dollar deposit accounts, CDIC also covers such things as money orders, deposit receipts, term deposits, GICs and debentures issued by its members. One caution here, though: term deposits and GICs are only covered if they're cashable on demand or have a fixed term of five years or less. So if someone offers you a GIC for longer than five years, think twice before you accept.

Some other important rules to keep in mind:

- Coverage is per financial institution. Spreading your money among different branches doesn't help, but using associated companies (see below) does.

- Although funds over the $60,000 maximum in one financial institution are not protected in theory, there are some ways around this. Some financial institutions have more than one corporate entity that belongs to the CDIC, so deposits with each are entitled to separate deposit insurance coverage. For example, Toronto-Dominion Bank, TD Mortgage Corporation and TD Pacific Mortgage Corporation are all CDIC members. Each corporate entity may therefore issue GICs which are protected by deposit insurance up to $60,000. So you could obtain $180,000 in coverage by spreading your money among TD Bank and its associated companies. In this way, you can greatly increase your CDIC protection without having to go to the trouble of opening accounts all over town.

• Another way to beat the $60,000 rule is to spread your deposits among various family members or qualified "persons," using the CDIC's broad definitions. For example, if you and your spouse have a joint deposit, it's a separate "person" for deposit insurance purposes. That means you could have a joint account with $60,000 along with individual accounts for each of you at the same financial institution and all the money would be protected — a total of $180,000 coverage. Add separate RRSPs for each of you, and your protection is now up to $300,000. A family which is serious about increasing coverage (and which has a great deal of money) could add hundreds of thousands of dollars in additional CDIC protection at the same institution by carefully managing their accounts and investments. Of course, this is largely theoretical because, if you had that kind of money, it's unlikely you would want to keep it all on deposit in the same place anyway.

• CDIC membership is restricted to banks, trust companies and mortgage loan companies. If the company is federally incorporated, it must be a member. But provincially incorporated companies may or may not have coverage. That's where you have to be especially careful.

• Credit unions are not covered by the CDIC. But provincial governments have their own insurance programs to protect depositors, some of which are actually better than the coverage offered by the CDIC. Manitoba, for example, provides unlimited coverage for credit union deposits. Ontario credit unions, however, have the same protection as CDIC members, a maximum of $60,000. If you deal with a credit union and you're not sure what protection you have, ask.

Now for the investments CDIC does *not* cover. Stocks, bonds, mortgages and mutual funds are excluded — I'll explain the significance of that shortly.

The contents of your safety deposit box aren't protected. Foreign currency deposits are also out, as we've already seen.

These restrictions are of special importance in terms of an RRSP or RRIF. The money in your plan is only covered if the funds are in the same kind of investment instruments that would be protected if they were outside an RRSP.

Suppose, for instance, the assets in your RRSP looked like this:

Cash	$2,000
Money market fund	6,000
GIC	5,000
Mortgage Fund	3,000
Bond Fund	2,000
Equity Fund	2,000
Total	$20,000

What's insured and what isn't?

Your cash is covered, assuming it's in Canadian currency. But your money market fund, which many people regard as the equivalent of cash, is not. This needn't be a cause for concern — most money market funds invest heavily in Canada Treasury bills, which are guaranteed by the federal government. Nonetheless, you should be aware of the distinction.

The GIC is protected, as long as its term doesn't exceed five years. So no problem there.

The mortgage, bond and equity funds have no insurance coverage — mutual funds are specifically excluded from CDIC protection, even if the fund is created and operated by a bank or trust company that's a member institution. So that's where you could conceivably run into trouble. If your mutual funds lose money because of bad investment decisions by the managers, you have no recourse. That's the chance you take when you make such investments. Failure of the financial institution itself shouldn't create a crisis for you, however, because your RRSP assets are held in trust, separate from the corporate assets. Still, you need to be aware of every possibility.

So out of the $20,000 in assets in this RRSP, only $7,000 — about a third — is actually protected by deposit insurance. That shows you how important it is to select RRSP investments that are as secure as possible.

One final point: if you are unfortunate enough to be caught in the failure of a financial institution, you may not get away scott-free, even with full CDIC coverage. I mentioned earlier in this chapter that when Seaway Trust was closed I lost some interest I would otherwise have been entitled to. Here's how it happened:

In June, 1984 the Supreme Court of Ontario issued an order formally winding up Seaway. The action was initiated by the CDIC and marked the first time the CDIC had ever petitioned a company into bankruptcy. By having the company wound up, the CDIC was able to immediately pay off all outstanding GICs. That meant people like myself who were holding long-term Seaway GICs at high rates of interest had them terminated prematurely. The three-year GIC at 13.25% which I had taken out on December 31, 1982 would normally have not matured until the end of 1985. Instead, by forcing Seaway into liquidation, the CDIC was able to pay off the certificate half way through its term.

As it happened, interest rates were much lower in mid-1984 than they had been when the original Seaway investment was made. Instead of getting 13.25% on my money for the eighteen months to the end of 1985, I was only able to re-invest at 10.75%. The result was a loss of about $600 in interest compared to what I would have made if Seaway had stayed in business.

So even though your principal may be fully protected by CDIC coverage, your interest entitlement won't be. It's something to keep in mind when you're making decisions on where to put your money.

Also keep in mind that if the financial institution where you keep your money should run into trouble, you may not be able to get access to your funds for several weeks, even though they're insured. CDIC has made arrangements for emergency funds in many cases (the Standard Trust collapse, for example), but you have to cope with bureaucracy to get the money and that could take several days.

It's a good idea to have another account at the bank or trust company across the street to use in an emergency. You never know!

Remember, take nothing for granted. There's too much turmoil in the financial world right now to take any more risks than you need to. You can never protect yourself completely from the unexpected. But the good wealth builder will do everything possible to minimize risk and protect his or her asset base. Knowing the ground rules of deposit insurance is an essential part of that process.

Understanding Mutual Funds

I've mentioned mutual funds several times in the past two chapters. You probably understand what they are but don't feel badly if you don't. For many people, the term "mutual fund" is something like the word "empathy" — they feel they *should* know what it means, but they aren't absolutely certain.

So if you're a bit vague on what mutual funds are and how they work, you've got lots of company. I learned that several years ago when the firm I was working for launched two mutual funds of its own. An employee meeting was held to explain the exciting new venture to everyone. Shortly after it began, the person chairing the meeting asked if there was anyone in the audience who did *not* know what a mutual fund was.

Predictably, no hands were raised at first. Then one daring woman raised hers. Another hand went up, then another. Before long, it was apparent that almost half the people in the room did not know what a mutual fund was. Would you believe that the main business of this particular company was financial education?

That meeting was a real eye-opener for me. I knew that only a relatively small percentage of Canadians invested in mutual funds. But I had assumed that just about everyone knew what they were all about. Now I know better — which is why I'm devoting this chapter and the next to explaining what mutual funds are and how people without a great deal of money to invest can use them as one of the early steps towards building wealth.

A mutual fund is simply a pooling of money for investment purposes. For example, suppose every reader of this book sent me ten dollars and asked me to invest it on their behalf. If 100,000 people did that, we'd have a million-dollar fund. As the manager, I would be required to report regularly to the shareholders (or unit holders, as they're also called) on how well we're doing. If the securities I bought for the fund's portfolio did well, we'd all make a profit and you'd probably send more money. If they did badly, you might decide to cash in your units for whatever you could get and write the whole thing off as a bad idea.

That, in a simplified way, is how mutual funds work. When you invest in a fund, you're really buying two things: a diversified portfolio in a particular investment area and professional investment management. In effect, you're getting a small stake in many different investments. The value of your units will move up or down depending on the performance of the investments held by your fund.

The type of investments you hold will depend on the kind of fund you buy and you may be surprised at the choices available. As this edition is prepared, there are more than 600 mutual funds in Canada and thousands in the United States. None is the same as any other — they differ in investment philosophy, the timing of their sales and purchases, the nature of their holdings, their volatility, and in numerous other ways. That's what makes picking a good mutual fund so difficult. With all the choices, how do you know where to begin?

I'll offer some guidelines on how to choose a good fund in Chapter Eighteen. For starters, let's take a look at some of the different types of funds currently available.

MORTGAGE FUNDS

We took a look at these in Chapter Fifteen, in the discussion on RRSP investments. Most mortgage funds invest in first mortgages on Canadian residential real estate; in other words, you're helping to finance other people's family homes. As we've already seen, these funds are relatively safe and are unlikely to lose money. However, the return on your investment is modest.

Some mortgage funds go beyond the single-family residential market to invest in industrial and commercial properties as well as apartments. The Great-West Life Mortgage Investment Fund is one example.

Mortgage funds are an excellent choice for the beginning investor who is looking for steady returns with no surprises. They tend to have low volatility and most can be purchased without any sales commission. Average annual rate of return for all Canadian mortgage funds for the ten-year period ending March 31, 1992 was twelve percent, according to the *Globe and Mail Report on Business.*

BOND FUNDS
These invest in bonds and debentures issued by governments, crown corporations, municipalities, utilities and private companies. With mortgage funds, this group is known collectively as *Income Funds* or *Fixed Income Funds* because of the income they generate through regular interest payments. Many people think of bond funds as being dull and ultra-conservative. They're certainly more stable than equity funds. But they can have major swings in their performance, depending on what's happening with interest rates, and that opens the way to capital gains as we saw in an earlier chapter. For example, units of the AGF Canadian Bond Fund produced a return of only 5.5% in 1990, a year of high interest rates. But in 1991, when rates sharply declined, the fund rewarded investors with a 20.4% return. So don't make the mistake of assuming bond funds won't have much price movement. They'll do very well when interest rates are dropping, because bond prices rise in that situation. Conversely, when interest rates are rising you're best to stay well clear of bond funds.

CANADIAN EQUITY FUNDS
These mutual funds specialize in Canadian stocks and they're very popular among investors, especially when things are hot in the stock market. They're an easy way for people who know little or nothing about stocks to get in on the action with minimal risk. But that

doesn't mean they're safe. When the stock market is strong, as it was in the mid 1980s, a well-managed equity fund can produce spectacular results. In 1985, for example, Mackenzie Financial's big Industrial Growth Fund posted a return of 28.1%. But when the market is wallowing, many stock funds have problems. In 1990, a bad year for most Canadian stock funds, Industrial Growth lost fifteen percent of its value.

The key with equity funds is to find one that performs reasonably well through good times and bad, keeping any losses in bad years to a minimum. The Vancouver-based Ethical Growth Fund is a good example; in the five years ending December 31, 1991 its performance record as reported by the *Mutual Fund Sourcebook* is shown below. To illustrate what that record means to you as an investor, I've assumed an original $1,000 investment, after sales commissions, and calculated the value of your fund units at the end of each year.

Year	Return	Value of Investment At Year-End
1987	10.9%	$1,109
1988	13.9%	1,263
1989	22.1%	1,542
1990	-3.1%	1,494
1991	10.9%	1,657

In five years, the value of a $1,000 investment made in Ethical Growth Fund at the beginning of 1987 increased by almost two-thirds. Not bad, considering that period included a terrible stock market crash in October, 1987 and a bad year for the markets in 1990.

But not all funds did anywhere near as well. Look what happened to someone who bought $1,000 worth of units in the Corporate Investors Stock Fund on January 2, 1987. Again, sales commissions are not taken into account.

Year	Return	Value of Investment At Year-End
1987	−22.8%	$772
1988	−12.9%	672
1989	10.0%	740
1990	−19.9%	592
1991	10.4%	654

In this case, the investor lost about one-third of his stake over the five years. Perhaps not surprisingly, the total amount of money invested in this fund fell from just under $40 million in 1987 to about $8 million in 1991.

You can make good money in equity funds but you can lose as well. That's why choosing the right fund is so important. A top-performing mutual fund will build your wealth; a poor one will diminish it.

AMERICAN EQUITY FUNDS

As the name implies, these funds specialize in U.S. stocks. Again, they can have spectacular advances in strong markets, sometimes increasing in value over fifty percent in a year. But they may be battered when the market collapses.

These funds have certain disadvantages. They aren't qualified for RRSPs or RRIFs except as foreign content and any dividends earned by the companies in their portfolio aren't eligible for the dividend tax credit.

But these negatives are offset by the broader range of investment possibilities available to the managers of these funds. The U.S. stock market is more diverse than the Canadian one, which is dominated by resource stocks. The manager of a U.S. equity fund therefore has greater latitude and more flexibility in deciding where to invest his money, along with access to some of the greatest companies in the world.

Long-term comparisons of Canadian and U.S. stock funds support the conclusion that American-based funds tend to do better for investors. The average ten-year annual rate of return for all Canadian stock funds to the end of March, 1992 was 10.4%, according to the *Globe and Mail Report on Business*. During the same period, American funds sold in Canada generated an average annual return of 13.4% — three percentage points more.

Those three percentage points translate into a huge difference in the value of your investment over time. If you'd invested $1,000 in the average Canadian stock fund in 1982, your units would have been worth $2,690 at the end of ten years. The same investment in the average U.S. stock fund would have been worth $3,517. Your profit would have been almost fifty percent more!

INTERNATIONAL EQUITY FUNDS

These invest in stocks from all over the world, in areas the managers see as having high growth potential. Best known is the Templeton Growth Fund, founded by the guru of investment fund managers, Sir John Templeton. Its track record is a model of consistency; only three times in the eighteen years from 1974 to 1991 did the fund's units lose money and in only one other year was the gain less than ten percent. Even though it's been around for a long time, the fund shows no sign of losing steam; it was up over thirty percent in 1991.

The Templeton Growth Fund invests globally. But some international funds specialize in a particular country or region of the world. Examples include Investors Japanese Growth Fund and the Global Strategy Europe Fund. During the 1970s and 1980s, Japanese funds made huge amounts of money for Canadians who chose to participate in that country's economic miracle. For example, $5,000 invested in the AGF Japan fund at the beginning of 1976 would have been worth almost $69,000 by the end of 1987. But then the Japanese stock market fell on hard times; over the next four years the value of your investment would actually have declined by more than $4,000, to just over $64,000. You'd still be way ahead on your original stake. But you would have done much better by redeeming your units in 1987 and moving your money elsewhere.

SECTOR FUNDS

These are funds which specialize in a particular type of stock — health care, energy, biotech, etc. Sector funds became immensely popular in the U.S. in the mid 1980s, with some mutual fund companies, such as the Boston-based Fidelity Group, offering dozens of them. They haven't caught on in a big way in Canada, mainly because our stock market simply isn't large or diverse enough to enable funds to concentrate on a single area. We do have a few, however, mainly in the resources area. Examples include the Cambridge Resource Fund and the Royal Trust Energy Fund. One non-resource sector fund is the AIC Advantage Fund, which specializes in mutual fund management companies.

The problem with Sector Funds is that they have a greater boom or bust propensity than the more broadly based stock funds. This is because if the particular industry in which the fund invests goes into recession, there's nothing to take up the slack. The record of Royal Trust's Energy Fund reflects this: down 18.1% in 1982 when the country was gripped by recession and the National Energy Policy; up 10.9% in 1985 after the Conservatives took office and there was renewed optimism in the oil patch; down 11.5% in 1986 as the international price of oil collapsed; up 37.5% in 1989 as the oil price recovered and optimism again appeared in the industry; down 12.4% in 1991 as the Gulf War failed to spur oil prices and an international oil glut became evident.

That kind of performance is typical of Canadian sector funds. They're really for more advanced investors who understand market timing and know when to move in and out.

PRECIOUS METALS FUNDS

This is a type of sector fund that specializes in such precious metals as gold, silver and platinum. These funds may hold the metal itself or shares in producing companies. As long as international inflation remains low, I don't see much prospect for big profits here during the nineties. They should be held only as a hedge against a major credit collapse, which would drive up the value of hard assets like gold. I don't see that as likely, but it's not completely outside the realm of possibility.

BALANCED FUNDS

These funds hold a variety of securities — stocks, bonds, debentures, mortgages, etc. The investment mix will vary depending on the fund managers and general economic conditions. When interest rates and inflation are rising, for instance, they may reduce their bond holdings and add equities. When stock markets appear overextended, they may take profits and build cash reserves. These funds are normally somewhat more stable than equity funds, but they are not immune to heavy losses in poor markets. They are most vulnerable during a period when interest rates are rising and stock markets are weak, a deadly combination that saddled many balanced funds with losses in 1990.

DIVIDEND FUNDS

These funds specialize in providing maximum dividend income by investing in high-yielding common stocks, such as BCE (Bell Canada) and preferred shares. The swings in these funds don't tend to be as volatile as in regular equity funds and the best ones have a respectable track record. They're especially good vehicles for people with large incomes who want to reduce their tax burden through the use of the dividend tax credit.

The best performer over the ten years ending March 31, 1992 was the Laurentian Viking Dividend Fund. Among other places, it's sold through Eaton's financial centres. Most of us don't normally think of a department store as a place to make investments, but this particular fund's track record may change a few minds. A $1,000 investment made at the beginning of 1982 would have grown to almost $3,400 over the decade to the end of 1991. And much of that profit would have received tax breaks through the dividend tax credit and the capital gains exemption.

MONEY MARKET FUNDS

These are a place to park your cash for a temporary period. They invest in high-grade, short-term notes, such as Treasury bills, banker's acceptances, certificates of deposit, etc. They are the safest type of mutual fund you can buy; no properly managed money market fund should ever lose money. As you might have guessed, the corollary of that is a comparatively low return on your investment most of the time. Your yield will be something close to current short-term interest rates — although, as with any other mutual fund, an astute management group can turn in an above-average performance.

There are times, however, when money market funds are one of the best places for your money. In 1990, for example, high interest rates and turbulent stock market conditions combined to make things rough for managers of fixed income and equity funds. Money market funds prospered, however, with some producing an annual return of over thirteen percent. With just about every other form of investment losing ground, that was an exceptional result, especially given the safety record of these funds.

There are many excellent money market funds in Canada and the differences between them are usually minuscule. I strongly recommend sticking with no load funds here. By nature, these are short-term investments. If you pay a commission to go in, the cost will significantly reduce your profit. Nor do you want to be in a position of having to pay a redemption fee when the time comes to move on.

One danger with money market funds is that you'll stay with them too long. Many people missed out on the great opportunities in the bond market in 1991 because they had done so well with money market funds the year before. They failed to realize that falling interest rates would reduce their money market returns while allowing bonds to score big gains. Don't fall into that trap.

REAL ESTATE FUNDS

These funds hold a variety of real estate related investments, including office buildings, apartments, shopping centres, medical buildings and retail stores. They have a tax advantage unavailable to other types of mutual funds in that rental income distributed to unit holders is sheltered by the use of capital cost allowance (depreciation on the buildings owned by the fund). For that reason, it's better to hold such funds outside an RRSP or RRIF.

Real estate funds are relatively new in Canada. They met their first real test in the recession of the early nineties, when property values fell in some parts of the country and many tenants went bankrupt, especially in the retail sector. As a result, a number of these funds declined in value; for the year ending March 31, 1992 the average gain of all Canadian real estate funds was only 2.7%.

The most serious problems were encountered by the Central Guaranty Property Fund. As unit values declined, many investors decided to sell. The fund was left without adequate cash to pay off unitholders and was forced to suspend redemptions for several months (the alternative would have been to sell some real estate at distressed prices, which would have compounded the problem). This sort of situation can create serious hardship if money is needed quickly. So if you want to invest in a real estate fund, do so only for the long term.

Those are the types of funds available to you. As you can see, they cover a broad range of investing options. Before we move on to consider how to use them most effectively as wealth builders, there are a few terms you need to understand.

FRONT END LOAD FUNDS

As I've already explained, a load fund is one that charges a sales commission. Front end load means the commission is paid at the time of purchase. For example, if you wanted to invest $1,000 in Trimark Canadian Fund, you would have to pay a maximum commission of nine percent. If that's indeed what you were charged, you'd end up with only $910 worth of fund units to your credit. The other $90 would go to pay the salesperson.

However, you'll rarely have to pay the maximum quoted fee. It's like buying an appliance; if you don't get a discounted price, it's probably because you haven't shopped around. Most mutual fund sales people will charge a lower rate, especially when business is slow. Even a small investor shouldn't be hit with a high commission. Set a maximum target of four percent; if you use a discount broker you may get the units for as little as two percent. Also, contact the fund manager directly. Some sell units direct to the public without any sales charge at all.

Not everyone will negotiate rates, however. Groups like Investors Syndicate and the life insurance companies use a set commission structure and won't deviate from it. So you have to know the policy of the company you're dealing with before you start to haggle.

BACK END LOAD FUNDS

These are funds that don't charge you anything when you buy, but may hit you for a fee when you cash in. They've become immensely popular in Canada in recent years, to the point that most fund companies offer some type of back end load option. The best known Canadian back end load fund is Industrial Horizon, which began the stampede away from traditional front end load funds when it was launched with a great fanfare of publicity early in 1987. It charges a 4.5% redemption fee if you cash in your units during the first year. That charge drops by half a percentage point a year, so that after you've held the fund for nine years the redemption fee vanishes. The idea, of course, is to discourage people from redeeming their fund units. If you plan to buy and hold for a long time, that's fine. But if you plan to move your money around, back end loads are an inhibiting factor.

You will also find that some back end load funds make up for the lack of an up-front sales commission in other ways. Some charge an annual "distribution fee." Other companies impose higher management charges on their back end load funds. So be careful when you buy; make sure you understand all the costs involved.

MANAGEMENT FUNDS

Every mutual fund has a management fee structure, which is usually expressed as a percentage of the total fund assets. So if a fund has $100 million in assets and charges a 1.25% annual management fee, the managers would receive $1.25 million a year for their services. This money comes out of the fund's holdings before they're valued and before distributions are made to investors. The money goes directly to the fund's managers, which means you may never be aware the money is being taken out. But those fees are cutting into your profits so you should consider them when you make your mutual fund investment decisions. Sometimes part of the management fee also pays for the expenses involved in running the fund, which can be quite high. But more often these expenses are an extra charge on fund assets.

Although all funds charge management fees, the range can vary considerably. For some money market funds, the cost can be less than one percent of asset value. At the other extreme, the managers of some international funds take more than three percent of the asset value for their fees and expenses.

Southam's *Mutual Fund Sourcebook* uses a measurement called a Management Expense Ratio which takes all fees and expenses into account and shows you how much it actually costs to run a fund. When you're dealing with hundreds of millions of dollars, these fees mean a big difference in the fund's profit and therefore to your return on investment. That's why it's a good idea to do some checking before you buy.

VOLATILITY

This is a term you must understand before you choose a mutual funds investment strategy. A fund's volatility is a measure of how likely it is to move sharply in response to what's happening in the stock or bond market. The most volatile equity funds will tend to score the best gains in a bull market and the worst losses when there's a market crash. A fund with a lower volatility rating will be more stable — the ups won't be as exciting; the downs won't be as gut-wrenching.

If you're investing for the long term, you'll probably want a fund with a low volatility rating. That means your chances of losing a substantial part of your investment will be lower in the event of a sudden decline in the market.

On the other hand, if you choose a mix-'em-and-move-'em fund strategy — one in which you keep switching from one fund to another in an attempt to take advantage of the hot areas — you'll probably want to look at more volatile funds. Just pray you can get out before the market goes down.

As you might expect from what you've read so far, the funds with the highest degree of volatility tend to be the sector funds, those that specialize in particular areas of the economy such as gold, energy and natural resources. The international equity funds also tend to rank high on the volatility list.

The least volatile funds are the money market funds, which are about as stable a mutual fund investment as you'll find. Mortgage funds, as again you might expect, are close behind.

RRSP/RRIF ELIGIBLE

The federal government has imposed some pretty tight restrictions on the type of investments you can hold in a Registered Retirement Savings Plan or a Registered Retirement Income Fund. If you're buying mutual funds for an RRSP or RRIF, you have to take this into account.

If a fund is listed in the paper as RRSP-eligible, that means you can hold it in your plan without restriction. Otherwise, you could have some problems.

Some mutual funds are not qualified for RRSPs and RRIFs under any circumstances. Your mutual fund sales person should advise you if this is the case with any fund you're considering. Others must be treated as foreign content. As such, they can't exceed sixteen percent of your plan's book value in 1992, rising to eighteen percent in 1993 and twenty percent in 1994. So if your RRSP has a book value of $10,000 in 1993, you can't hold more than $1,800 worth of foreign securities in it.

Typically, these funds will be those which specialize in foreign investments, such as U.S. or international equity funds. If you're considering any of them for your RRSP, see if they come under the foreign content rule. Not all will; in recent years some enterprising fund managers have created mutual funds which, while heavily invested in what appear to be foreign assets, are fully eligible for RRSPs and RRIFs. An example is the Royal Trust International Bond Fund, which invests in bonds denominated in foreign currencies issued by Canadian governments and corporations and the World Bank. Under tax rules, all such issues are considered Canadian content for RRSPs and RRIFs.

NET ASSET VALUE

This is the value of each unit of a fund at any given point in time. Sometimes you'll see two net asset values shown, one of which is labelled "fully diluted." That simply means that all potential shares have been taken into account, including those that might be issued at a future date as a result of people exercising outstanding warrants, allowing for purchase of shares at a specific price for a certain time.

OPEN END FUNDS

Most mutual funds are open end. This means they will continue to issue new units from their treasury. In other words, there's no limit on the number of units that can be held by the public. Holders of units in an open end fund can cash them in at any time for their current net asset value.

CLOSED END FUNDS

These funds sell a fixed number of shares at the outset; after that you can only buy them from another investor, normally on the stock exchange. So only a limited number of shares exist and that number never increases. Closed end funds haven't been very popular in recent years because they tend to trade at below their net asset value. That means you can buy them on the stock exchange for less than they're really worth, something that doesn't happen with open end funds. As a result, some closed end funds have converted to open end in order to improve the return to investors.

Those are all the basics you need to know for starters. Now that the homework is done, let's get on to the fun part — finding some mutual fund strategies that will make you money.

Building Wealth With Funds

The first mutual fund I ever bought was AGF Special Fund. Perhaps it would be more accurate to describe it as the first mutual fund I was ever sold; it's a time-worn cliché in the industry that most mutual funds are sold, not bought. Although that's no longer as true as it once was, it should be enough to put you on your guard when it comes to mutual fund purchases.

It was the late 1960s. My father had recently passed away, leaving me a small amount of money. Most of it went towards the down payment on our first home in west-end Ottawa. But there was a bit left over and I decided to try my hand at investing.

Mutual funds go through cycles of public favour and disfavour. In the past, these cycles tended to coincide with what was happening in the stock market, since most people equated mutual funds with stocks. So in the late sixties, funds were hot. Then the markets hit hard times in the early seventies and investors deserted them in droves. Funds only returned to public favour in the roaring bull market of the mid-1980s, when everyone wanted to hitch a ride on a stock market that seemed destined to go nowhere but up — until the crash of October, 1987 brought us all back to earth.

In recent years, Canadian investors have become more knowledgeable about mutual funds and how to use them. Although there is still a great deal of confusion and uncertainty where funds are concerned, more people now understand that investing in mutual funds doesn't automatically mean investing in the stock market. Money market funds, little understood a decade ago, have become immensely popular with Canadians, who pour billions of dollars into them every year. More people are showing interest in conservative mortgage fund investments and bond funds have also been attracting greater interest as a result of their strong performance in 1991. In short, we're learning more about mutual funds and, as we do, we're discovering more ways to profit from them.

When I made my first foray in mutual funds back in the sixties, it was a different story, however. Few people — including me — understood what mutual funds were or how they worked. Investment decisions were made on the basis of sales promotion, not knowledge.

I can't remember exactly how I became involved with AGF (which has since become one of the major players in the mutual funds industry in Canada). I do recall their sales literature: it was full of impressive-looking graphs and terrific performance claims. In that regard, nothing much has changed over the years.

I had $1,000 available, quite a bit of money at that time, especially since I was making less than $15,000 a year. With the terrific track record the AGF funds had already established, I figured I couldn't lose. And the salesman who sold me the fund did everything he could to reinforce that impression.

Sigh. If only I'd known then. . . . It didn't occur to me at the time that, with the stock market at one of its periodic highs, it might not be the best time to buy a volatile equity fund, which AGF Special was. Mistake number one. Nor did I worry about the nine percent front end load. The salesman assured me I'd earn it back within months and the record of the fund was so good his argument seemed perfectly logical. It never even occurred to me to negotiate the fee. Mistake number two.

You can guess what happened. The market went into a tailspin a few months later. I watched in horror as the value of my fund units dropped. I never considered taking advantage of the lower price and investing more. Mistake number three.

The value of my holdings fell by around twenty-five percent

(including the front end load) before bottoming out. I almost panicked and cashed in my units at one point, but I held on with the idea of waiting it out until I at least got my money back — a classic mistake of beginning investors. In this case, however, it worked. The units finally recovered their original value and, with great relief, I sold them in February, 1973. Mistake number four.

My net profit after holding the fund for about four years was $23.63. Not exactly a sterling performance.

But if I'd held on at that point, this would be a different story. I'd be telling you about my first great investing success, not giving you a terrible example of what *not* to do. If I had not drawn out the money but simply left it in the plan without investing any more, the units in AGF Special Fund which were worth just over $1,000 when I sold them in 1973 would have increased in value to over $16,000 by the end of 1991!

Mind you, it would have taken strong nerves to hang in. The fund dropped by 18.5% in 1974 and by another 3.9% in 1975 before turning around and recording a series of spectacular gains which included profits of around fifty percent in each of 1979 and 1980.

But that's the way mutual funds work. Either you pick a good one with solid management and stay in it over the long haul. Or you trade in and out of them like stocks, trying to catch the hot ones on the way up. More experienced investors can try that route; I don't recommend it if you're just starting out.

The 1980s saw a huge revival of interest in mutual funds, or *investment funds* as they're also called, and this has continued into the nineties. Sales of new units hit record levels both in Canada and the U.S. By early 1992, Canadian mutual funds had over $55 billion under management.

There were a number of reasons for this incredible growth, ranging from strong stock markets in the mid-eighties to the public's discovery of money market funds as an alternative to savings accounts in the early nineties. The growth of RRSPs and RRIFs created a huge pool of retirement money, an increasing portion of which has been directed into mutual funds. As well, investors became more demanding. They wanted a better return on their money than a savings account or a GIC would offer, especially when they read reports of big money being made in the markets. Perhaps the most important element of all in the fund industry revival was performance. Some mutual funds did remarkably well during the 1980s and early nineties, with growth rates that once would have seemed unattainable to the ordinary investor.

We've already looked at some of them, but here are a few more examples.

Bullock American Fund, which I strongly recommended to readers of my *MoneyLetter* columns, put on a dazzling display over the three-year period from 1989 to 1991. An aggressive fund, which specializes in companies on the leading edge of change, it seemed to do everything right during that time. A $1,000 investment (after commission) made January 2, 1989 almost tripled in value in just three years, to $2,852.

Investors Special Fund, which invests in smaller companies with above-average growth potential, didn't produce quite as good a result, but then neither did anyone else. A $1,000 investment in the fund made in early 1989 would have grown to over $1,650 by the end of 1991, a two-thirds increase in value in three years.

A more conservative $1,000 investment in the Altamira Income Fund (another of my *MoneyLetter* picks) made in early 1989 would have grown to over $1,500 in value by the end of 1991.

So there were ways to make money in mutual funds, even during a period that was extremely tough on many investors.

However, not all funds did well by a long shot.

Mackenzie Financial, one of the giants of the mutual fund industry, fell on hard times during this period. Their Industrial Equity Fund was especially hard hit; $1,000 invested at the start of 1989 was worth only $732 by the end of 1991. Even their flagship Industrial Horizon Fund, the largest mutual fund in Canada, produced very mediocre results. A $1,000 investment at the start of 1989 was worth only $1,051 at the end of 1991, a gain of barely five percent in three years.

That doesn't mean the Mackenzie funds won't come back. Even the best fund managers can go through a rough streak. But these results illustrate how important it is to pay attention to what your investments are doing and take appropriate action if required.

Beginning wealth builders need to adopt a patient and conservative approach towards mutual funds. Funds will have their ups and downs, that's inevitable. But if they're solid and well managed, they'll pay off in the long run for those who set up a regular investment program and stick to it through good times and bad.

This doesn't mean you should never withdraw your money or switch funds. If your particular fund is consistently underperforming the industry average for its group, you should certainly move to one that is doing better. But don't pull out just because of one bad year, especially if the whole fund industry is going through a difficult time. If anything, that's the time to increase your contributions, to take advantage of low unit prices.

Enough of the preliminaries. Now let's get into some specific strategies you can use.

CHOOSING A FUND

Your initial choice of a fund is critical. You want to get involved with a company with a good track record, strong prospects for the future, a good reporting program, first-rate customer service and strong management. How do you find the right one?

1. *Assess the economic climate.* If possible, avoid buying into a fund just when the type of security it invests in is about to go through a cyclical decline. For example, if interest rates appear to be on the way up, don't rush to buy a bond or mortgage fund; you may be able to pick it up six months from now at ten percent less. If the stock market appears to be peaking or is in a clear-cut bear phase, stay away from equity funds. Again, you'll probably be able to buy them more cheaply in six months.

This doesn't mean you should try to outguess the markets every step of the way. But for your initial fund purchase decision, at least give it a try.

If you're not sure just what's happening, start with a money market fund and watch for a while. You can switch into some other type of fund when you're more comfortable about where conditions are heading.

2. *Check out the fund's performance.* Spend a couple of hours with one of the business papers, reviewing their mutual fund performance tables. Look for a combination of good results and consistency. If a fund has shown a solid record of growth over the past ten years, the odds are in your favour that pattern will continue — although, of course, nothing is guaranteed. The tables will tell you how the fund has performed over the past three months, six months, one year, three years, five years and ten years. (The *Globe* also provides two-year results).

The performance record is important, but you have to look beyond it. Consider the trend pattern by looking closely at the annual compound rates of return. If they're highest over the ten-year period and declining as the time span gets shorter, it could be a warning that the fund isn't performing up to earlier standards. I prefer to see an improvement in the performance pattern.

For example, one of the top ten-year performers among Canadian equity funds as of March 31, 1992 was the Trans-Canada Equity Fund, with an average annual compound rate of return of 13.8%, according to the *Globe and Mail Report on Business.* Very impressive, at first glance — well above average for this category. But look more closely. The five-year average annual rate of return is only 0.85% — barely above average. The three-year figure shows an average annual *loss* of 1.7%. The two-year figure shows an average annual loss of 2.9%. The one-year result is a drop of 8.15%, during a period in which the average Canadian equity fund advanced by 2.9%.

All these numbers are sending a message. Trans-Canada Equity clearly was an excellent performer at one stage. But recent results have steadily deteriorated and the trend line is not showing any signs of improvement. In a situation like this, you should be wary of making a commitment. Better to search out a fund that has a more encouraging growth pattern.

One that might have caught your eye that same day was the National Trust Equity Fund. Its ten-year average annual compound rate of return was 11.4% — respectable, but well below that of Trans-Canada Equity. The five-year results showed a turnaround, however. The National Trust fund averaged 3.3% a year compared to Trans-Canada's less than 1% return. The National Trust result may not appear great, but it was well above the average of all Canadian equity funds over what was a difficult period for everyone. The three, two and one year results for National Trust Equity continued to show strong improvement. Even the six-month return to the end of March, 1992 was well above average. In short, this fund is on a positive trend line — the managers are clearly doing something right. That doesn't guarantee the pattern will continue into the future, of course. But as a beginning fund investor, you're much better off picking a horse that seems to be gathering speed than one which appears to be about to pull up lame.

3. *Be cautious about buying new funds.* The rapid growth of the mutual fund industry has led to the introduction of literally hundreds of new funds in recent years. Some offer exciting new investment opportunities, but don't be in too much of a hurry to buy in. I've seen many new funds fall flat on their faces and a lot of money lost as a result. Remember, there's no track record to guide you when you buy a new fund. You're investing mainly on faith; you have no clue as to the fund's performance. It could turn into a world-beater, but it could also be a dog.

When you buy a new fund, you're often buying hype. New funds are frequently heavily promoted to the investing public; the Industrial Horizon Fund and the Hume Funds were two prime examples during the eighties. As we've seen, Industrial Horizon still hasn't lived up to its promise while the Hume Funds are no longer in existence, having been swallowed by Altamira after a disappointing performance.

Of course, heavy promotion doesn't mean a fund won't succeed. But hype is a poor substitute for a proven performance record when it comes to making a selection.

There are some cases when buying a new fund can make sense, however. For example, when the investing public made it clear it preferred back end load funds over the traditional front end load fund, many companies launched back end load options. The Trimark Select funds were an example. The Trimark Select Canadian Fund was launched in late 1988. It was managed by the same people who ran the older Trimark Canadian Fund and employed the same investment disciplines. The only difference was in the commission structure and the management fees. In this case, anyone who preferred a back end load could comfortably buy into the Trimark Select Canadian Fund, even though it had no track record of its own at the time. It's interesting to note that since the fund was introduced, there has been little to choose between the Trimark Canadian Fund and the Trimark Select Canadian Fund in terms of results.

4. *Give preference to no load funds at the outset.* This doesn't mean you should automatically rule out all load funds. But if you're just starting out and don't have a lot of money to invest, load charges can be a drain on your assets, while potential redemption fees may lock you in to a bad decision. Until you have a better understanding of mutual fund investing, it's preferable to have the flexibility to switch to something else without cost.

There are many good no load funds around to get started with, especially in the money market and fixed income categories. However, finding a good no load equity fund is more difficult; most of the high-performing stock funds involve a commission either going in or coming out.

Once you've cut your teeth on no load funds, you can begin adding some of the better load funds to your portfolio. There's nothing wrong with paying a sales commission to invest, as long as you're getting value for money. Be sure to negotiate for a reasonable fee, but don't lose sight of reality. Recognize the level of service you're receiving from the sales person and be prepared to compensate him or her for it. If a financial planner has spent hours working with you to develop a comprehensive investing strategy, you should expect to pay a somewhat higher commission than if you bought the same fund through a no-frills discount broker. Just be sure it's reasonable in the circumstances.

5. *Choose a fund that meets your objectives.* If you're like most Canadians, your number one priority is safety of capital. If that's the case, start with funds that hold relatively safe investments —

you can check which ones they are in the previous chapter. Stay away from the more aggressive funds. They may have more growth potential but they're also higher risk.

You should also consider your financial requirements over the next few years. For instance, if you think you may have to cash in soon to buy a house or for some other need, a low volatility fund with minimum potential loss becomes an even greater priority. In these circumstances, a money market or mortgage fund would be a good option. With a high volatility fund you run the risk of being caught in a downturn just when you need the cash.

The portfolio-building strategy outlined for your RRSP in Chapter Fifteen is equally valid here, if you're just starting out. Begin modestly, protect your capital base and only add higher risk funds to the mix as you progress.

6. *Find out the costs.* There are all kinds of fees associated with mutual funds beyond any sales commissions you may pay. Some companies charge you to switch from one fund to another in the same family. Some funds have a one-time set-up or registration charge. Some funds levy a cancellation charge if you pull out. Some back end load funds will hit you for an annual "deferred sales charge" or "distribution fee," which can be as high as 0.6% of the total value of your assets (Bullock American does this). There can also be administration fees, withdrawal fees, certificate fees and more. Be sure to ask before you sign on. Also, read the simplified prospectus you'll receive before finalizing any fund purchase; you'll find a special section explaining all the costs in detail. If you don't understand any of them, ask questions.

7. *Inquire about the reporting system.* Most funds will send you a quarterly performance report, while a few report monthly. The more frequent your reports, the better. Check before investing.

8. *Find out about the fund's managers.* They should be solid people with a good reputation in the financial community. A knowledgeable broker or financial planner can help you here; he or she should know the investment philosophy of any major fund man-

ager. The management team is extremely important in your selection of a fund; they're the people you're trusting to look after your money. Some are very good, with proven track records. Others are mediocre or unknown quantities. Ask yourself which type you prefer.

MANAGING YOUR FUNDS

Making the initial fund selection is only the first step in using mutual funds to build wealth. From then on, it becomes a matter of skilful financial management if you're going to make the most of your investments. Here are some guidelines that may help as you move forward.

1. *Diversify.* Just as you wouldn't consider putting all your money into one stock, don't stay with just one fund. Introduce more funds into your portfolio as soon as possible, preferably of different types. This allows you to spread your risk — if you only hold equity funds and the stock market falls, you're going to take a beating. A basic mutual fund portfolio would include an equity fund, a bond or mortgage fund and a money market fund. This combination gives you stock market participation, interest play in the bond/mortgage fund and what amounts to a cash position in the money market fund. Once you have that structure in place, you can add extra funds if you wish.

Don't go to the other extreme and over-diversify, however. Building a large mutual fund collection is not a good strategy. The more funds you have, the more work that's involved in monitoring them. And the more difficult it is to maintain a regular investment program. Find a comfortable balance.

2. *Establish a fund investment plan and stick to it.* As we've already seen, regular contributions to a well-managed fund will pay off over the long haul. This technique is known as *dollar-cost averaging*. It simply means putting a specific amount of money, say $500, into a fund at regular intervals. In this way, the cost of your units is averaged out over the years to somewhere between the fund's high and low points. In a volatile fund, this will smooth the peaks and valleys of

price movements, because you'll be adding more units for your money when prices are low, fewer units when they're high.

3. *Never turn your back on your money.* Monitor the performance of your funds on a regular basis and compare the results to others in the same group. That's easy to do; just check the monthly reports in the financial papers. Pay particular attention to the average for the group, which you'll find at the end of each section. If you discover you're in a fund that continues to underperform the average for more than six consecutive quarters, it may be time to consider a switch to one with a stronger record.

4. *Avoid leveraging.* During the mid-eighties, when the stock markets were going crazy, borrowing to invest in mutual funds became the rage. I know of people who took out huge mortgages on their property to invest in mutual funds, with hopes of making a big killing.

The attraction was obvious. Not only were you in a position to increase your return on investment, you also got a tax break to make the prize even bigger.

So widespread did the practice become that in 1986 an estimated thirty percent of all mutual fund sales in Canada were paid for with borrowed cash. That amounted to something on the order of $800 million. The situation finally reached the point where the Ontario Securities Commission, the watchdog of the investment industry in the province, felt obliged to issue a warning about the dangers of borrowing money to invest in funds.

As I discussed in Chapter Twelve, there's nothing wrong with borrowing to invest. In fact, it can be a smart decision in the right circumstances. But timing is critical because, as we've seen, leveraging magnifies your risks. If you borrow to buy equity funds when the stock market is high and the economy then turns sour, you could end up in serious financial trouble. That's probably why Sir John Templeton, the dean of fund managers, offered these words of advice on a visit to Toronto in mid-1987, a time when the markets were high: "Do not have heavy debts against investments in mutual funds."

We've become more cautious about using leveraging in recent years. The stock market crash of 1987 and the recession of the early nineties have resulted in a more conservative approach to mutual fund investing. But when the stock market goes on another roll, which it inevitably will, we'll once again see people going over their head into debt in the hope of making a fast buck.

Beginning wealth builders should avoid leveraging, except in situations like a home mortgage. Save that strategy for a future time when you've acquired some investing experience and understand all the risks involved.

5. *Consider fund "families."* The explosion in the mutual fund industry in recent years has been accompanied by the creation of dozens of mutual fund "families." These consist of several mutual funds run by the same company. A small fund family may consist of only three or four funds; a large one, such as MacKenzie Financial, may have more than twenty.

Fund families offer investors an opportunity to switch their assets from one fund to another at minimal cost, perhaps even free. This is a valuable privilege, especially as you become more experienced in money management. There may be times, for example, when you want to protect profits made in equity funds by switching part or all of the assets into a money market fund. If you're operating within a fund family, this type of transfer can be arranged quickly and easily, usually with just a phone call. If you're dealing with a no load fund group, there will be no expense involved in this. If the group charges load fees, you'll have to negotiate a switching cost with your sales representative. However, it should never exceed two percent.

Fund switching is really a game for more seasoned investors who have a clear understanding of the business cycle and its effect on different types of assets. But even beginners may wish to do it occasionally when clear-cut situations present themselves. For example, if you've just made a lot of money on a bond fund because of falling interest rates, protecting some of your profits by switching a portion of your holdings into a money market fund or an equity fund makes excellent sense.

Mutual funds are a good way to start an investment portfolio and you should seriously consider them when you feel the time is right, both inside and outside an RRSP. Just remember, they're like any other investment. You have to select them carefully, monitor them regularly and treat them as long-term holdings. If you follow the strategies I've outlined and do your homework carefully, mutual funds should add considerably to your wealth over time.

CHAPTER 19

Who's Afraid of the Stock Market?

Don't gamble. Take all your savings and buy some
good stock and hold it till it goes up, then sell it. If it
don't go up, don't buy it.
— Will Rogers, 1924

It's hardly news that Canadians are ultra-conservative when it comes to money. Traditionally, we simply haven't been risk-takers. We've always had a fascination for people who are, from the empire-building era of the Hudson's Bay Company to the international deal-making of Conrad Black. But few of us are willing to assume that degree of risk with our own financial resources. If it came down to a hard choice, I suspect a majority of Canadians would rather bury their money in the back yard than put it into a risky investment, even though that investment might have significant growth potential.

This element in our national psyche probably explains why, until very recently, only about half as many Canadians as Americans owned stocks, on a proportionate basis. As recently as the early eighties, a study carried out by the Toronto Stock Exchange revealed that less than fifteen percent of Canadians owned stock in one form or another. The TSE called that "worrisome" and said that something had to be done to encourage people to overcome their "undue concern with risk, and their lack of understanding about stock investment."

Well, much has happened in the decade since and many more Canadians now own stocks, directly or indirectly. We went through a roaring bull market in the mid-eighties, which attracted a lot of people into the market for the first time. Mutual funds, many of which invest in stocks, became popular, bringing more Canadians into the market via that route. The federal government encouraged more people to invest in stocks by implementing a lifetime $100,000 capital gains exemption. In the 1992 budget, Finance Minister Don Mazankowski sharpened the focus of that exemption by decreeing that real estate gains would no longer be covered — in effect, telling Canadians to put more money into stocks if they wanted to get the tax break.

Several provincial governments also introduced tax advantages for the purchase of shares in companies located within their boundaries, with Quebec's program the most ambitious. It turned out to be a great success at the outset but ran into serious problems when a combination of weak markets and poor economic conditions caused a number of companies which had issued shares under the scheme to experience difficulties. Many investors ended up losing money, which only goes to prove that you should never make an investment decision purely on the basis of a tax break.

The sharp drop in interest rates in 1991 further contributed to the flow of more money into the stock market, either directly or through mutual funds. When a GIC paying twelve percent matures and you're offered only eight or nine percent to renew, it encourages you to look for other options. Many people found them in stocks with high dividend yields. Because of the effect of the dividend tax credit, a preferred share yielding 7.5% will actually leave more in your pocket, after tax, than a GIC paying 9.5%. As interest rates declined, more Canadians discovered this fact and shifted their money accordingly.

A solid stock market performance in 1991 further encouraged this trend. Despite the wretched state of the economy, the TSE 300 Total Returns Index actually gained twelve percent during the year. Part of the reason was anticipation by investors of better times ahead once the recession ended. But there were also some good profits to be made in certain sectors.

Interest-sensitive stocks — banks and utilities — tend to do well in a climate of falling rates. In the case of the banks, it's because declining rates relieve the pressure on borrowers, thereby diminishing the risk of loan defaults. Lower rates also attract more business for the banks by encouraging people to borrow to finance homes, cars, furniture and appliances. Utilities benefit from declining rates because they normally carry heavy debt loads, the result of the large capital expenditures required to provide telephone, power, gas distribution and similar services. As rates decline, the burden of servicing their debt is also reduced.

As a result, 1991 saw significant gains in the price of many of these types of issues. For example, Bell Canada Enterprises, which is normally about as far from a volatile stock as you'll find, opened 1991 trading at $39.50. By year end, the price had soared to $47.63 — a gain of 20.6%. With the $2.60 annual dividend taken into account, anyone who held the stock through the year enjoyed a profit of 27.2%. Not bad for a blue chip holding in a rough year for investors.

Or consider the Bank of Montreal. It began 1991 trading at $29.13. By the end of the year, it had surged to $43.75 — a gain of 50.2%. With dividends taken into account, the total return to a Bank of Montreal shareholder in 1991 was 57.8%!

These are both conservative companies, the kind most Canadians would naturally gravitate towards. When investors realized what was happening, more money began to flow into the markets.

Many investment experts expect the mid-nineties will be a new golden age for stocks, similar to the explosion in prices we saw in the mid-eighties. There are a number of reasons behind these predictions. The recession of 1990-92 forced companies to cut out deadwood and improve productivity, thus placing themselves in a stronger position for the years ahead. Inflation is expected to be moderate during the nineties, a good sign for the economy. Low inflation usually means low interest rates, which encourages people to spend. A lower Canadian dollar makes Canadian goods more competitive on international markets — a fact which was reflected in stronger exports in early 1992.

The optimists expect our international trade will continue to strengthen, as new agreements are forged. Meanwhile, the end of the Cold War will switch the world focus to more productive activities than weapons building.

Whether all this will come to pass, only time will tell. If it does, however, look for another rush of first-time buyers into the stock market, as greed overwhelms our deep-seated fears of risk-taking.

Unfortunately, many of these novice stock buyers probably shouldn't be in the market at all. They'll be attracted by tax breaks and dreams of a quick buck, but they'll know virtually nothing about what they're getting into. As Andrew Sarlos, one of Bay Street's most canny money managers, observed at the height of the last great bull market in the mid-eighties: "Many of these people probably don't even know that stocks can go down. They think up is the only direction that exists."

Well, stocks can go down — sometimes a lot. Sure, there are great profits to be made. But there is also large loss potential for the naive or the unlucky.

Don't interpret this as a suggestion that stocks are to be avoided at all costs. That's not the case. It's more a matter of priorities. There are other places where you should direct your money first. Then, when the time does come to venture into the stock market, you should do so cautiously and with a clear understanding of what you're getting into.

Let's pause for a moment here and review the priorities a good wealth builder should have in place before thinking about stocks.

Number one is the family home — acquiring one and paying down the mortgage.

Number two is an RRSP, because the tax breaks make this a unique wealth building vehicle.

Number three is some interest-bearing investments, like savings certificates or GICs. These enable you to gain an initial feel for money management without putting your capital at undue risk.

Number four is mutual funds. You're now adding an increased element of risk to your assets, in the hope of generating better returns. But your risk level is still relatively low, especially if you use the plan I outlined to build a mutual funds portfolio.

Number five would be bonds, mainly because I think they are easier for most people to understand and be successful with than stocks. As I said in Chapter Ten, the key to profitable bond investing is getting the interest rate trends right. There are many more variables when it comes to investing in stocks.

Let me be clear here. I'm not suggesting you have to complete each stage before you move on to the next. It isn't a case of paying off the family home before you set up an RRSP. You should be gradually developing a range of assets as you go.

Rather, the above list should be used as a guideline on how to progressively add different assets to your holdings. Which brings me back to stocks.

I would not suggest the beginning wealth builder get involved with the stock market directly until he or she has had some experience with more basic types of investments. I would especially recommend holding one or more equity-based mutual funds for a period of time. This can be an excellent way to learn about the stock market, especially if the fund has a good reporting system. The Altamira Funds are among the best in this regard; they publish a periodic newsletter which discusses the buy and sell decisions made by the fund managers and the rationale behind them, and analyzes the appropriate investment strategies for the future. This kind of information will provide you with valuable insights into how the professionals make investment decisions. You have to take the time to read and digest it, however; too often mutual fund investors simply throw away their reports unread. What a waste of potentially valuable information!

Your reports will also provide a summary of the fund's holdings, usually as of the end of the last quarter. This gives you an opportunity to see how professional money managers deal with diversification by spreading their risk among a variety of stocks in various market sectors. You'll also receive information on how much of the fund's holdings are in cash. Watch that percentage closely; the higher it is, the more nervous the fund managers are about general market conditions — and the more nervous you should be too, if you're thinking of striking out on your own.

As you approach the point where you feel you may want to go into the stock market, pay even closer attention to the financial press. Read the investments sections to see what brokers are recommending. Pick some of the stocks that sound pretty good and start developing your own phantom portfolio. Make notes on what the recommendation predicted would happen to the stock's price and see which ones pan out over a period of time.

The phantom portfolio stage is extremely important for the first-time stock market investor. Make your selections carefully; pretend you're really putting your money at risk. Track the performance of your stocks at least weekly. Make sales when you think it's appropriate and note the gains or losses. Add new stocks when it appears a buying opportunity has presented itself.

Judge the results realistically. If you're consistently losing money in your phantom portfolio, analyze why. Is it because the entire market is down? If so, are your stocks doing better or worse than the index average? If you're doing better, be encouraged — your stock picking instincts are good. It's just a question of honing your market timing instincts.

As you're monitoring your phantom portfolio, tune into what's happening to the markets generally, especially the Toronto Stock Exchange and the New York Stock Exchange. Read the daily reports in the financial section of your newspaper on what the indexes are doing. Find out whether the market is in a bull (advancing) or bear (declining) phase. Develop a sense of what the financial professionals are saying and thinking.

You can further develop your stock market acumen by becoming a member of an organization. The Canadian Shareowners Association, which has its headquarters in Windsor, Ontario, is especially recommended. It's a non-profit group which promotes the fundamentals of good stock selection through a variety of educational materials and a monthly magazine. You can contact them at 1090 University Avenue West, Windsor, Ontario N9A 5S4. Their phone number is (519) 252-9965.

Once you've learned enough to feel comfortable about investing real money, begin by dipping your toe in the water. But don't rush; wait for the right moment.

There is, of course, no perfect time to buy stocks. But some periods offer better prospects for gains than others. Ironically, it's not always the time when euphoria is sweeping the market that the best profits can be made. In fact, undue optimism may be the harbinger of disaster, as the crashes of 1929 and 1987 demonstrated. Long-time stock market watchers know that times when doom and gloom is everywhere can be the most rewarding of all. Everyone has heard stories of how fortunes were made by those with the courage and the foresight to buy stocks like General Motors when they were at their low point during the Great Depression. But there are more recent examples of cashing in on a doomsday scenario.

In mid-1982, for instance, there was serious concern North America was tumbling into another Depression. The economy was in a tailspin. Long-established companies were closing down. Those firms that survived were chopping staff right and left in an effort to reduce overheads. Middle-class families who had never before faced serious financial difficulties suddenly found themselves in real trouble as salaries were frozen and second jobs lost. In a phrase, things were in a helluva mess.

The stock market responded accordingly. Prices of top-quality shares were way down. There was fear they would fall even lower, perhaps to levels seen in the thirties.

That's when smart investors bought. They picked up shares of Torstar Corporation, publishers of the Toronto Star, in the $8 to $10 range. Five years later, in mid-1987, they were trading at around $35. They bought Lac Minerals, the big gold producer, for less than $5 a share. By mid-1987, those shares were selling for over $40. Imperial Oil stock could be had for a bargain price of between $20 and $25 a share. Five years later it was worth over $75.

Obviously, the first-time investor is going to have difficulty deciding exactly when to jump in. The temptation is to enter the market when enthusiasm is high. You tend to get swept away in the psychology of the moment — the madness of crowds can cast a spell on all of us.

But you must exercise patience. Your first stock purchase is a critical one in the wealth building process. If you get badly burned, it may turn you off the market for years, perhaps forever. It's happened to others. If that should occur, you'd be cutting yourself off from one of the most exciting, and most lucrative, wealth building techniques around. That's why it's so important to give yourself every opportunity for success the first time out.

Here are some thoughts that may help you in the initial timing decision.

1. Be patient. Wait for the right moment to make a purchase. Don't feel that if you don't buy now the stock will double over-night; it rarely does.

2. The best possible time to enter the market is after a lengthy downturn, when indexes are showing signs of starting to move up and the economy seems to have bottomed out.

3. Don't enter when stocks are at an all-time high. They may move higher, sure. But your risk potential is much greater in that situation.

When you do decide to go in, move cautiously. You will have put some money aside for stock investments at that stage; don't invest it all at once. Get a feel for what you're doing. Talk things over with your broker (more on that in the next chapter). Explain your strategy and get him or her on-side.

I strongly suggest that you begin by assembling a modest portfolio of top-quality blue chip stocks. There'll be a temptation not to go this route, for a couple of reasons. First, blue chip stocks tend to be expensive. Beginning stock investors often feel more comfortable with $5 stocks than with $50 ones. There's the nagging feeling that it's easier for a $5 stock to double than for the $50 stock to reach $100. Well, it isn't so. It's the value and performance of the company that's important. And when you buy a blue chip stock with a proven track record, that's what you're getting.

You may also be drawn away from the blue chips by the stories of huge profits made from penny mining stocks on the Vancouver Exchange. It's true, that does happen occasionally. In fact, I have a close friend who was fortunate enough to make an investment of about $12,000 in a gold mine called Stikine on Vancouver Island and then watched in amazement as his shares skyrocketed to a value of more than $240,000! But for every gold stock that strikes it rich, a hundred others will fail. There are times when playing the penny stocks can be fun and maybe even profitable. But not when you're just starting out.

Beginning stock market investors are also frequently attracted to "concept" stocks — those based on a great idea, usually in some leading edge technological area, such as satellite broadcasting or virtual reality. The problem with concept stocks is that all they have going for them is an idea — no product, no sales, no profits. I lost more than my share of money on these things before I woke up to the fact they were just penny mines in another form, all dream and no substance.

Another reason I favour blue chip stocks is that they usually pay dividends. These are cash distributions made to shareholders out of company profits and they can be an important part of the financial return on your stock market investments. I like dividend-paying stocks because they provide two ways to make a profit, rather than just one. If a stock does not pay a dividend — and many don't — the only way you can make any money is through a capital gain, if the share price goes up. I prefer to improve the odds with dividends.

But blue chips, you may be muttering as you read all this. Boring.

Think so? Well, you saw what happened to the shares of BCE and Bank of Montreal in 1991. Stocks don't come much bluer than that. Here are a few more examples.

Bombardier. This Quebec-based company has become one of the world's leading manufacturers of a wide range of transportation vehicles. In 1991, Bombardier's class B common stock gained 85.4% in value, from $15.38 to $28.50.

Magna. One of the world's premier suppliers of auto parts, the company's class A stock zoomed from $2.75 at the start of 1991 to close the year at $19.50. It didn't stop there; by May, 1992 it was trading at more than $32!

Northern Telecom. The undisputed leader of Canada's high-tech industries, it began 1991 at $32.50; ended at $52 — a sixty percent gain.

Seagrams. The big distiller moved from $102 to $131.50 a share in 1991, a 28.9% gain. As if that weren't enough, the stock also paid a $2 per share dividend.

The point is there's plenty of action in blue chip stocks — and a lot of money to be made. So don't be lured by the siren call of cheap shares or highly-touted juniors. Stay with the big boys, at least at the start. If you time your market entry properly, you'll reduce your chance of a major loss first time out — and you may find yourself with a tidy profit faster than you expect.

Don't put all your money into a single stock. If you haven't got enough cash to buy shares in, say, four or five companies, hold off until you do. No mutual fund manager would dream of putting all his or her assets into one stock, no matter how good its prospects. Too risky. You're in the same position. Regardless of how good a stock may appear to be, don't let everything ride on it.

Spread your initial stock selections across several market sectors. Don't load up in one area, such as oil or gold. We've already discussed the high volatility rate of sector mutual funds, those which concentrate in a particular segment of the economy. Don't create a similar situation for yourself in your stock selections.

Here's an example of how you might go about starting a stock portfolio. Please note I'm *not*, in any way, recommending you purchase the particular stocks mentioned. I'm only using them as examples of companies in different sectors.

For starters, decide which sectors of the economy you'd like to be involved with financially. There's a broad range of choices: the forest industry, mining, real estate, oil and gas, banks, steel, breweries, high technology companies, financial services, management companies, communications firms, pipelines — the list goes on and on. The Toronto Stock Exchange has fifty-two indexes and subindexes which allow you to track the current performance in each of the main sectors; the financial section of your newspaper should carry them.

Some sectors do better than others at certain stages in the business cycle. We've seen how interest-sensitive stocks perform well in a recessionary environment characterized by falling rates. Natural resource stocks, on the other hand, tend to perform best in the late phases of an economic boom. Stocks of consumer products firms will do best in the early stages of an economic recovery, when consumer confidence is strengthening. If you have a good broker, he or she should be able to advise you on which sectors appear to offer the best prospects at the time you're ready to enter the market.

Let's say, for example, that after reviewing the situation you decide you want to begin with investments in the management, communications, integrated oils and bank sectors. Your next step is to review the leading companies in those areas to see which appear to combine the best dividend yield with the greatest growth potential. Try to narrow the selection down to three in each group.

In the management sector, you might find that your choice comes down to Brascan, Power Corporation and Canadian Pacific. Among the integrated oils, Imperial, Shell and Petro-Canada may look like the best bets. In the communications sector, Maclean-Hunter, Thomson Newspapers and CHUM Ltd. may seem attractive. Among the banks, you may settle on Toronto-Dominion, Bank of Montreal and CIBC as the leading candidates.

Now comes the toughest part of all. Choosing which stocks to actually buy.

Ask your broker to supply you with research reports on the companies in the sectors you've chosen which his firm is recommending. Read them over carefully — brokerage research reports are written in a language all their own; if they appear to be damning a stock with faint praise ("appears to have overcome recent difficulties"; "may have long-term profit potential"), avoid it.

Look for such things as a steady improvement in revenue and net income (profit) in recent years. See what's happening to the earnings per share (EPS); that will tell you how well the company is doing in relation to the total number of shares outstanding. Check the price/earnings ratio (the ratio between the price of the stock and the earnings per share) and see how it compares with competitive companies. In general, a low price/earnings ratio makes a stock more attractive. As long as the company is sound, a low p/e ratio suggests the stock price is not overvalued in comparison to similar firms.

See what the brokerage house has to say about dividend payouts.

A stock with a good dividend and a solid payment history will tend to hold up better in a market downturn.

Finally, see how strong the brokerage house is in its buy recommendation. Is the report giving the stock lukewarm approval or is the tone one of genuine enthusiasm?

Also, read the financial press carefully for any references to the companies you've selected. Is there a new scare on loan defaults at the banks because a major developer has run into financial trouble — as happened to Olympia and York in early 1992? If so, see which banks could be most affected and take that into account when you make your decision. Watch for new earnings reports on the firms in which you're interested. See if anything unusual is happening.

While you're doing all this, track the prices of the candidate stocks in the paper and see how they're performing. If there's any sign of weakness, ask your broker if there's any particular reason for it. It may be just a case of profit-taking, in which case there's a buying opportunity for you.

Once you've done your homework, start buying. But remember, do so gradually. You don't have to place all your orders in the same day. You may spread your initial purchases over a month — perhaps even longer if you're nervous about the general state of the market. In the meantime, keep a close watch on what's happening to the companies you selected for purchase. A new report or a sudden price run-up may affect your decision. If so, don't be afraid to change course and switch to your second choice.

Finally, a word about selling. Some people never sell. They consider themselves to be in the market for the long haul, through good times and bad. So they buy a stock and hang on to it through its peaks and valleys.

This kind of long-range investing approach is perfectly valid and can be very profitable — if you buy and hold the right kind of stocks. However, many stocks simply don't lend themselves to the sit-back-and-watch-it-grow approach. Remember the stocks I told you about earlier in this chapter, the ones that made such terrific gains between 1982 and 1987? Well, by early 1992 every one of them was trading well below the mid-1987 price. Torstar was in the $22 range, its profits having been hard hit by the recession. Lac

Minerals could be had for $7 and change, reflecting the fall in the price of gold and the loss of one of the company's major mines in a legal action. Imperial Oil was trading at around $40, thanks to low international oil prices and an oversupply situation. In other words, if you'd continued to hold on to these stocks, you would have lost most of the profits you made between 1982 and 1987. Far better to cash in and move on to new opportunities

The reality is that no stock, no matter how solid and blue chip, is going to rise forever, at least not in a straight line. When the market falls, as it inevitably does, so will the bluest of the blue chip stocks. Good stocks will eventually recover. But why hang around for the ups and downs when you could be making more money somewhere else? Furthermore, I don't like going through the gut-wrenching process of watching my profits get wiped out and having to wait for months, perhaps years, to rebuild them. There are better ways.

By all means, take a long term view when you buy your first stocks. Approach the investment with the idea it's something you would be prepared to hold for several years. That's one way to avoid taking a get-rich-quick approach to the market, which has been the downfall of many investors before you. But even as you buy your first shares, be aware that somewhere down the road, you'll sell them — just like you'll eventually sell your home.

Initially, I was reluctant to sell any stocks. If they went down, I wanted to hold on until I at least recovered my money. If they went up, I was afraid that if I sold they'd rise still more. But as I became more knowledgeable about investing, I found myself selling more frequently. And sooner rather than later. I've taken to heart a comment from Bernard Baruch: "Repeatedly in my market operations I have sold a stock when it is rising — and that has been one reason why I held on to my fortune." Now, I rarely hold a stock for more than two years. I take my profits (or my losses) and move on.

In doing so, I've missed some opportunities. Stocks that I've sold for a fifty percent profit would have produced a hundred percent return if I hadn't let them go. I once sold a stock after tripling my money in less than a year, only to see it triple again in value. But I've also had situations where I sold a stock for a big gain and then watched as it fell back to my original purchase price — or even below.

Laidlaw is one example. Many Canadians made a lot of money on this trucking/waste management/school bus company during the 1980s. I was one of them. I started buying shares in Laidlaw in 1985 at $12 a share. They performed well and I continued to add to my holdings at various prices until 1988. The stock split several times and continued to gain in value through the late eighties. When I had almost tripled my original stake, I decided to take some profits and began to sell. I disposed of my final Laidlaw holdings in 1989, at $22.25 a share (at that point I held 4.5 shares for every share I had purchased in 1985, because of stock splits. So each original share was now worth over $100). The stock had done remarkably well, but there were some straws in the wind that made me uncomfortable about the future. The stock went up after I sold (it always happens that way!), hitting a record high of $28.38 in June, 1990. But Michael DeGroote, the driving force behind Laidlaw's exceptional growth, had by now sold control of the company to Canadian Pacific Ltd., and shortly thereafter severed his relationship with the firm. That news did not sit well with shareholders. Neither did subsequent events which saw earnings results below expectations, problems with acquisitions, some bad press and news of serious contamination at one of the company's dumping sites in Quebec. By April, 1992, this one-time high-flyer was trading for less than $12 a share, having actually fallen to below $9 at one point. In retrospect, I got out at just about the right time.

Remember: nobody ever went broke taking a profit. Once you've developed a feeling for the market, be prepared to sell at an appropriate time. When you buy a stock, set a profit target for it. When it reaches that point, collect your earnings happily and don't worry about leaving some money on the table for the next person who comes along.

And, although you don't want to think about losing money, you should also set a loss target. If the stock drops to that level, dump it, unless there's some very strong reason to hold on. I admit, locking in a loss is the hardest decision a wealth builder faces. You always cling to the hope it might come back. Don't fall into that trap.

I speak from experience here. Let me tell you my classic story about holding a stock too long.

The company was called Nu-West. It was an aggressive, western-based real estate firm that rose to prominence in the Alberta economic boom of the 1970s. I bought 1,000 shares in the late seventies at about $8, on the recommendation of a broker friend.

The stock performed wonderfully well. Within a year it was trading at over $13 and I was delighted. Prospects for the company still looked great. But, applying my rule of taking profits when the target is met, I decided to sell. Because I had 1,000 shares, though, I compromised. I only sold half. I've been kicking myself ever since!

Alberta's economic miracle came to a sudden end. Nu-West, which had borrowed heavily to finance its growth, found itself in deep trouble. The stock began to tumble. But did I sell? No way. I stupidly sat and watched as it dropped through $10, then $8, then $6.

How could you be so dumb, you ask? Good question. You find yourself applying different rationalizations along the way. When it fell to $10, I dismissed it as a temporary price correction. The company was going through a tough period. But Alberta and Nu-West would come back. Anyway, I had the profit from the initial 500 shares; I could afford to wait out the downturn.

When the stock hit my original purchase price of $8, I clearly should have dumped it. That would have protected my profit from the 500 shares already sold. But I held, still expecting a rebound.

By the time the stock was down in the $4 range, I knew I'd made a bad mistake. But at that point I figured it couldn't drop much lower. All the downside potential was gone. Hah!

Nu-West tumbled to a quarter a share. That's right, 25¢! And would you believe I still had those lousy 500 shares? Looking back on it, I wonder where my mind was at that point in time.

The final indignity came when the company reorganized, changed its name to N-W Group and moved to the States. Stockholders voted to recall outstanding shares and replace them with new ones. Those who didn't have enough shares to meet the minimum requirement for this share amalgamation would receive a cash payment instead. I was in that category. My cash payment amounted to less than $200. That was all I received for shares which had originally been purchased for $4,000 plus commission and which I could have sold at one point for $6,500. The only good part about it was that the debacle was finally over.

About the only positive thing in this whole experience is that it gave me a genuine, true-life horror story to tell all you emerging wealth builders.

So let me say it again. If your stock drops to your loss target — which should probably be set at twenty-five to thirty percent below your purchase price — get out unless you have some overwhelming reason not to. If it drops forty percent, sell, regardless of your good reasons. Someone knows something you don't. Whatever you do, don't ride the stock down and watch your losses mount. Salvage what you can and live to fight another day.

The stock market is like anything else in life — the more you know about it, the less afraid of it you'll be. Stocks are tricky and potentially dangerous investments. But they can also be immensely rewarding — if you approach them carefully and with respect.

CHAPTER 20

Your Broker is Your Buddy — Sometimes

A friend in the market is better than money in the chest.
— Thomas Fuller, 1732

Since I ended the previous chapter with a horror story, let me begin this one with another.

During the winter of 1985, I was keeping a close watch on the stock of a small company based in London, Ontario. The name of the firm was Cableshare and it had developed what appeared to be a revolutionary new method of selling merchandise. It was a shop at home technique called Touch 'n Shop, and I had been knocked out when I went to a demonstration of the technology.

The system was based on interactive video discs. It operated by using cable TV and a touch tone phone. People who were hooked up to it could browse through thousands of items of merchandise, watch demonstrations, do price comparisons among several stores and place orders for home delivery.

Some of the applications were highly innovative. You could plan a vacation to Bermuda by calling up videos of various hotels on the island, with details of their available services and price ranges. If you wanted to look for a new home, Touch 'n Shop could select all the current listings in your price range within your preferred area and bring photos, interior and exterior, up on your screen. You could select those that really interested you for a visit and eliminate the rest. The system even contained a mortgage payment calculator which would work out the carrying costs of any house on the basis of the down payment you planned to make.

Like I said, knockout stuff!

Moreover, Cableshare was thirty-seven percent owned by J.C. Penney, the huge U.S. retailing giant. Penney was handling the marketing of this exciting technology, which meant it had an excellent chance of making big inroads in the States.

Everything was still in the drawing board stage, of course. Apart from some tests, there was no proven commercial application of the technology. The company had no sales to speak of, no profits, not even a real product yet. There were no guarantees that people were about to change long-established buying patterns, which they'd have to do if the Cableshare idea was to fly in the marketplace. In short, a classic concept stock — but what a concept!

So the stock was a pure speculation. But I thought it was a pretty good one.

I felt it was priced a bit too high, however, so I watched it over a couple of months. I'd made up my mind that if it went below $6 a share, I'd buy.

On March 5, 1986, that happened. The stock slipped to $5.75. I phoned my broker. The nightmare began.

My broker was out of town. But he had an assistant, a young lady with a pleasant-sounding voice. He'd told me previously that any time he wasn't available I could safely place my orders with her.

So I did. I asked for a thousand shares of Cableshare, at a price of $5.75 or better. She acknowledged my order verbally and our conversation ended.

Now I should explain something at this point. I'd dealt with this particular broker for several years prior to this incident.

We had developed a rather casual relationship; he never phoned me back on an order unless there was a problem. If I didn't hear from him, I automatically assumed all was well and a few days later a confirmation of the trade arrived in the mail. Sloppy. I don't do it any more. You're about to find out why.

For the next couple of days, I checked Cableshare prices in my morning scan of the TSE listings. It continued trading at $5.75 on fairly large volume. So it never occurred to me there may have been some difficulty filling my order. I assumed I owned a thousand shares of the company.

Then the stock started to move. It quickly rose to over $7. In the meantime, I noticed I hadn't received my confirmation slip. So I called. And that's when it all hit the fan.

The assistant told me she'd only put in a "day" order. That's a stock order that automatically expires at the end of the trading day, unless it's renewed. I'd never used day orders, only what are called open orders, which means they're valid until filled or cancelled. My broker knew that. The subject had never come up in my brief conversation with the assistant so it never occurred to me that she might do otherwise.

But she did. At the end of that particular day, the order expired automatically with only a hundred shares purchased.

I was livid. I don't think I've ever been so angry in my life. The stock was now trading at $7.50, which meant I'd been done out of a profit of almost $1,600 by the error. Bad enough, certainly. But there's more.

When my broker got back, he tried to placate me. He said the stock was still a good buy at $7.50 and I should pick up the other nine hundred shares at that price. But after having carefully watched the stock and waiting for just the right moment to buy, I was too angry to do that. No way was I going to pay out $1,600 when I should have had the shares at $5.75.

Well, Cableshare really started to move. When it reached $9 in about a month, I decided to dump my hundred shares and take a fifty percent profit. The fact was, I was so disgusted by the whole affair I just wanted it out of my portfolio.

That upward move turned out to be just the beginning. By early June — just three months after I had placed my buy order — the stock was trading at over $60 a share! That's right, $60. If my order had gone through as I intended and I'd held on during the rise, my original investment would have been worth over $60,000 at that point — a ten-fold return.

I still have bad dreams about it.

This is a rather lengthy story, but it's an important one because it contains several lessons about dealing with brokers.

Lesson one: Just because you've been dealing with a broker for a period of time, don't take anything for granted.

Lesson two: Whenever you place an order, make sure all the details are clear. And if you intend it to be an open order, say so.

Lesson three: Ask your broker to call you back with verbal confirmation that a transaction has been completed. If you haven't heard from your broker by the end of the day, you place the call.

Lesson four: Don't let your emotions get in the way of a good investment decision. My broker had tried to persuade me to buy more Cableshare at the higher price but I'd been so angry I refused to listen. That ended up costing me far more than the original botched order.

A stockbroker can be worth his or her weight in gold to you. Good brokers provide sound advice on when to buy and sell and what stocks are appropriate for you at any given point in time. They can send you research reports prepared by the company's analysts. They can advise you of hot new issues that are about to hit the market and make sure you get some. They can tell you about good tax shelter offerings — and bad ones. In short, a good broker can make you a lot of money — just as a bad broker can lose you a lot of money through poor advice, ignorance or account churning. (Churning is a commission-generating technique practiced by unscrupulous brokers. It involves encouraging clients to buy and sell more often than necessary. Since each transaction generates a commission, the more activity there is in an account, the bigger the pay-off for the broker.)

Most important, a good broker will take a long-range view. He or she will realize that your greatest value is as a satisfied client, whose business will grow as your personal wealth increases.

Obviously, the trick is to find yourself a good broker. And believe me, it's not easy. It took me years.

There are five key points to look for when it comes time to select a broker. I call them the Five Ps: Personality, Philosophy, Patience,

Prudence and Profits. Let's look at each.

Personality: It's extremely important to find a broker with whom you feel comfortable and whose personality meshes with yours. After all, you're embarking into a new area about which you know very little. You'll probably feel somewhat intimidated at the outset. You need a broker who will relate to you, guide you along, take a little more time explaining things and generally make you feel good about what you're doing. You don't want someone who's going to leave you feeling brow-beaten and nervous.

I remember when I was out searching for a new broker some years ago. I was given the name of a real fireball at one of the largest brokerage houses in the country — a man who'd made fortunes for his clients. I called for an appointment and went to see him.

The meeting was a disaster. The fellow talked faster than a machine gun. He showed no interest in my needs or concerns; instead he monopolized the time by pontificating on his own views on investing. At the end of the meeting he handed me some documents to read and told me if I was interested in becoming one of his clients to call. Needless to say, I never did. He was undoubtedly brilliant and I happen to know he's still doing very well for his clients. But the personality fit just wasn't there. I like to talk freely with a broker, not be subjected to ego tripping whenever I call.

So be sure you're comfortable with the personality of any prospective broker before you sign on. If you're not, keep looking — there are plenty of others out there.

Philosophy: There are almost as many different investing philosophies as there are brokers. You'd better find one that thinks more or less like you do, or you're going to end up being very unhappy.

Some brokers believe in taking big risks, because when they pay off the returns are spectacular. Others prefer conservative investments with modest growth potential but low downside risk. Some brokers believe in building solid, long-term portfolios. Others think that the active trader stands the best chance of profiting. There are brokers who put a great deal of emphasis on proper diversification of your holdings. There are others who pay no attention to that at all, focusing entirely on the strength of individual stocks and not worrying whether you have too much concentration in a particular sector. And the list goes on.

Before you talk to any broker, you should decide what your stock market approach is going to be. If you decide you want to begin with conservative stocks in a well-diversified portfolio, with a view to turning them over as profit objectives are met, then you should look for a broker who shares that philosophy. Otherwise, you and he are going to be in a constant state of turmoil and indecision.

Patience: As a beginning stock market investor, you *must* find a broker who has the patience to work with you. That means he or she will devote a little more time than you might otherwise expect to explaining new terminology, discussing possible trades and outlining alternatives. A little hand holding is going to be needed at the outset; make sure you find someone who's prepared to do it.

Prudence: You want a broker who's going to treat your money as if it were his or her own. That means someone who is careful, who assesses the risk in any situation and makes sure you know about it before you go in, and who generally keeps his or her eyes open for potential trouble, such as a major market correction. If a prospective broker gives you the impression of being a little too much of a high flyer, pass. He or she is unlikely to bring the caution and prudence you need to the relationship.

Profits: The most important P of them all. A broker may have all the other virtues I've outlined, but if he or she can't make money for you, forget it. In the end, it's performance that counts. If you end up with a bunch of dogs in your portfolio, any good rapport you may have established with your broker is going to collapse pretty quickly in any event.

Of course, you're really not going to know how effective a broker is in generating profits until you've dealt with him or her for a while. But there are ways of testing the water first. When you're interviewing prospective brokers, ask what they're recommending to clients and why. Then track those stocks for a while and see how they do. You might also ask for some examples of past successes — with trading slips to back up any claims, of course.

One broker I know has a sign on the wall that pretty well sums it up: "Our clients don't come to us so they can sleep well. They come to us so they can eat well."

So those are the Five Ps to look for. Now, how do you go about conducting your broker search?

To begin with, allocate some time. You should select a broker as carefully as you would a doctor, dentist or lawyer. That means doing some proper research and having some interviews. Don't decide you're too busy and grab the first broker who can talk in coherent sentences; you'll regret it later.

Next, give some thought to the type of brokerage house you want. A bigger firm will have a number of advantages: a larger research department, better opportunities to participate in new issues and larger inventories of bonds, strips and mortgage-backed securities are a few. A smaller firm will probably track fewer stocks but may monitor those it follows more closely. And you may get more personalized service.

Once you have some idea of the type of brokerage house you'd prefer, you can begin the search for a specific broker. Start by asking friends and acquaintances for recommendations. Who do they use, are they happy with the person, why or why not? Don't just get a phone number to call. Do a little probing. See how well their brokers fit with the Five Ps.

If you can't come up with any good leads this way, your task is obviously going to be more difficult. But you should still be able to locate the right person.

Contact several brokerage firms in your area. Start the conversation by inquiring whether they're actively interested in small retail accounts. Some houses concentrate on institutions and very large individual investors only; you'd be wasting both their time and yours to go any further with them.

The method of dealing with prospective new clients varies from one brokerage firm to another. But typically when you phone for the first time, you'll be connected with the broker of the day. That chore is rotated among all the brokers in the office, so the person you get depends strictly on the luck of the draw. Give the broker of the day some good background. Explain your position, the amount of money you plan to invest at the outset, and provide an idea of the type of person you want to work with. If the broker you're talking to doesn't feel you and he would make a good fit, he should suggest another name for you to contact. But it doesn't always happen that way. New brokers just starting out are sometimes so hungry for clients that they'll jump through hoops in an effort to persuade you that they're exactly what you're looking for. If you're uncomfortable with the broker of the day but are still interested in the firm, call back, ask to speak to the manager and explain your concerns. If she's sincerely interested in you as a prospective client, she should come up with one or two other names for you to contact.

If you find a broker that comes across well over the phone, arrange to set up a meeting. You might even consider taking him to lunch; you'll often pick up a lot more insights after a second glass of wine than you will by spending an hour in the broker's office.

Obviously, you want to concentrate on seeing how well he measures up to your Five Ps. But get some nuts and bolts information as well. Ask for copies of the firm's research reports. Find out their commission structure. Get a sample of the reports they send clients and determine how frequently you'll receive them. While your comfort and confidence level in the broker is the most important element in your decision, these are all factors to take into account in making a final choice.

So now, let's assume you've done it. You've made a selection, signed all the necessary papers to set up an account and you have a broker of your very own. Your first reaction may be a new sense of status ("I spoke to my broker today, and she said. . ."). Your second one may be a sense of disappointment (How come she never calls?). The third one will likely be elation or despair, depending on how well your first investments perform.

Whatever your feelings about the broker, remember you haven't gotten married. There's no lifetime commitment involved. In fact, you've really only completed the first step in the broker selection process.

You may have picked a crackerjack. On the other hand, the person could be a dud. You won't know for sure until you've worked with him or her for a while. Here are some of the things to watch for:

Attentiveness: A good broker should call you periodically with suggestions — good suggestions. He should review your account with you regularly, at least once a quarter. He should return your phone calls promptly. He should advise you when orders are filled and if there are any problems. He should ensure you're on the firm's mailing list for research reports. All of these things tell you he's interested in you and your business. If he's not performing up to standard, you should discuss it with him and, if matters don't improve, look elsewhere.

Churning: I've already explained what churning is. If you begin to feel that's what your broker is doing, switch in a hurry.

New issues: Brokerage houses are involved in *underwriting* new stock issues. This means the firm purchases new securities from a company and then resells them to institutions and the general public. The underwriting function can be a mixed blessing for you as an investor. Sometimes a new issue can produce spectacular profits in no time. I bought units which consisted of one share and half a warrant in a Quebec-based shipping company called Socanav when they were issued at $5 in the fall of 1986. Within weeks they were trading on the Toronto Stock Exchange for $7.50. Needless to say, I was more than happy with a fifty percent gain in that short space of time.

A more recent new issue that turned out well for investors was Trimark Financial, the mutual fund company, which I recommended in *The MoneyLetter.* Shares were offered to the public for the first time in April, 1992. Trading began on the Toronto Stock Exchange April 21. Within weeks, the shares had topped $15 and investors were ecstatic.

Often, however, new issues bomb. I've seen them drop twenty-five percent from issue price in the first day of stock exchange trading. Even issues that look like almost certain winners are not immune. When the federal government began selling off shares in Petro-Canada in June, 1991, the stock seemed like an excellent buy at an issue price of $13. After all, the government was promoting it heavily to ordinary Canadians. Surely they would price it at a level that would almost guarantee a profit. The Conservatives had enough problems; they wouldn't want the added burden of thousands of people blaming them because they'd lost money on shares in a crown corporation. And Petrocan was a huge company with tremendous assets.

All very logical. So I went in for a couple hundred shares myself and recommended the stock to *MoneyLetter* readers. Sigh. You can't win 'em all!

As it turned out, the issue couldn't have been timed worse. Shares of integrated oil companies hit the skids as petroleum prices dropped and heavy operating losses piled up. The price quickly skidded to eleven bucks and by May, 1992 was in the nine dollar range.

That's not the type of investment you need, which may help explain why I've become so wary of new issues.

The problem here is that when you come to the bottom line, your broker is a salesperson. She is employed by the company to sell products and generate commissions. If the broker is good at the job, both she and the company make money and are happy. If not —well, let's just say that Bay Street has been doing a lot of downsizing in recent years.

When the brokerage house underwrites a stock, your broker may have a genuine conflict of interest. She has an obligation to her firm to help move the stock out — and the less attractive the issue, the more of it she's likely to be called upon to sell. On the other hand, she has an obligation to you, as a client, to make the best possible recommendations. The two don't always coincide.

As a result, you may find your broker constantly trying to sell you new issues of dubious quality. That's a situation you don't need and shouldn't tolerate. It won't happen with a good broker — one who realizes that *you* pay the commissions and that a long-term relationship will be far more profitable than any one sale. But not all brokers understand that.

During your first meeting with your broker, you should clearly state what relationship you wish to establish regarding new issues her firm underwrites. You may say you don't want to hear about any of them — the potential conflict of interest is too serious. You may ask her to advise you of all of them, so that you can make your own decisions. Or you can ask to be advised only of those she genuinely believes are potential winners — and make it clear that her track record on these particular calls will be of special interest to you as you evaluate the business relationship.

If, as you work with the broker, you feel you're not being well-served on new issues — either because you're not being offered a crack at the good ones or she's pushing too many duds — talk it over. If things don't improve, discuss the matter with the manager and ask to have your account reassigned within the company. Moving to another firm should only be a last resort. Many brokerage firms now charge a transfer fee for switching your account elsewhere (imagine being charged because you're dissatisfied with the level of service — it's the ultimate insult!). Also, the transfer of an account can sometimes take weeks, during which time your assets will be frozen and you won't be able to trade. Better to stick it out where you are if at all possible.

Performance: No broker is going to be right all the time — infallibility is the exclusive prerogative of only one Being in the universe and He doesn't happen to be in the brokerage business. So don't expect that every recommendation you receive is going to turn to instant gold. What you *do* have a right to expect is a reasonable batting average. Your broker's suggestions should be profitable more often than not, and the net result of all gains and losses should be decidedly in your favour.

I keep a scorecard on which I track all stock trades. I note the source of each recommendation and how it turned out. That way I can easily see how my brokers are doing. If I find a situation in which performance is starting to lag, I'm much more cautious about accepting recommendations from that particular broker.

When you're dealing with your broker, remember you're in a

give-and-take situation. His only income results from the commissions which his accounts generate. If you're not doing a lot of trading, you won't be contributing much to his take-home pay. That's all right, certainly at the outset. But recognize the situation and don't impose unduly on his time. Do your own homework, read the research reports that come in and generally keep informed. When you do need input, make sure it's for matters of substance — not trivial questions. If your broker is good, he'll appreciate your discretion and be more prepared to spend a few extra minutes when you do call.

Finally, a brief word about discount brokers. As you read the financial pages or watch TV, you'll see advertisements for firms offering to handle your stock trades for a fraction of the cost charged by the full-service brokerage houses. The two leading names are Green Line Investor Services (operated by the Toronto-Dominion Bank) and Marathon Brokerage.

There's no gimmick here. The discounters are for real. You can actually have your trades done for as much as eighty-five percent off the rate you'd pay at a regular broker. You may wonder, then, why I don't recommend you do it.

The reason, in a word, is advice. The discount brokers are strictly order takers, nothing more. You tell them what you want and they'll execute the trade for you at a bargain price. That's terrific — if you know exactly what you're doing. If you don't, you're asking for trouble.

I once read a letter in the *Report on Business* which described the kind of problem that can arise. The reader had purchased a thousand warrants of Gulf Canada through the TD Bank's Green Line Investor Service. The warrants offered an opportunity to acquire an interest in all of Gulf's holdings, which extended well beyond oil and gas. But they had to be exercised by July 1 of that year. The reader failed to recognize the significance of that date — and because he had purchased the warrants through a discount broker, he had no one to advise him. As a result, he allowed the deadline to pass without exercising his warrants — and lost $20,000!

Let me hasten to add that there's no guarantee a full-service broker would have done better. Some are not as conscientious as they should be, no question. But the reader would have stood a better chance of a full-service broker picking up on the expiry date, especially if they discussed the status of the account periodically, as you should do.

That's why I firmly believe that if you're just starting out, you need the hand holding of a regular broker. Even if you have some firm ideas of what you want to buy, it's always useful to have someone to bounce them off. You need good research reports and advice on when to take a profit and run. The discount brokers don't provide it.

Once you've developed some experience in the stock market and have more business to offer, you can open a second account with a discount broker to handle those trades you don't feel you need advice on. But until then, I suggest staying away. Remember the old adage: you get what you pay for. Brokers are no different.

Keeping Some for Yourself

The promises of yesterday are the taxes of today.
— Mackenzie King, 1931

Let me begin this chapter with a question. How much of every dollar you earn do you think goes out in taxes?

I'm not just talking about income tax here. I want you to consider the whole range of taxes you pay: provincial sales taxes, property taxes, gasoline taxes, liquor taxes, tobacco taxes, the GST — everything.

Take a moment to think about it. Write down your answer on a piece of paper.

Ready? Okay. According to a calculation prepared by Vancouver's Fraser Institute, the average Canadian has handed over almost 54¢ of every dollar earned in 1991 to our various levels of government. Put another way, you get to keep only 46¢ of every dollar.

When you've recovered from that shock, think about this: Americans pay far less in taxes than Canadians. A recent study done by Robert D. Brown and Rick Gimbert of the chartered accounting firm of Price Waterhouse Canada found that a married couple earning $50,000 each in New York City would have been assessed $18,300 in federal, state and social security taxes in 1989. A comparable couple residing in Montreal would have paid $34,800; a Toronto couple $30,100; a Calgary couple $29,700. (Sales and other consumption taxes were not included in the calculations.)

That's a heck of a gap. If you look at it in percentage terms, the

Toronto couple paid sixty-four percent more in taxes than the New York couple in 1989. The gap has probably widened since. If you've ever wondered why the United States is so attractive to many successful Canadians, there's a large part of the answer.

The plain fact is that the tax burden in this country is stifling. The Fraser Institute has its own unique way of driving home that point to Canadians. Every year the Institute calculates what it calls Tax Freedom Day — the day when you've worked long enough to pay off all your tax obligations and can start enjoying your money. You'll be depressed to learn that for the 1991 tax year, the average Tax Freedom Day across Canada was July 16. For Ontario residents, it didn't happen until August 2!

If you're looking for someone to blame for this mess, start with the politicians. They've allowed government spending to get completely out of hand, with the result that our national deficit is atrocious, despite repeated promises to bring it under control. Until our elected representatives screw up the courage to make some real spending cuts, the situation is just going to get worse.

What does the debt level have to do with high taxes? Well, in 1970, the total cost to the federal government for interest payments to service the national debt amounted to just six percent of Ottawa's revenues. By the 1992-93 fiscal year, the cost of interest payments on the debt had risen to over $40 billion — over thirty percent of total projected revenues. The cost of financing the public debt was up about $10 billion from three years before. Clearly, the situation is not getting any better!

There are only two ways to deal with a situation like that — cut spending or raise taxes. So far, the politicians have cringed at the idea of any serious cost cutting. We've heard a lot of rhetoric from Ottawa, but nothing more. So our tax bills continue to go up and Canada becomes less competitive as each year passes. This onerous tax burden is important to the aspiring wealth builder. Clearly, the more the government grabs in tax, the less that's available for investment and wealth building. And so, by extension, the longer it's going to take to achieve our wealth objectives.

That's why minimizing the tax bite has to be part of the basic strategy of every wealth builder. It's not much good making all the right investment decisions if the government is going to turn around and grab a big chunk of your profits back from you.

Unfortunately, it's becoming increasingly difficult to protect your money from the long arm of government. Ironically, the Progressive Conservatives under Brian Mulroney (who, from a philosophical point of view, should have been encouraging wealth creation) were the major culprits in closing off the escape hatches. From the moment they were first elected in 1984, the Tories began systematically closing down tax shelters, introduced a minimum tax, eliminated many deductions and exemptions, cracked down on legitimate tax avoidance and generally played havoc with traditional tax planning strategies.

The Conservatives also hit us in another, more sneaky, way when they put an end to full indexing of personal exemptions and tax brackets. As a result, we're no longer protected against the tax impact of the first three percent of increases in the cost of living. Indexing only cuts in after that. So if inflation rises four percent, the adjustment of the tax brackets is only one percent. If it rises three percent, there is no adjustment at all. This formula also applies to the tax credit system and to a number of other tax-related calculations.

Most people don't understand the full implications of this. It's too technical and the numbers seem too small to worry about. But, in fact, this partial indexing costs taxpayers a great deal of money.

Let me illustrate. Suppose you live in Ontario and have a taxable income of $28,000 a year. Your total non-refundable tax credits work out to $1,200. For the 1991 tax year, your combined federal/provincial tax bill would have been $5,447, not including surtaxes and assuming no provincial government tax credits.

Now let's say that for the next five years, inflation increases at a rate of three percent a year. Your income increases at exactly the same pace, no more, no less.

At the end of five years, you've stood still financially. Your salary went up — your taxable income is now just over $32,460 a year. But since prices went up at the same rate, your money isn't buying any more than it was before.

But look what happens to your tax bill! I've illustrated the result below, assuming no changes in the federal and provincial tax rates (good luck!) and not allowing for surtaxes. To keep everything consistent, I've also assumed a continued $1,200 worth of tax credits.

	1991	1996
Taxable income	$28,000	$32,460
Tax credits	1,200	1,200
Tax payable	5,447	7,113

Look at that result closely. Your buying power hasn't gone up one cent. But your tax bill is $1,666 higher! Now do you think that partial indexing isn't significant?

Every Canadian taxpayer is being hit by this. The amount will vary, of course, depending on your income and which province you live in. But, unless your income is so low you don't have to pay tax, or unless politicians get serious about spending cuts, expect to give governments a lot more money in the years ahead. The Conservatives built an automatic tax increase into the system that will hit you progressively harder each year, probably without your even realizing it.

The tax reform program introduced by then-Finance Minister Michael Wilson in 1987 knocked the props from under all sorts of valuable tax-saving techniques. It's true that federal tax rates were lowered in the process, but provincial governments have been moving to snatch back any savings we realized. On balance, wealth builders fared very poorly under the Tory government.

So, unfortunately, I can't offer as many tax-saving tips as I could have a few years ago. There are some left, though, and because they're so precious, you should do everything possible to take advantage of them. In this chapter, I'll deal with some tax-saving ideas that are applicable to your general income. In Chapter Twenty-two, I'll discuss those that relate strictly to your investments — the heart of your wealth building activities.

Let's start with some basics. The first step in reducing the amount of money the government grabs from you each year is to do some tax planning. This doesn't have to be overly complicated, at least at the outset. It's really just a case of organizing your affairs so that you attract less tax than you otherwise might.

For example, you should estimate in January how much your maximum RRSP contribution is likely to be for the year ahead. Divide the total by twelve and budget that amount each month to be set aside. That way you won't be caught short when RRSP time rolls around (which, inconveniently, falls shortly after Christmas, if you haven't already noticed). Many people fail to make their maximum RRSP contribution, and so don't get the full tax break, because they didn't put enough money aside during the year. Basic, perhaps, but important.

Your start-of-the-year tax planning should include a careful review of the income of all members of the family, including any children, to see if there are any income-splitting opportunities available. Obviously, any time you can switch income from a higher tax bracket to a lower one, you're going to come out ahead. I briefly discussed some income-splitting ideas in Chapter Five; you may wish to go back and review them. Generally, income-splitting opportunities are greater if you have a family business, whether on a full or part-time basis. That allows you to employ several members of the family and split the business income between them in the form of salaries or dividends. It doesn't have to be anything elaborate. I know of a woman who runs a small catering business from her home, specializing in hot and cold *hors d'oeuvres* for private parties. She and her daughter handle the food preparation, her teenage son does the deliveries and dad keeps the company books. All of them get paid according to the amount of work they do, effectively dividing the company's revenue among four people for tax purposes.

Another factor to take into account in your tax planning is the timing of income. If your only source of revenue is a weekly pay cheque, there isn't much you'll be able to do here. But if you have some income that allows for flexibility in when you receive it — commissions, bonuses and dividends from a family company are examples — you may find it advantageous to defer some of it until the next tax year. You have to stay on top of the latest tax developments to make that decision, of course. But, as a good wealth builder, you'd be doing that anyway. As an example, Finance Minister Don

Mazankowski announced in the February, 1992 budget that the federal surtax would be reduced in two stages. The first cut would be in July, 1992, the second in January, 1993. Anyone with some flexibility on when to receive income might decide to take a dividend or commission in January, 1993 rather than December, 1992 on the basis of that knowledge, knowing that the federal surtax on 1993 income would be less. (The risk, of course, is that other income taxes will be raised in 1993. But in tax planning, you have to operate on the basis of what you know, not on the possibility of what might be.)

Your start-of-the-year tax planning should give consideration to the nature of your investments and the type of income they're likely to generate. I'll go into this in more detail in the next chapter but it's important it be on your checklist.

If you plan to purchase any tax shelters, you should work out just how much money you can effectively shield from Revenue Canada by doing so. Be sure to take account of the Alternative Minimum Tax in the process. I haven't explored the subject of tax shelters in depth in this book because most beginning wealth builders won't need them yet. But if you're an exception, be sure to plan carefully before you commit any money.

Your tax planning review should include a close look at any outstanding loans you may have. Remember, you can only deduct interest costs on loans incurred for investment or business purposes. If you have any consumer loans outstanding, you should see if there's any way they can be made tax deductible. For instance, you might own units in an equity mutual fund which are worth more than the outstanding balance on your consumer loan. Sell as many units as are needed to obtain the money to pay off the debt. Then, if you wish, take out a new loan and invest the proceeds in new mutual fund units. Your debt load is exactly the same — only now the interest is tax deductible.

Here's one more idea for your start-of-the-year exercise. Do a preliminary calculation of your income tax for the previous year. If it turns out you have a refund coming — especially if it's a large one — you need to do some careful thinking.

A large tax refund may be gratifying. But what it really means is that you've been providing the government with an interest-free loan for many months. That's money that could have been earning more cash for you, even if you'd only held it in a daily interest savings account.

Frankly, I don't like loaning money to the government free of charge and I doubt many people do. If Ottawa wants to borrow from me, let them do so with CSBs or Treasury bills and pay market rates of interest.

This abusive practice results from Revenue Canada setting the source deduction levels too high; in other words, more than necessary is taken off your weekly pay cheque. Unfortunately, there's not a lot you can do about that except write your MP to complain and copy the Minister of Finance. But there is a little-known procedure which can be used in certain situations to lessen the withholding tax and thus reduce the amount of the interest-free loan you so graciously give Ottawa each year. I can't guarantee it will work for you. But I've made it work for me on occasion, so it is possible.

Revenue Canada has a provision which allows you to apply for a reduction in the withholding at source if you expect to receive a large refund next year. It's not widely publicized and the rules on who can get it are somewhat vague. There's also a fair amount of bureaucratic hassle involved. And it only works if you're having tax deducted at source from your income. But it's available if you want to try it. This technique is only effective if you make use of it at the beginning of the tax year, however. That's why it's essential that you consider it in the context of your overall tax planning strategy.

Here's how it works.

Look over your tax plans for the year ahead and see whether there's anything in them that would entitle you to make a claim of this type. Some examples: advance payments to an RRSP (you'll need to provide a receipt), alimony or child support payments, rental or investment looses, substantial charitable donations and investments in legitimate tax shelters. If any of these apply, you have a case.

To get things going, write a personal letter to the chief of the source deduction department at your district taxation office. Explain why you want your source deductions reduced and include the necessary documentation to substantiate your claim. Be sure to provide all the basic information the tax people will need, such as your social insurance number and the name and address of your employer.

There's a buzz phrase you should also include in your letter — "undue hardship" — as in "not obtaining this tax relief would cause me undue financial hardship." This kind of tax break is supposedly reserved for those who would be seriously hurt financially if it were not granted. But the tax people tend to be quite liberal in their interpretation of that term, so don't let it deter you.

Your letter will be reviewed and you may get a phone call from someone at Revenue Canada with further questions. Don't panic if that happens; it's just routine. If your request is granted, you'll get a letter to that effect and your employer will be advised. Your exemption will be increased, less tax will be withheld at source, and presto, you'll have more money to spend — or save — each month. Of course, you won't get a big tax refund a year later — but that only means you've managed to eliminate that interest-free loan to Ottawa.

So much for general tax planning. Now let me give you a few ideas on how you might save some money when the time comes to complete your return.

I'll begin with some advice you may not like: prepare your own tax return. Only about half of Canadians do their own tax form. The rest have it prepared by someone else. More than a quarter of all taxpayers pay to have it done, often by street corner tax preparation services which charge relatively modest fees. Be aware, you get what you pay for.

Most tax preparation firms provide decent training for their staff. But even with this training, the person who does your return will not normally be a high powered tax professional. More likely, it will be a housewife or student who's picking up some extra cash with part-time work. Their knowledge of the tax laws and regulations may be very rudimentary. And, at the low fees they charge, they're certainly not going to devote a lot of time to studying the intricacies of your particular situation and looking for unusual ways to save you money.

The only person who will be truly motivated to spend the time to save your tax dollars is you. That's why I strongly urge you to devote the hours necessary to learning the tax rules and completing the returns for yourself and the members of your family. If you wish to have them double-checked later by someone else, fine. But do the planning and thinking yourself.

What should you look for? Here are some ideas.

Every year, thousands of people lose out on money that is rightfully theirs by failing to take advantage of all the tax credits and deductions available to them. That's not so surprising because, with all the tinkering that's been going on with the tax system, it's almost impossible for the ordinary person to keep track of what's permitted and what isn't. Your best bet is to be aware of the most common errors or omissions others make in completing their return — and then be sure you don't do the same thing.

One of these is the equivalent-to-married credit, which I'll refer to as ETM for short. Some tax experts contend it wins top prize as the most overlooked tax credit available.

This is a tax break especially designed for single parents. It allows unmarried or legally separated people to claim what amounts to a married tax credit if they support a dependant who lives with them. Usually, that means a child, although there are other possibilities. For example, the dependant could also be a parent or grandparent you're supporting at home. Also eligible are other relatives under eighteen, for example a niece or nephew, or a disabled relative of any age.

Single parents very often miss out on this one by claiming the child credit instead of the ETM. That can be a costly mistake. For example, a divorced woman with a young child could obtain a basic federal tax credit worth $890 in 1992 by claiming the ETM on her return. She would also have her surtax reduced as a result. With provincial tax taken into account, her total tax benefit in 1992 worked out to around $1,400. If she claimed the child credit instead, her total tax saving would have been slightly more than $100.

Technically, the dependant is supposed to be living with you but Revenue Canada has been somewhat relaxed on this. For instance, if you qualify for the ETM but your child attends boarding school, you can still claim the credit as long as the child lives with you when school's not in session.

But remember, you're only allowed one ETM credit. If you're a single parent with two children, only one qualifies. The other would get the standard child tax credit for the 1992 tax year. (It disappears after that, when the new Child Benefit plan begins in 1993. The ETM remains, however.)

By the way, if you've read this with dismay because you could have made an ETM claim in the past but didn't, contact Revenue Canada. In 1991, the federal government announced a new taxpayer fairness package that allows you to go all the way back to 1985 to claim money to which you were rightfully entitled.

Another area of the tax return that gives many people fits is the spousal transfer. And no wonder. It is quite complicated to work out. But if your spouse has a low income and is disabled or over sixty-five or attending school or receiving a pension cheque, you'd better learn the rules.

As of 1992, the age credit was worth a basic reduction of $592 in basic federal tax, plus savings in surtax and provincial tax. The basic disability credit was worth $720, while the pension income credit reduced basic federal tax by $170.

In the 1992 budget, the government announced increases in education credit. Full-time students may now claim a credit of $80 for each month they're attending a post-secondary institution, which works out to a reduction in basic federal tax of $13.60 a month. Since most students are in classes eight months a year, that translates into a federal tax reduction of about $109 a year. Surtaxes and provincial taxes increase the total value of that reduction to the $170 range.

Tuition fees may be claimed as a credit up to the total amount spent. However, the total amount of education and tuition credits transferred to another person may not exceed $680.

If your spouse qualifies for any of these but can't make full use of them because he or she doesn't have enough taxable income, you can claim them. A typical example would be an older couple living on pension income. The wife is over sixty-five and receives just over

$3,000 a year in pension money as her only income. She won't be liable for any tax, but she has tax credits available worth about $750 in reduced basic federal tax.

Her husband can make use of those credits by completing Schedule Two of the General Income Tax Return. There are several lines to be filled out but the money saved is worth the effort.

For a younger couple, a transfer of credits might save tax in cases where one spouse is attending university while the other works. Check out all the possibilities; I hate to see a perfectly good tax credit go to waste. We have so few of them!

One other point before I leave transfers. Unused tuition and education credits and the disability credit can also be transferred to a supporting parent or grandparent. So if you have a child in university who can't make use of these credits, claim them yourself.

Another frequently misunderstood tax credit is the one relating to medical expenses. An estimated 500,000 Canadians claim this credit each year. But many of those aren't getting as large a tax break as they should. And there are thousands of others who could be making a claim but don't know how to structure their tax affairs to be able to do so.

The basic rules are fairly well understood. You can only claim those medical and dental costs which exceed three percent of your net income or (in 1992) $1,614, whichever is less. That means if your net income works out to $30,000, only those costs in excess of $900 ($30,000 x 3%) are eligible. If your net income was $60,000, any costs in excess of $1,614 could be deducted. (That figure is adjusted each year under the partial indexing formula.) Your basic federal tax credit is seventeen percent of the eligible amount. Either spouse can claim all the medical expenses incurred by the family, unless costs for children are involved. The expenses can cover any twelve-month period that ends in the tax year for which you're filing the return.

So much for the basics. Now here are some angles to look at.

First, you can include any premiums paid to a private health insurance plan as part of your medical expenses. That means if you belong to a group plan at work and pay all or part of the premium yourself, you can add that amount to your medical costs. Just ask your employer to tell you what your share was. Payments made for special medical coverage while you're travelling outside Canada may also be claimed.

Second, it isn't automatic in two-income families that the higher earner should claim the medical costs. In fact, quite the contrary. It will usually be advantageous for the lower-income spouse to do so. The three percent rule means the lower-income person will have a larger deduction to claim. And the way the tax credit is structured, it doesn't matter what tax bracket the claimant falls into. The value of the credit will always remain seventeen percent of the eligible amount.

Let me give you an example. Let's take a two-income family in which the wife has a net income of $40,000 a year and the husband, who works part-time because he's studying for a degree, has $20,000. They have eligible medical/dental bills totalling $1,500.

If the higher income wife should make the claim, the return would look like this:

Net income	$40,000
Total expenses	1,500
Exempt medical expenses (3%)	1,200
Eligible expenses	300
Federal tax credit (17%)	$51

If the lower income husband makes the claim, however, the result changes significantly:

Net income	$20,000
Total expenses	1,500
Exempt medical expenses (3%)	600
Eligible expenses	900
Federal tax credit (17%)	$153

As you can see, by a simple reorganization of the way in which the medical expenses are claimed, this particular family saves over $100 in basic federal taxes. Once surtaxes and provincial income taxes are taken into account, the total tax advantage of going this route is in the $160 range.

If you have children and are claiming medical expenses for them, this flexibility isn't available to you for their costs, unfortunately. The rules state that the higher-income spouse must claim medical expenses on behalf of dependent children.

Let's look at another area: disability. If you or anyone in your family is disabled, you know that the impact goes far beyond the physical and mental anguish involved. Any kind of serious disability involves a severe financial strain as well. I know; we have a daughter who is profoundly deaf. She's done remarkably well in overcoming her handicap and is living a reasonably normal life. But there's been a lot of expense involved in making that possible: costly hearing aids, a captioning decoder so she can enjoy TV, special equipment to enable her to use the telephone, an alarm clock that shakes her bed to wake her, a strobe light that alerts her to a crying baby, just to mention a few.

But for many years, she was not considered to be officially disabled for income tax purposes. In that regard she was in exactly the same position as people suffering from mental retardation or severe cardio-respiratory failure or a variety of other debilitating conditions. The expenses were all there, but the tax relief wasn't.

Finally, however, the government changed the rules, extending the disability tax credit to thousands of people who couldn't use it before and providing much-needed tax relief in the process. You're now considered to be disabled if you have a severe impairment that markedly restricts you in the activities of daily living.

You have to have your doctor complete a form which confirms that you or a family member falls into this broader definition of disabled. But the reward is considerable; the disability tax credit is worth a $720 reduction in your basic federal tax payable.

As I mentioned before, this credit can be transferred to a spouse or supporting parent or grandparent if desired.

Although the change got a fair amount of publicity at the time it was announced, many eligible people are probably still not aware of it. If you think anyone in your family should be claiming it, get hold of Form 2201 from Revenue Canada and get your doctor to fill it out.

These are only a few examples of frequently overlooked claims and strategies. There are many more — in fact, entire books have been written on the subject. If you want to explore the possibilities in greater depth, I suggest you get hold of a specialized tax guide. Just be sure it's Canadian; U.S. tax guides are worthless in this country. You should also consider subscribing to a newsletter on the subject; *The TaxLetter*, published by Hume, is the best one I know of.

I admit it's a complex area. But it will be worth your while to devote some time to it. After all, why give the government any more than you absolutely have to, especially when the system seems to make it almost impossible for you to win. You *can* win though — if you learn the basic facts and devote the time and energy needed to do your tax return yourself. I'm not saying it will be fun — but it may be profitable.

Tax-Efficient Investments

Anyone may so arrange his affairs that his taxes shall be low as possible; he is not bound to choose that pattern which will best pay the treasury; there is not even a patriotic duty to increase one's taxes.
— Judge Learned Hand, 1951

It's no accident that the basic building blocks in my wealth program are a home and an RRSP. It just so happens they're the most effective tax shelters still around.

To build wealth in Canada, given our high tax rates, you have to construct your plan in a way that minimizes the impact of taxation on your money. Every dollar you are required to hand over to governments is one less dollar that's available to you for investment and growth.

The younger you are, the more important this becomes. I've already stressed the significance of compounded growth in an investment program, but let me remind you of it again in a tax context. Let's say you're twenty-five years old and you plan to be financially independent by the time you're fifty-five — that's thirty years from now. Assuming you were able to invest for an average ten percent after-tax return per year, every $100 in taxes paid today means you will have $1,745 less in your investment portfolio at age fifty-five. (Those compound interest numbers always seem astounding, but they're correct. If you don't believe me, try it yourself on a calculator.)

That's why I lay such stress on developing your wealth building program in such a way as to shield your money from taxes wherever possible, with your home and your RRSP as starting points.

The family home allows you to build tens, maybe hundreds of thousands of dollars in equity over the years, entirely tax free. There's no ceiling, no restrictions. The capital gain you make on your principal residence doesn't even come under the $100,000 lifetime exemption limit. It's over and above that. And by using devices like the home equity line of credit (which I described in Chapter Twelve) or a reverse mortgage, you can gain access to that tax-free money whenever you want. It doesn't have to remain locked away until the house is sold.

As for RRSPs, I don't have to reiterate their wealth building power. Just keep in mind that it's all made possible because the income earned inside the plan is tax sheltered until it comes time to take the funds out.

After the home and the RRSP, however, your tax-sheltered choices start to thin out. But there are still some techniques you can use to legitimately keep money out of the hands of Revenue Canada and in your own pocket.

If you have children, a Registered Education Savings Plan (RESP) is one option worth considering. I discussed these briefly in Chapter Five. Although you don't receive any tax deduction for money contributed to an RESP, income earned inside the plan compounds tax free until the student needs it for post-secondary education. Given the financial constraints on governments, I expect the cost of a college degree to rise substantially over the next decade. The result will be that a growing number of talented students may be deprived of higher education for financial reasons. An RESP is one way to help ensure your children won't be in that group. But if you want to set up a plan, go back and read my comments on switching beneficiaries in Chapter Five. And get the program in place as soon as possible after the child is born. You're allowed to contribute up to $1,500 a year per child, but there is no retroactivity. If you miss a year, the opportunity is gone for good.

One of the problems with RESPs is that younger people — who still tend to have the most babies — simply don't have any money left to fund a plan after making mortgage payments and contributing to an RRSP. One way around this is to ask the grandparents to set up a plan. The money they invest on the child's behalf simply amounts to an interest-free loan, because they can withdraw their capital from the RESP tax-free at any time. Assuming that money would otherwise be invested in a taxable security, such as a GIC, this makes the real cost of the RESP contribution relatively small. For example, suppose a grandparent is in a forty-five percent tax bracket and could be earning nine percent interest on $1,500 if it were not invested in an RESP. The actual after-tax cost of the contribution to the grandparent, in terms of lost interest income, works out to less than $75 a year!

Another way of tax-sheltering some savings for the future is through a home ownership savings plan. The federal government abandoned its program several years ago, but Ontario still has a provincial plan in place. It's designed to help low and middle-income families buy their first home. If you're single, it only works if your income is under $40,000 a year; married couples may have family income up to $80,000.

It works like this. As long as you or your spouse has never owned a home, you may contribute up to $2,000 a year to a plan for five years (a maximum contribution of $10,000). Married couples may each have a plan. You receive a tax credit for your contribution, which decreases as your income rises. For example, a couple with a combined income of $40,000 who each contribute $2,000 to their plans (a total of $4,000) will receive an Ontario tax credit of $1,000. Either person may claim the total credit on their return. If their income is $50,000, the tax credit for a combined $4,000 contribution drops to $750. At the $60,000 income level, it falls to $500 and continues to decline until it reaches zero at $80,000 combined income.

As a bonus, participants in the plan also get a refund of any Land Transfer Tax paid on the purchase of a home, provided they pay less than $200,000 for the property. If the purchase price is under $150,000, the full amount of the tax is refunded; between $150,000 and $200,000, the refund is based on a sliding scale which reduces as the cost of the house goes up. So, for example, eighty percent of the Land Transfer Tax will be repaid on a $160,000 house, but only twenty percent on a $190,000 property.

The Ontario program is temporary. You must open a plan by

December 31, 1993 to take advantage of it. All funds must be removed and used to buy a house by December 31, 1999, otherwise you'll have to refund any tax credits you claimed plus interest.

Home ownership plans, education savings plans and RRSPs are ways of tax-sheltering some of your savings for specific future needs. Now let's look at some ways you can invest money outside structured programs like these and still get a break from Revenue Canada.

Let's start with the $100,000 lifetime capital gains exemption.

This is an intriguing story. When the Finance Minister of the day, Michael Wilson, first announced the plan in his 1985 budget, it looked like it was going to be an absolute bonanza for wealth builders. Canadians, Mr. Wilson proudly told the House of Commons, were going to be allowed to accumulate half a million dollars in capital gains over their lifetimes, tax free! I still remember where I was at that moment (some people remember where they were when presidents were shot; I remember budgets). It was in a hotel room in Niagara-on-the-Lake. I was attending a business conference but broke away to watch the speech on TV. When Wilson got to the capital gains part, I thought I had died and gone to heaven!

Since that magical day, it's all gone downhill. Hardly a year has gone by when the value of this exemption hasn't been eroded in one way or another. I've developed a theory about the whole farce. It goes like this:

When Wilson arrived at his office the morning after the budget speech, the top mandarins from Finance were waiting for him. It turned out they'd made a few miscalculations. The half million dollars was going to cost the federal Treasury far more than they'd anticipated. Something had to be done.

Well, a new Finance Minister could hardly do a complete about-face overnight. So they came up with a plan. Over the next few years, they'd gradually chip away at the exemption until it became almost worthless. But they'd do it in such a subtle way that no one would notice.

The first step was to reduce the maximum we'd be allowed. Instead of half a million, it was scaled back to $100,000, except for the sale of farm property or shares in a small business. That was only twenty percent of the original amount, a huge reduction. But since few Canadians ever expected to make even $100,000 in capital gains during their lives, no one complained.

Emboldened by the acceptance of that step, Finance went forward with phase two. This involved the introduction of an incredibly complex calculation known as the Cumulative Net Investment Loss (CNIL). I'll spare you the gory details here; you'll find them in my book *Low-Risk Investing* if you're feeling masochistic some day. Suffice to say that CNIL is a device for limiting your access to the capital gains exemption if you claimed any investment expenses (such as interest on borrowed money) or losses after January 1, 1988. It also creates a bureaucratic impediment to claiming the exemption because you must file a completed CNIL declaration with your tax return if you want to escape tax on a capital gain — even for small amounts.

The third blow to the capital gains exemption came in the 1992 budget. Mr. Wilson had since moved on to greener pastures, but his successor, Don Mazankowski, continued the assault by announcing that real estate gains would no longer be eligible for inclusion under the capital gains exemption. At one blow, that knocked out about half the exemption claims being made every year.

All that's left now is for some future government to end the whole charade by eliminating the exemption entirely. That would certainly not surprise me, so you should take advantage of the remnants of the plan that remain while you can.

And what happens if the exemption is abolished? Are we simply back to where we were before it all started?

Not by a long shot. In fact, wealth builders would have been far better off had the Tories never dreamed up the idea in the first place.

The reason is that, as part of an unstated quid pro quo for the exemption, the tax rate on unsheltered capital gains has increased significantly. Until 1987, only half your capital gains were taxable — the rest belonged to you. Now you'll pay tax on seventy-five percent of your taxable profits. The difference is significant. Here's how someone in a forty-five percent tax bracket is affected:

	Old System	Current System
Gross capital gain	$1,000	$1,000
Non-taxable portion	500	250
Taxable portion	500	750
Tax @ 45%	225	338

As you can see, the tax rate on capital gains not covered by the exemption has effectively been increased by fifty percent! That's a high price to pay for a program that was supposed to encourage more Canadians to invest in their country.

Since you're going to end up paying more taxes eventually, you should make every effort to take advantage of what remains of the capital gains exemption while it's still around. With real estate gains no longer eligible, stocks, bonds and mutual funds are the main vehicles for achieving this.

The desirability of accumulating capital gains is one reason why I've stressed the importance of diversifying your investments as you move forward. Too many people never get beyond GICs and CSBs, neither of which normally have any capital gains potential (there have been occasional exceptions with both, but they're rare). At some point, you need to add investments to the mix which can generate capital gains, following the plan I outlined in earlier chapters. That $100,000 lifetime exemption may be a shadow of its former self but, as I write this, at least it's still there for the taking; don't pass up the opportunity to use it.

And if you're entrepreneurial and think you'd like to start your own small business, remember you can still get up to $500,000 tax free when you sell it. Now there's a good incentive to get you going!

After the capital gains exemption, the most important tax break for investors outside a registered plan is the dividend tax credit. A lot of people have either never heard of this tax credit or have only a vague idea of how it works. Believe me, it's worth the trouble to find out more.

There are two philosophical reasons for this particular tax break. One is to encourage more Canadians to invest in our own industries. The other is to recognize the fact that when companies pay dividends on their stocks, that money comes out of after-tax profits. In other words, corporation income tax has already been paid on that money. The dividend tax credit goes some way (although not all the way) towards ensuring that money isn't taxed twice.

Like the capital gains exemption, the dividend tax credit has been watered down in recent years. As a result, it's nowhere near as valuable as it once was in reducing tax. But it's still better than nothing and you'd be smart to take advantage of it.

Here's how it works. Let's assume you own shares in Bell Canada Enterprises (BCE Inc.) and have received $100 in dividends. You're going to pay substantially less tax on that money than if you'd received it as GIC interest. But you're going to have to jump through some hoops first.

As a first step, you'll have to *gross-up* your dividend income on your tax return by twenty-five percent. Grossing-up is one of those little tax wrinkles Ottawa dreams up to complicate our lives but, believe me, it's much harder to explain than it is to do. In fact, you probably won't have to do any of this at all, since all the numbers should be on the T5 slip you receive from the company paying the dividends. Still, it's useful to understand how it all works.

Grossing-up involves increasing your dividend income artificially for tax purposes to an amount that theoretically approximates the before-tax income originally received by BCE. The purpose of this strange exercise is to enable Ottawa to then give you credit for the tax BCE paid on the income before dividends were distributed to you and other shareholders. The idea is to avoid double-taxing the same money.

The grossing-up process produces the *taxable amount of dividends*, to be shown on your return. In this example, the grossed-up amount of your $100 dividend will be $125.

Let's assume you're in the twenty-six percent federal tax bracket — the middle range. The federal tax payable on your dividend is calculated on the grossed-up (or taxable) amount. So in this case, you'd be liable for basic federal tax of $32.50 ($125 x 26%).

Now for the good part. You get a tax credit against that amount of 13.33% of the grossed-up dividend (not the actual amount you received). In our example, that would amount to $16.67 ($125 x

13.33%). That credit is deducted from the tax payable, so your net tax on your $100 dividend will be $15.83. If your provincial tax rate is fifty-two percent of the federal tax payable, the total tax on your dividend (excluding any surtaxes) will be $24.06 ($15.83 x 152%).

Compare that to your tax on comparable interest income. The example below makes the point:

	Dividend	Interest
Amount received	$100.00	$100.00
Gross-up	125.00	100.00
Gross federal tax (26% bracket)	32.50	26.00
Dividend tax credit	(16.67)	n/a
Net federal tax	15.83	26.00
Provincial tax @ 52%	8.23	13.52
Total tax payable (excluding surtaxes)	$24.06	$39.52

As you can see, the tax advantage of dividend income over interest is considerable. That means that you could select dividend-paying investments, such as preferred shares, which actually appear to have a lower return than an interest-bearing alternative, and still come out ahead after tax.

Suppose, for example, you had $2,000 to invest. You were faced with a choice between a bank preferred stock paying a 7.5% dividend and a one-year GIC paying nine percent. The GIC might look like the better alternative. But is it, once you've taken taxes into account? Let's take a look. Note that the following calculations don't apply in Quebec, which has its own dividend tax credit formula.

	Stock (7.5% Dividend)	GIC (9% Interest)
Annual return	$150.00	$180.00
Gross-up	187.50	180.00
Gross federal tax (26% bracket)	48.75	46.80

	Stock (7.5% Dividend)	GIC (9% Interest)
Dividend tax credit	(25.00)	n/a
Net federal tax	23.75	46.80
Provincial tax @ 52%	12.35	24.34
Total tax payable (excluding surtaxes)	36.10	71.14
After-tax return	113.90	108.86
Percentage return after tax	5.7%	5.4%

As you can see, you're better off after tax choosing the stock, even though at first glance it would appear to pay a lower return.

Now here's a point that's extremely important for beginning wealth builders who are not yet earning a lot of money. *The lower your income, the more tax-efficient the dividend tax credit becomes.* Let's look at the same example again, but this time assume you're in the lowest federal tax bracket (17 percent).

	Stock (7.5% Dividend)	GIC (9% Interest)
Annual return	$150.00	$180.00
Gross-up	187.50	180.00
Gross federal tax (17% bracket)	31.88	30.60
Dividend tax credit	(25.00)	n/a
Net federal tax	6.88	30.60
Provincial tax @ 52%	3.58	15.91
Total tax payable (excluding surtaxes)	10.46	46.51
After-tax return	139.54	133.49
Percentage return after tax	7.0%	6.7%

As you can see, the percentage of after-tax return on your investment increased significantly for both interest and dividends in the lower tax bracket. Also, the gap between the actual net revenue received from the two investments widened — in the twenty-six percent bracket, your after-tax dividend income was $5.04 more than the after-tax income from the interest-bearing investment. In the seventeen percent bracket, that difference widened to $6.05. That might not seem like a lot. But applied to larger amounts and spread over several years, it adds up.

What all this means is that you must take the tax consequences into account in assessing your investment options. Examine the before-tax rates of return, find out your tax bracket and calculate the probable after-tax results. If they're relatively close, or even if there's a slight advantage for the interest-bearing alternative, you may still decide on the dividend-paying stock. That's because shares carry the possibility of capital gain, which many interest-bearing investments do not.

In making that decision, however, remember that the capital gains potential of shares will differ depending on whether you select preferred or common stock. Preferred shares offer limited capital gains potential. Any gains you do realize will be tied to interest rate movements; preferreds operate in much the same way as bonds in that regard. The major capital gains potential is in common shares, however they won't normally offer as high a dividend yield as preferred shares. You'll have to decide where your priorities lie.

There's a downside risk when you invest in stocks, of course. Even a blue-chip stock with a solid record of dividend payments can drop in value in a falling market. But if you select wisely, and avoid buying when the market is at its peak, you can minimize that risk.

Also, remember that only Canadian stocks qualify for the dividend tax credit. Foreign stocks do not.

If you do go the dividend route, don't overdo it. You can't use a dividend tax credit to generate a refund; the best you can do is to reduce your taxable income to zero. And if you're in a high income bracket, the Alternative Minimum Tax may come into play. If you make over $40,000 a year and have a lot of dividend income, check this potential booby-trap carefully.

One other caveat. If you're considering investments within an RRSP, the after-tax calculations won't apply because all the income is tax-sheltered. In that case, go for the investment with the best total return.

There are two other ways to invest that may save you some tax dollars. One is to use real estate mutual funds. As I mentioned in Chapter Seventeen, they offer a tax advantage in that rental income distributed to unit holders can be tax sheltered, in whole or in part, through the application of capital cost allowance (CCA), which is simply a tax write-off for depreciation on buildings and certain other assets owned by the fund. The result is that a significant portion of the income received from a real estate fund will be tax-advantaged. There's a catch, however. If you cash in your units, you'll have to repay a portion of the tax you saved. Each fund has a different formula for recovering this money; ask for a thorough explanation before you invest.

The other alternative is a limited partnership. These have been aggressively sold to high-income earners, especially professionals, for many years, with mixed results. Some have made good money for investors, others have been disasters. They're not suitable vehicles for beginning wealth builders and I suggest you not consider them until you've put a firm financial foundation in place and gained considerable experience in making investment decisions.

I wish I could offer more ideas on how to protect your money from big government but there's been a systematic move in recent years to reduce the tax sheltering opportunities available. So let me summarize the list of the top half-dozen tax efficient investments for beginning wealth builders:

Number one: Your home. Unlimited capital gains potential. Does not effect lifetime capital gains exemption.

Number two: Your RRSP. Tax-free growth for as long as the plan is in force. Funds are taxable at your marginal rate when withdrawn.

Number three: If you have children, an RESP. No tax deduction for contributions, but tax free compounding within the plan. Capital withdrawals are tax-free, interest withdrawals are taxed in the student's hands.

Number four: A tax-sheltered home savings plan, if one exists in your province.

Number five: The capital gains exemption. Tax-free gains up to

$100,000 on profits in stocks, bonds, mutual funds and other securities (but not real estate acquired after March, 1992). For the sale of farm property or a small business, the exemption is $500,000.

Number six: Dividends. The dividend tax credit makes them the most effective type of investment income once the capital gains exemption has been exhausted.

There they are. Good luck.

It's Hard to Get Good Help These Days

Distrust interested advice.
— Aesop

Don't be surprised if there comes a time when you want to throw up your hands and scream for help. It's a natural reaction. Starting and maintaining a wealth building program isn't easy. And even though I've tried to provide both general guidelines and specific examples in this book, you'll undoubtedly run into a situation at some point that isn't covered here. It's to be expected; everyone's personal circumstances are different. The question is: Where do you turn for good advice?

When the time comes to ask this question, you might be comforted to know you're not alone. I'm asked it all the time, on hotline shows, in question periods after speeches and in my mail. Sometimes total strangers call me up out of the blue to ask for assistance in finding an advisor they can trust.

It's not an easy question to answer.

The right advisor will depend to a large extent on the nature of your problem. You shouldn't go to a lawyer or bank manager for investment advice, for example, although a great many people do. They aren't trained to deal in such matters. Your broker is not usually the best person to ask about a tax problem, for the same reason. Nor is your insurance agent normally the best source of impartial advice on an RRSP.

Going to the wrong expert for advice is not just an unproductive way to spend your time and money. It could actually end up costing you a bundle, as a result of improper counselling.

I once received a call from an Ottawa businessman which both flattered and shocked me. He had heard me talking about money on CBC radio and, on no more knowledge than that, asked if I'd undertake to manage his money for him.

"How much?" I asked.

"About one million dollars," he replied.

My immediate reaction was that it was a put-on. But as we talked further, it turned out it wasn't.

The man's story was a prime example of how financial advice from the wrong person can be disastrous. He had spent most of his adult life developing what became a very successful business. About a year prior to his phone call to me, he had sold it and walked away with just over a million dollars in cash. Like many successful business people, he knew virtually nothing about investing; his whole life had been devoted to making his company a success. So when he suddenly found himself with more money than he'd ever dreamed of, he didn't know what to do with it.

So he turned to a financial expert for help. In this case, it was his accountant, the man who'd helped him in business matters and looked after his tax returns for many years. Unfortunately, the accountant might have been terrific at financial statements, but he was no investment expert. Faced with the prospect of finding somewhere to place a million dollars, he chose the safest, most conservative route possible — he put all the money into Treasury bills.

Now, this was in the mid-eighties, at a time when interest rates were at their lowest point in a decade while the stock markets were in the midst of their biggest run-up since the 1920s. But because all the money was in T-bills, the businessman didn't get any part of that action. His return on the million dollars was about seven percent over that year. Sure, the money was safe. But he would have liked to have done a little better than that.

I'm not in the personal money management business, but I gave him some names of people he could contact. I also strongly suggested he do so without delay. The poor investment advice he'd received had already cost him many thousands of dollars; the faster he rectified the situation, the better off he'd be.

That's why it's so important to seek advice from the right qualified person.

Some people think that's their bank manager. Not so, unless the advice you're looking for relates to borrowing or to one of the specific products offered by the bank. There are tight restraints on the type of financial advice bank personnel can give. When they have strayed beyond the bounds, the results haven't always been auspicious. In one case a few years ago, two widows actually ended up suing their bank after the manager approved loans for them to invest in a speculative cattle deal. When it collapsed, they lost everything. They launched legal action, claiming they hadn't been properly advised — and the courts agreed with them.

Lawyers tend to be another favourite source of financial advice, perhaps because of a misconception that, since they're highly educated, they must know about handling money. Most of them don't; they only know about law. There are some exceptions, of course, particularly among lawyers who specialize in tax policy, business organization and personal contract negotiations. But if you want to use a lawyer for financial advice, make sure he knows what he's talking about and that he has proven credentials in the specific field in which you need help.

Insurance agents are another popular source of advice. But keep in mind, their main interest is in selling you their products. If the financial guidance they offer seems to put heavy emphasis on the services they're selling, consider any potential conflict of interest before making a decision.

Too often, people in search of financial help find they've inadvertently set themselves up as a target for a sales pitch on a dubious investment, tax shelter, insurance policy or something similar. If the person doing the planning has a vested interest in selling you something, be on your guard.

One of the newest and fastest-growing professions in Canada is financial planning and more people are turning there for help. There are some excellent financial planning services available — but be careful. Although there's been a lot of talk, there are few regulations governing the operations of financial planners in most provinces; Quebec and Alberta are notable exceptions. As a result, in many parts of the country anyone, qualified or not, can hang out a financial planner sign. Their fees can vary widely and there's no guarantee that the highest fee will produce the best results. To complicate matters further, many self-styled financial planners are not that at all. They're well-trained salespeople who use financial planning techniques to build a case for selling you their products.

My personal experience with financial planners has been limited to two occasions, neither of which was encouraging. I described one of these in Chapter Sixteen, when I told you about the recommendations that caused me to put money into Greymac Trust and Seaway Trust just before the Ontario Government closed them down.

The company that made those suggestions was a well-known and highly reputable Toronto firm, which was being paid a lot of money for its services. Yet even that wasn't enough to protect me from bad advice. That same company, by the way, also recommended that I make some major insurance purchases, including a disability insurance program that would have cost several thousand dollars a year to carry. When I questioned this, I discovered that the firm — which, remember, was being paid a fee to advise me — was also an agent for the insurance company in question and stood to receive a commission if I agreed to the proposal. The recommendation *may* have been perfectly valid. But, given that kind of conflict of interest situation, it was hardly impartial.

My second experience with financial planners came a few months later, when I was searching for a tax shelter in an effort to protect some money from Revenue Canada. I asked my banker for some suggestions and he had high praise for the thoroughness and integrity of this particular firm. Fortunately, I had no problems with them. I purchased my tax shelter without a hitch. But I *could* have had trouble — I was just lucky. The company also suggested that I buy a number of other investments, many of which they had developed and promoted themselves. A couple seemed tempting. But in the end I decided against them. A few months later, I read in the paper that the financial planning company was in trouble and that people who had bought some of the investments I turned down were in danger of losing a great deal of money. After I breathed a sigh of relief that it wasn't me, I began to pay closer attention to what was happening in the financial planning community.

I've been watching it evolve for several years and I'm generally encouraged by what I've seen. There are still some bad planners around, people who will buy a portfolio of equity funds for a widow who really needs low-risk, income-producing investments like mortgage-backed securities. A few planners I've encountered put too much emphasis on dubious tax shelters or encourage clients to leverage their investments to an extent that is totally inappropriate.

But most of the financial planners I meet these days are well-trained men and women who are highly conscious of their responsibilities and the need to do a good job for clients. This is particularly true for those operating in smaller communities. As one planner who works in the British Columbia interior told me: "If you put one client into a bad deal, the whole town will know about it tomorrow and your business will be finished. It certainly focuses your mind!"

What can you expect from a good financial planner? Just about every type of financial service. A good planning organization should review your current financial situation and make recommendations for reducing debt, setting up a retirement savings plan, cutting taxes and developing an investment strategy. They may prepare your tax returns, if you wish. Depending on the planner, he or she may also handle securities purchases for you. Many financial planners are licensed to sell mutual funds and are agents for GICs. Some also have an insurance license. A few — but the number is growing — also hold a brokerage license, which enables them to purchase stocks and bonds on your behalf.

In fact, the line between financial planners and brokers is starting to blur. At one time, the two professions were quite distinct. But now financial planners are starting to edge into the brokerage business. On their side, brokers are offering more comprehensive investment advisory services than in the past — some brokerage houses now refer to their representatives as "financial advisors" or "investment advisors," instead of as simply "brokers." And many brokers now do a big business in mutual funds, an area they largely ignored in the past.

Here's an example of what a financial planner might do for you. A Vancouver woman I know was left with a fairly sizeable inheritance after her husband died unexpectedly. She had no idea how to handle the money in such a way as to ensure she could keep her home and maintain her lifestyle. So she contacted a financial planner. He put together a comprehensive program that included recommendations for investments that would provide her with the cash flow she needed. He also showed her some of the techniques we looked at in Chapters Twenty-One and Twenty-Two for reducing her tax liability. His work wasn't cheap — she was charged $1,200 for the plan. But she came away with a sense of security and the feeling she had received excellent value for money.

The Canadian Institute of Financial Planning is making an effort to establish standards for the profession and offers courses to help financial advisors improve their knowledge and skills. They also have an introductory course suitable for beginning investors. You can contact them at 80 Bond Street, Toronto, Ontario M5B 1X8 (phone 416-865-1237).

The Canadian Association of Financial Planners will assist you in finding a financial planner in your area. There's a chapter in every province or you can write to their national office at Suite 1111, 120 Eglinton Avenue East, Toronto, Ontario M4P 1E2 (phone 416-481-1225). They'll send you a roster of all certified financial planners in your province which will include information on their rates and how they're paid. That's especially useful because it will enable you to identify which planners sell insurance, mutual funds or tax shelters. Also request their *Consumer Guide to Financial Planning*, which contains suggestions on what to look for in a planner and questions to ask before you make a decision.

Here are some other tips on finding a good planner.

1. Ask friends and relatives for their input. See if any of them have ever worked with a financial planner. If so, get all the details: the kind of work they had done, the cost, their degree of satisfaction, any problems or concerns they may have had. The best guarantee of a good choice is the endorsement of someone you know and respect.

2. Know your objectives. Don't go into the first meeting with a fuzzy mind. If all you can say is "I need help," you're setting yourself up for some potentially bad advice. Have a clear idea of just *what* kind of help you need. You're much more likely to get what you want if your opening comment is something like: "I've just inherited $250,000 and I would like a plan that will protect that capital and give me $20,000 a year in after-tax income."

3. Decide which type of planner you want. A fee-for-service planner will charge you for his or her time, either on an hourly basis or at an agreed-upon flat fee for preparing your plan. A planner who receives compensation in the form of sales commissions may prepare a plan for you free, or at a much reduced rate. However, you must not lose sight of the fact that this type of planner will expect to receive some purchase orders from you in return.

If you choose a planner who operates on a commission basis, you'll usually be offered a range of investment products to choose from, usually mutual funds. But be aware that the recommendations will probably be restricted to those which will pay the planner a commission. He or she is unlikely to mention mutual fund companies like Altamira or to recommend funds offered by the banks and trust companies because most of them are no load — which means no sales commission. A conscientious planner will acquire a no load fund for your account if you ask, as a good will gesture. But don't look for such funds on the planner's recommendation list.

On the other hand, a free comprehensive financial plan, if it's well prepared, is a valuable inducement to do business with a firm. You'll have to decide where your priorities lie.

Some financial planners offer both types of service, depending on your preference.

The roster you'll receive from the Canadian Association of Financial Planners contains all the information you need to identify the income source of a planner. For instance, one roster entry may read: "Fees — none." Then it will go on to say something like: "Licensed to sell the investment funds of. . ." At that point it will list the names of whatever companies the planner represents. You know immediately from that type of listing that this planner will have an interest in selling you mutual funds. If that's not a problem, fine. But just understand where the planner is coming from and realize that the free plan he prepares for you will likely be weighted to particular products which his company represents.

In contrast, another roster entry might read: "Fees — $110 an hour. The company is not licensed to sell any financial products."

That's your classic fee-for-service planner. There are no hidden interests at work, but you'll pay for their services.

Fee-for-service planners are *not* cheap. After all, the good ones are well-trained people who probably have years of experience in some type of financial work and who may have completed a long and complicated program of courses. The Association says you should expect to pay between $50 and $200 an hour for a good one. A bare-bones, computer-generated plan will run you about $150 and that won't include any follow-up help. A full-scale, custom-tailored plan will cost between $500 and $5,000, depending on how complicated your financial affairs are. At those prices, be certain you really need the advice before you go.

Even though a planner is billed as being fee-for-service, double-check by asking whether he or she accepts commissions from any source. Full disclosure up-front will put you in a better position to evaluate the objectivity of the program that's prepared for you.

Major chartered accounting firms that charge on a fee-for-service basis are another source of top-quality, independent advice. However, their field of expertise tends to be more in the area of tax planning as opposed to investment strategy. Don't go to them unless you've got a lot of money. The minimum cost for them to sit down with you will likely be $2,000 and up for a comprehensive plan. For a more targeted plan, such as a retirement savings program, expect to pay in the $750 range. A few trust companies, most notably Royal Trust, have experimented with financial planning. However, results have been disappointing and it appears that future services in this area may be directed primarily at high-income clients. The banks are not into financial planning yet, and here again it appears that high-end people will be the main target if they do move.

4. Interview prospective advisors. Before making a choice, inter-

view a few candidates for your business. Most financial planners will not charge for an initial meeting. Ask about background and experience, what courses the planner has completed and whether he or she belongs to a recognized industry association. Ask for references and follow up by contacting them. Satisfied clients are the best indicator of competence.

While you're at it, get a sample of the type of report you'll be receiving. Look it over carefully and make sure you'll be able to understand it. Also decide whether you'll be able to implement the recommendations yourself or will need the planner's help on an ongoing basis. Most planners expect the business relationship will be a long-term one; very few will be comfortable with giving you a one-shot plan and saying good-bye. During the interview, consider your reaction to the planner. You should feel comfortable with the person and come away with the feeling he or she is really interested in your problems. If you don't end the interview feeling enthusiastic about working with the planner, you'd better look elsewhere.

Also, try to find out just what the person's strengths and weaknesses are. Don't expect a planner to be an expert in everything. Just because she can put together a terrific tax strategy that will save you thousands of dollars doesn't necessarily mean she should be advising you on what stocks to buy. For that kind of specialized advice, an investment counsellor might be more appropriate.

While you're interviewing planners, they'll be interviewing you. They'll want to know about your needs and objectives. They'll be trying to get some idea of your priorities — whether your emphasis is on establishing an income flow as opposed to saving taxes, for example.

They may also be trying to assess what type of person you are. Financial planners in the United States have faced a rash of lawsuits from disgruntled clients claiming they were badly advised. If the planner feels you're the type who might try something like that if things don't go well, he may reject your business. Or you may be asked to sign a release, absolving the planner of liability if things go wrong.

Once you've made a selection, do yourself a favour by not

wasting the planner's time. Remember, every hour spent on your project is costing you money if you choose a fee-for-service planner. So do some advance preparation to make the task as easy as possible. Don't show up with a shoebox full of unsorted documents, dump them on the planner's desk and ask him or her to make sense out of them. Believe it or not, I know of cases where just that sort of thing has happened. Avoid it, unless you're prepared to pay for the extra hours it will take to piece together the whole mess.

You'll minimize your costs by summarizing all the relevant information on a sheet of paper and making copies of the important documents before your first planning meeting. Be sure to take along copies of pay slips, your latest tax returns, mortgage information, a list of your assets, a summary of your liabilities (including up-to-date information on the interest rate being charged on any loans you may have) and anything else you think may be useful. All of this will be a tremendous help to the planner and will get things moving quickly.

This type of advance preparation is a good idea even if you decide not to use a fee-for-service planner. Just because a plan will be prepared "free" doesn't entitle you to impose unduly on the planner's time. You'll get better results, and establish a stronger rapport, if you do your homework first.

There are six things you should expect the planner to do for you:

1. Clarify your current financial situation. You should receive a clear snapshot of where you stand right now in terms of your income, assets, debts, taxes, retirement savings and cash flow.

2. Identify your objectives. If you aren't sure exactly what you need, the planner should help you identify priorities and time frames.

3. Identify problems. The planner should be able to pinpoint any potential difficulties in achieving your goals and offer other solutions.

4. Provide a written report. This should contain recommendations and various options to consider.

5. Assist you with implementation. The report is just step one. It has to then be made to happen. The planner should play a key role in that process.

6. Review your plan. No plan is for a lifetime. Conditions change. Expect to meet with the planner periodically (perhaps once a year) to review progress and update the plan.

When the report is done, don't accept the recommendations unquestioningly. Review the final plan with a critical eye to see if it truly meets your objectives. Make sure you're comfortable with any investment recommendations and that you fully understand the direction and details of the program. If some of the advice contradicts what you've read in this book, ask why. Be sure the arguments are well reasoned and make sense to you.

Obtaining a comprehensive financial plan from a competent person can be useful if you're unsure about how to proceed. But take the time to learn something about financial and investment fundamentals first. That way, you'll be better able to articulate your needs — and you'll be much less vulnerable to bad advice or a plan that is ill-suited to your personal requirements.

CHAPTER 24

Building Wealth in the Nineties

The golden age is not in the past, but in the future.
— E.H. Chapin

For the aspiring wealth building, the beginning of the nineties looked like a disaster.

Doom and gloom were everywhere. We were heading into a new Depression. The men and women of today's generation would have a lower standard of living than their parents. There wouldn't be enough jobs to go around. The outlook was bleak and getting bleaker.

And, indeed, the early years of the nineties were tough. The recession of 1990–92 threw many people out of work, pushed others into accepting wage freezes or even salary cuts to keep their jobs and forced thousands of Canadians to delay major purchases, from cars to homes.

Hardly a day seemed to go by when the nightly news didn't feature yet another story about an Ontario plant closure. The Alberta oil industry was hard hit by weak international prices. Newfoundland, where life is tough at the best of times, was socked by vanishing cod and the unhappy realization that the giant Hibernia project might not be economic until some distant future time. In B.C., American tariffs and a rising tide of environmentalism rocked the forest industry.

We weren't alone in our troubles. In the U.S., General Motors shocked the nation by announcing it would close several plants and eliminate tens of thousands of jobs. In Japan, the economy staggered as the Tokyo stock market went into freefall. Germany was forced to push interest rates to previously undreamed-of levels to help raise money to finance the economic rebuilding of the old German Democratic Republic. Further east, the former Soviet Union faced economic collapse.

It was a chaotic time. It was a normal time.

Much as we long for tranquillity, it never happens, at least not for long. If you wait for ideal conditions before you make a move, you'll never succeed financially. The world is a turbulent place, economically and politically. The intelligent wealth builder accepts that reality and tailors his tactics and strategies to meet the situation.

It's impossible to predict how events will unfold over the rest of this decade. There are too many uncertainties, both economic and political. The separation of Quebec, for example, would have a profound influence on the financial life of all Canadians, should it occur. But as this is written, there is no way of knowing how the whole constitutional scenario will unfold.

So how do you plan for the nineties, in the face of such uncertainty? Carefully — but optimistically.

History teaches us that bad economic times are inevitably followed by boom periods that may continue for many years. The exact timing can't be predicted. But the movements themselves can, as surely as night follows day.

As I see it, there are four phases in each economic cycle that the wealth builder must recognize and plan for. Perhaps the easiest way to understand them is to compare them to an ordinary day. They are:

Phase one: darkness. This phase is typified by an economy in recession. Unemployment is high, corporate profits are low, consumer confidence is weak. Housing starts fall, car sales are low, retailers go bankrupt, real estate prices weaken, office accommodation goes begging. Inflation and interest rates are usually quite high at the start of this phase, then fall rapidly throughout. The stock market will normally drop at the beginning of this phase, then wallow aimlessly for a period before starting to rise as the darkness phase approaches an end. This was the phase we experienced in 1990–91.

Phase two: daybreak. The first rays of light begin to appear. The economy shows signs of stabilizing, unemployment stops rising and starts to level out. Consumer confidence gradually starts to return. Retailers begin to report modest improvements in sales. Housing prices stop falling. Inflation is low, as are interest rates. The stock market starts to show some clear signs of life, in anticipation of the coming recovery.

Phase three: midday. The sun is shining and all is well with the world. The economy is humming again, unemployment is falling, consumers are coming out of their shells and buying cars and appliances. Inflation starts to edge up, as do house prices. The stock market takes off and more investors decide to plunge in. Labour unions begin receiving higher settlements. Vacancy rates fall. Corporate profits improve dramatically. Cicadas buzz in the trees, and it's endless summer.

Phase four: twilight. The day has been so glorious, we aren't really conscious of nightfall fast approaching. But there are plenty of signs around. The government has declared inflation to be a major problem. Short-term interest rates are high. Commodity prices are soaring — oil, copper, wheat, aluminum, potash, timber. House prices in Toronto and Vancouver have begun to move back into the stratosphere, as have prices for cottages in Muskoka and condos in Whistler. The stock markets are setting all-time records. Younger people believe that prices have nowhere to go but up. The world looks like its heading for a new Golden Age.

And then it all unravels. The world is dark again.

There's no way of knowing precisely when we move from one phase to another; the passage isn't as clearly defined as the periods of a day. So I cannot give you a timetable for the nineties. You'll have to devise that yourself, based on your observation of events and your reading of evolving conditions.

The successful wealth builders in the nineties will be those who recognize the changing phases and who arrange their affairs to take advantage of them. Each phase requires its own financial strategies. Your ability to build personal wealth for the balance of this century will depend on how well you plan for each phase and then implement your program using the principles contained in this book.

Following are appropriate strategies for each phase for conservative and aggressive wealth builders.

DARKNESS

Conservative: A time for defensive measures. Build cash reserves to protect yourself in the event of job loss. Debt should be reduced or, preferably, eliminated entirely. The greater your debt load, the more vulnerable you are in the darkness phase. Investments should be concentrated in low-risk areas. If you have some money saved, this is a time for wheeling and dealing in retail shopping; almost everything is on sale. Bond and mortgage funds offer the best profit opportunities for conservative investors during this phase. Low interest rates make cash holdings unattractive; any cash not required for your emergency reserve should go towards reducing loan balances. This is an opportunity to lock in low mortgage rates for the long term. Conversely, GIC and similar interest-bearing investments should be for one-year terms only. Avoid the stock market.

Aggressive: The darkness phase offers tremendous opportunities for more aggressive wealth builders. This is an excellent period to buy a home — cheap prices and low mortgage rates combine to make real estate more affordable than in any other phase. Vacation properties in popular areas should also be cheaper than at any other time. As the darkness phase deepens, the ability to acquire a big ticket item like a car at a giveaway price improves. For investors, the capital gains potential in bonds at the start of this phase offer a great wealth building opportunity. Leveraging increases this profit potential, with added risk. The deeper into the darkness phase we move, the lower stock prices become, creating a buying opportunity. Use bond profits to take advantage of this. Avoid cash investments; interest rates are low and there is no profit potential.

279

DAYBREAK

Conservative: Ease up on savings, but don't deplete the emergency fund. Continue to reduce outstanding debt. If you haven't yet locked in your mortgage for the long term, do so now. If you need a new car, get it now; as conditions improve the good deals will vanish. Reduce your holdings in bond and mortgage funds; put some of the profits into equity funds (but no more than thirty to forty percent of your investment portfolio). Move your cash into money market funds, which will gradually produce better yields as interest rates stabilize.

Aggressive: Stocks offer terrific growth potential. Build your equity holdings, but with care. Stick with solid equity funds or shares in large, well-established companies. They'll do very well in a rising market. Avoid speculative issues, especially during this phase. There is too much easy money to be made in blue chips to be taking unnecessary chances. Investment real estate may also offer potential in this phase. There will still be some bargains around, a hangover from the darkness phase. Avoid bonds at this point; interest rates will begin to rise soon and bond prices will be adversely affected.

MIDDAY

Conservative: Use salary increases and investment profits to reduce your mortgage. This phase normally offers the greatest potential to achieve this. Avoid the temptation to build new debt. Good times typically encourage people to spend beyond their means to improve their lifestyle; don't fall into that trap. Rising interest rates will make it increasingly more expensive to carry that additional debt and reduce your ability to pay down the mortgage. If you have stock market investments, begin taking profits as we move further into this phase. Keep cash reserves in money market funds. Stay away from bonds.

Aggressive: A time to take profits from your earlier moves. The real estate market will heat up. When it reaches the point people are almost panicking to buy, sell any investment property. The more aggressive investor may even contemplate selling his or her home and cottage, with the idea of buying back later. Stock market profits should be taken as the Midday phase moves along. Put your cash into money market funds, which by now should be providing excellent returns. If you've done any leveraging, use this opportunity to take profits and pay off outstanding loans. Waiting too long in this situation could be a disaster.

TWILIGHT

Conservative: Time for renewed caution. High interest rates make the cost of carrying any debt very expensive; pay off everything you can. Cut down on purchasing, especially big ticket items. Avoid buying a house at this time; you'll probably overpay by thousands of dollars. Mortgage renewals should be short term; don't lock in current high interest rates for the next five years. On the other hand, if you're a GIC investor, do lock in five-year rates now — they're probably at or near their cyclical high. Those close to retirement should purchase annuities or long-term RRIFs while interest rates are high. If you still have any stocks, take your profits. Money market funds are the best place for your investments during this phase.

Aggressive: Even aggressive wealth builders should pull in their horns during this phase. Darkness is coming; it's a time to consolidate your position and wait for the next great opportunity. Sell your stocks and real estate, if you haven't done so. Like the conservative wealth builder, keep your money in high-yielding money market funds. This is not a time to be taking risks. The economic world is about to unwind and you don't want to be exposed when it happens. Sit tight and wait. Your time will come again.

There you have it — your wealth building strategies for the nineties. As I said earlier, you'll have to work out the timing. But don't worry about being too precise. Each phase will last for some time; you'll have ample opportunity to read the signs and take appropriate measures. As long as you remain alert to what's happening around you and act accordingly, you have an excellent chance of success.

CHAPTER
25

Now It's Up to You

> *There are two kinds of people: those who don't do what they want to do, so they write down in a diary about what they haven't done, and those who haven't time to write about it because they're out doing it.*
> — Richard Flournoy and Lewis R. Foster — *The More the Merrier,* 1943

I've done as much as I can.

The preceding chapters should give you two of the three essential ingredients you need to begin a lifetime wealth building program.

You have the basic knowledge, the information you need to acquire before you start. You should by now understand such key concepts as budgeting, risk and return, compound growth, income splitting, leveraging, tax shelters, after-tax returns and diversification. I hope you've grasped the relationship between interest rates and bond prices, understood the difference between constructive and destructive debt, and mastered the implications of the dividend tax credit. And you've come to grips with the fundamentals of mutual funds, stocks, term deposits and mortgages.

The second ingredient in the mix is technique, and you are now acquainted with that as well — at least to the extent necessary to get started. You know how to set up and carry out a program for purchasing a home and paying off the mortgage quickly. You know how to accelerate the wealth building process by keeping a large portion of your investment money out of the government's hands. You're aware of the basic techniques for setting up and managing an investment portfolio. You know how to improve the odds that the mutual fund you select will outperform most of the others in its category. You know where to look for professional help, and what criteria to apply in the process. And you know what sources to use regularly for relevant information.

As I said, two of the three essential ingredients: knowledge and technique.

But it's like baking a cake. If *all* the ingredients aren't there, in the right proportions, it will end up a disaster. Leave out the egg, or the sugar, or, heaven forbid, the flour, and even your dog will turn up his nose at it.

I can't provide that third essential ingredient. Only you can. If you can't, or won't, then I'm sorry to tell you the time you've spent reading this book will be wasted.

What is this magical final ingredient?

Motivation.

Let me repeat, because it is so essential.

Motivation.

Even more specifically, *motivation to action.*

It's not just a matter of genuinely wanting to acquire wealth. Most of us do. That's why lotteries have become such an integral (and destructive) part of our social fabric.

But lotteries are relatively painless. A buck or five gives you a crack at millions. Never mind that the odds are better that you'll be struck by lightning; there's always a chance. After all, someone has to win!

And, who knows, maybe you'll get lucky. But the more likely result is that you'll throw away thousands of dollars on useless tickets over the years.

Wealth building, by contrast, is *not* painless. As I said at the beginning of this book, it requires dedication and hard work. The necessary motivation isn't just the desire to acquire wealth. It's the commitment to actually *do* something about it. If you don't have that, the cake will never get baked.

On the other hand, if you *do* act, the chances you will succeed are a heck of a lot better than if you just keep buying lottery tickets. No guarantees, of course. But life doesn't offer many of those anyway.

Consider this, though. Suppose you were offered a $10,000 bet.

The idea would be to pick which of two people would have accumulated the most wealth twenty years from now. One of them will spend $50 a week on lottery tickets over that time. The other will use that same $50 a week to set up a dedicated wealth building program. Which one do you want to bet on?

If you chose the lottery player, you might luck out. But he'd better win the big one because if the wealth builder manages only a ten percent return each year, he's going to be sitting with over $150,000 in assets when the time comes to declare the bet winner. I know which one I'd pick.

In Chapter Two, I offered what you may have felt at the time was a rather facetious bit of advice. I told you to *begin*. Now I'm saying it again.

Our lives are full of unrealized good intentions. We all have books we intend to read, trips we're someday going to take, people we mean to tell we love, sensations we'll eventually get around to experiencing, projects we'll start tomorrow. A thousand events waiting for a beginning.

Add wealth building to that list and I can almost guarantee it won't happen. And years from now, it will end up on another list we all have: the "If only I'd..." list.

You *must* make a start. Now!

Let me tell you one last story.

Every aspiring writer dreams of one day producing a novel. I was no different. All through the early years of my journalistic career, I told anyone who would listen about how I would someday write a novel that would dazzle the literary world. My poor wife must have heard the boast a thousand times; it's a wonder she didn't divorce me.

But the years went by and there was no novel. The intent was always there. But there was never any time. There was always another election campaign to cover, or some new international flare-up to write about, or a fascinating new political figure to profile. The novel would have to wait.

And then I turned forty. Everyone has a different reaction to that event; mine was pretty traumatic. I suddenly realized I was an overstressed, overweight male entering the coronary zone. While my health was good, I'd seen too many friends and acquaintances suddenly stricken to feel comfortable. And the idea kept going through my mind: what if I died tomorrow? My last thought might well be that I'd never accomplished the one thing I'd set my heart on since I was a kid. I'd never written that novel.

That's what it took to motivate me to action — the realization that my life was probably more than half over and it was time to put up or shut up. There still wasn't any time to write — but I *made* time. I got up before six every morning and wrote for a couple of hours before leaving for work. I spent evenings and weekends hashing over plot, characters and dialogue with my friend and co-author Tony Aspler.

The books that were eventually published didn't exactly rock the North American literary establishment to its foundations. But that didn't matter. I had done what I really wanted to do. The novels were there on my bookshelves, all the evidence I needed of the achievement of my personal objective.

But it only happened because I finally stopped dreaming and began. And it was tough at first. Six pages of manuscript one day, four the next, five the next. Putting together more than 400 pages seemed like an impossible objective. But as I plugged away at it, the file folder got thicker. And then, one day, I was done. The novel was finished.

Wealth building works in much the same way. Ten dollars here, twenty there, maybe a hundred occasionally. It seems at the start you'll never get anywhere. But if you have the self motivation to begin and the determination to stay with it, you'll eventually start to see the results. And then one morning you'll wake up and you'll have it. Not a pile of money, because, remember, money is only a means to an end. No, what you'll wake up to is the ultimate satisfaction of knowing you've achieved what you set out to do: that you've created a life for yourself and your loved ones that offers all the material and spiritual rewards you've ever dreamed of.

That's *real* wealth!

Good fortune!

INDEX